"This wonderful book explores to depth the unending unconscious effort of human beings trying to recover unity and harmony in their own sense of self. It investigates how to repair the split and lacks which detached minds from bodies, creating tragic feelings of subjective discontinuity and alienation. An innovative experiment of scientific cross-fertilization, by merging creatively for 14 years two different analytic perspectives thanks to the joint theoretical-clinical research of a 'resilient' British-Italian working group, generates here a fascinating, unexpected and much more integrated vision on the soma-psyche issue. This book confirms the immense power of cross-fertilization in psychoanalysis, and I enthusiastically recommend it to the readers."

Stefano Bolognini, Past President of the International Psychoanalytical Association

"*When the Body Speaks* is based on a series of dialogues held along 14 years between analysts from the British Psychoanalytical Society and the Italian Psychoanalytical Society. This highly interesting book shows how building bridges between different psychoanalytical Societies and perspectives can produce new interesting ideas on the complex issue of the body–mind relationship. Issues such as the role of the senses in psychic life, the body as 'a way of being,' the maternal body and its availability to the infant, the role of metaphor in connection to the body and the place of the analyst's body in analytic treatment are just some of the subjects touched upon in this book which together with detailed description of clinical material of the analysis of children, adolescents and adults, make *When the Body Speaks* intellectually stimulating as well as extremely helpful for anyone interested in psychoanalysis and in clinical practice in general."

Catalina Bronstein, Fellow and Training Analyst, British Psychoanalytical Society and Visiting Professor, Psychoanalysis Unit, University College London

"Edited by Don Campbell and Ronny Jaffè this fascinating and lively book deals with sensoriality and bodily issues into the analytic material, it aims to a deeper understanding of the human somatopsychic unity. *When the Body Speaks* is the result of years of dialogues between Italian and British psychoanalysts who met from

2001 to 2013. A specific aspect of the topic is tackled in each chapter. Distinguished authors present clinical cases that illustrate their way of being in touch with their own body–mind unit when working, thinking, and interpreting to the patient. Affected and concretely transformed by a psychosomatic disease the body can also be invasive in the clinical material and this can distort the countertransference. Faced with the patient's body on the couch the analyst needs to listen to his own bodily counter-transferential reactions and try to work through his blind spots or scars. Remarkable survey!!"

Marilia Aisenstein, Training Analyst with the Hellenic Psychoanalytic Society and the Paris Psychoanalytic Society, Past President of the Paris Psychoanalytic Society and of the Paris Psychosomatic Institute

When the Body Speaks

This book is based on the work done by a group of British and Italian psychoanalysts who have been meeting twice yearly since 2003 to study clinically the relationship between the mind and the body of their patients.

The analytical dyad became the focus of a dialectical movement between body and mind and between subject and object. Containing contributions from a range of distinguished British and Italian analysts, this book covers such key topics as somatic symptoms, the embodied unconscious, bodily expressions of affect, sexuality, violence, self-harm, suicide attempts, hypochondria, hysteria, anorexia and bulimia, and splits and fragmentation associated with the body. The theoretical understanding is inspired by various psychoanalytic theoreticians, including Freud, M. Klein, Winnicott and Bion and their theories on sexuality, infantile sexuality, libido, aggressiveness, death instinct, Oedipus complex and mother–child relationship.

Offering new advances in theoretical thinking and practical applications for clinical work, this book will be essential for all psychoanalysts and mental health clinicians interested in understanding serious mental disturbance that is represented in the body.

Donald Campbell is a Distinguished Fellow and Past President of the British Psychoanalytical Society and former Secretary General of the International Psychoanalytical Association.

Ronny Jaffè has been President of the Milanese Centre of Psychoanalysis since 2016. He is a Training Analyst (SPI IPA), former Vice President of the European Psychoanalytical Federation (2007–11) and former member of the IPA Ethical Committee (2012–19). He is the author of several publications.

THE NEW LIBRARY OF PSYCHOANALYSIS
General Editor: Alessandra Lemma

The New Library of Psychoanalysis was launched in 1987 in association with the Institute of Psychoanalysis, London. It took over from the International Psychoanalytical Library which published many of the early translations of the works of Freud and the writings of most of the leading British and Continental psychoanalysts.

The purpose of the New Library of Psychoanalysis is to facilitate a greater and more widespread appreciation of psychoanalysis and to provide a forum for increasing mutual understanding between psychoanalysts and those working in other disciplines such as the social sciences, medicine, philosophy, history, linguistics, literature and the arts. It aims to represent different trends both in British psychoanalysis and in psychoanalysis generally. The New Library of Psychoanalysis is well placed to make available to the English-speaking world psychoanalytic writings from other European countries and to increase the interchange of ideas between British and American psychoanalysts. Through the *Teaching Series*, the New Library of Psychoanalysis now also publishes books that provide comprehensive, yet accessible, overviews of selected subject areas aimed at those studying psychoanalysis and related fields such as the social sciences, philosophy, literature and the arts.

The Institute, together with the British Psychoanalytical Society, runs a low-fee psychoanalytic clinic, organizes lectures and scientific events concerned with psychoanalysis and publishes the *International Journal of Psychoanalysis*. It runs a training course in psychoanalysis which leads to membership of the International Psychoanalytical Association – the body which preserves internationally agreed standards of training, of professional entry, and of professional ethics and practice for psychoanalysis as initiated and developed by Sigmund Freud. Distinguished members of the Institute have included Michael Balint, Wilfred Bion, Ronald Fairbairn, Anna Freud, Ernest Jones, Melanie Klein, John Rickman and Donald Winnicott.

Previous general editors have included David Tuckett, who played a very active role in the establishment of the New Library. He was followed as general editor by Elizabeth Bott Spillius, who was in turn followed by Susan Budd and then by Dana Birksted-Breen. Current members of the Advisory Board include Giovanna Di Ceglie, Liz Allison, Anne Patterson, Josh Cohen and Daniel Pick.

Previous members of the Advisory Board include Christopher Bollas, Ronald Britton, Catalina Bronstein, Donald Campbell, Rosemary Davies, Sara Flanders, Stephen Grosz, John Keene, Eglé Laufer, Alessandra Lemma, Juliet Mitchell, Michael Parsons, Rosine Jozef Perelberg, Richard Rusbridger, Mary Target and David Taylor.

A full list of all the titles in the New Library of Psychoanalysis main series is available at https://www.routledge.com/The-New-Library-of-Psychoanalysis/book-series/SE0239

For titles in the New Library of Psychoanalysis 'Teaching' and 'Beyond the Couch' subseries, please visit the Routledge website.

When the Body Speaks

A British–Italian Dialogue

Edited by Donald Campbell and Ronny Jaffè

LONDON AND NEW YORK

First published 2022
by Routledge
2 Park Square, Milton Park, Abingdon, Oxon OX14 4RN

and by Routledge
605 Third Avenue, New York, NY 10158

Routledge is an imprint of the Taylor & Francis Group, an informa business

© 2022 selection and editorial matter, Donald Campbell and Ronny Jaffè; individual chapters, the contributors

The right of Donald Campbell and Ronny Jaffè to be identified as the authors of the editorial material, and of the authors for their individual chapters, has been asserted in accordance with sections 77 and 78 of the Copyright, Designs and Patents Act 1988.

All rights reserved. No part of this book may be reprinted or reproduced or utilised in any form or by any electronic, mechanical, or other means, now known or hereafter invented, including photocopying and recording, or in any information storage or retrieval system, without permission in writing from the publishers.

Trademark notice: Product or corporate names may be trademarks or registered trademarks, and are used only for identification and explanation without intent to infringe.

British Library Cataloguing-in-Publication Data
A catalogue record for this book is available from the British Library

Library of Congress Cataloging-in-Publication Data
Names: Campbell, Donald (Psychotherapist), editor. | Jaffè, Ronny, editor.
Title: When the body speaks : British and Italian psychoanalytic chapters on the body and mind / edited by Donald Campbell and Ronny Jaffè.
Description: Abingdon, Oxon ; New York, NY : Routledge, 2022. | Series: New library of psychoanalysis | Includes bibliographical references and index. |
Identifiers: LCCN 2021008383 (print) | LCCN 2021008384 (ebook) | ISBN 9781032055541 (hardback) | ISBN 9781032055534 (paperback) | ISBN 9781003198079 (ebook)
Subjects: LCSH: Mind and body. | Psychoanalysis.
Classification: LCC BF161 .W458 2022 (print) | LCC BF161 (ebook) | DDC 153--dc23
LC record available at https://lccn.loc.gov/2021008383
LC ebook record available at https://lccn.loc.gov/2021008384

ISBN: 978-1-032-05554-1 (hbk)
ISBN: 978-1-032-05553-4 (pbk)
ISBN: 978-1-003-19807-9 (ebk)

DOI: 10.4324/9781003198079

Typeset in Bembo
by Deanta Global Publishing Services, Chennai, India

Contents

The history of the British-Italian group
and acknowledgements   xi

Appreciation   xv

About the authors   xvi

Introduction   1
Donald Campbell and Ronny Jaffè

1 Traces of the early relationship in the corpus of
Freud's work: A re-reading   19
Giuseppina Antinucci

2 The "psychoanalytical" body and its clinical
implications   41
Sarantis Thanopulos

3 Transmission of somatic and sensory states in the
psychoanalytic relationship   63
Ronny Jaffè

4 Perfume   84
Mariapina Colazzo Hendriks

5 Access to the embodied unconscious through
reverie and metaphor   105
Benedetta Guerrini Degl'Innocenti

6	The body in psychoanalysis *Cristiano Rocchi*	125
7	The body in the analytic consulting room: Italian-British conversations *Barbara Piovano*	146
8	When the body speaks: Bodily expressions of unrepresented affects *Luigi Caparrotta*	169
9	A skin of one's own: On boundaries, the skin, and feminine sexuality *Patricia Grieve*	191
10	"Seized with a savage woe": Attacks on the vitality of the body in a suicidal young man *Joan Schächter*	209
11	Physical violence and its depiction by a male adolescent *Donald Campbell*	229
12	The hidden secret – ego distortion in facial deformity: Some reflections on the analysis of an adolescent boy *Bernard Roberts*	249
	Afterthoughts *Donald Campbell and Ronny Jaffè*	266
	Index	275

The history of the British–Italian group and acknowledgements

Luigi Caparrotta and Mariapina Colazzo Hendriks

A British–Italian psychoanalytical exchange was initially conceived by Donald Campbell when he was President of the British Psychoanalytical Society (BPAS) in 2000, and he proposed it to Loredana Micati, Secretary of the International Relations of the Italian Psychoanalytical Society (SPI) at the time. The Italian President of SPI Fausto Petrella happily endorsed this new enterprise. Subsequently, the scientific secretaries of the two societies, Sheilagh Davies and Stefano Bolognini, invited Luigi Caparrotta, a Fellow of the British Society, and Mariapina Colazzo Hendriks, a Member of the SPI, to organise and set up the first dialogue between the two societies to be held in London in March 2001 and then to be held every two years, and alternatively hosted by the BPSA in London and by the SPI in different Italian Psychoanalytical Centres. Donald Campbell, President of the British Society and SPI President Domenico Chianese took part in the early Dialogues.

Mariapina and Luigi, both Italian born, were influenced by British psychoanalysis in different ways. Although exposure to psychoanalysis during Mariapina's two-year stay at the Tavistock Centre in London had been abruptly interrupted, that experience led to her embarking on a psychoanalytic training in Milan in 1987. She was interested in revisiting her earlier links with psychoanalysis in London. Luigi left Italy in order to work in psychiatry in London and gravitated to the psychoanalytic training at the British Psychoanalytical Society in 1982. For his part, Luigi wished to deepen his connection with the Italian psychoanalytical world. From these different perspectives, Mariapina and Luigi organised annual Dialogues between Italian and British colleagues.

Stefano Bolognini's opening address to the first British-Italian Dialogue in March 2001 illustrated the reasoning behind this exchange and gave a brief excursus of the history of the SPI. Excerpts from Bolognini's speech are quoted below.

> Italian Psychoanalysis owes a great deal to the British, who we have deeply studied; great British [psychoanalytical] masters have trained several Italian analysts, through treatment and supervision [while] their books were widely read by all of us. Certainly, with the exception of Eugenio Gaddini, Franco Fornari and Ignacio Matte-Blanco, who was born in Chile, but developed most of his theories during his lifetime in Rome, Italian psychoanalysts are little known to their British colleagues, so I would like to briefly describe our institutional and scientific reality. The SPI was founded in 1932, but under the Fascist Regime it was suppressed; after World War II, a few Italian psychoanalysts eventually reorganised it. With constant growth the actual number of members is 650 with 300 candidates [in 2001]. Our Society is composed of ten Centres, where local scientific life develops: this organisation, due to the Italian geographical shape, allows us to differentiate clinical and theoretical characteristics that are specific for each centre .... The multifaceted view is the main characteristic of contemporary Italian psychoanalysis, differentiating it from other national trends (like the French, for instance), characterised by a more uniform perspective. We consider this variety a source of richness and not an effect of pure imitation, because it enriches the internal dialogue among colleagues, [thus] producing new and promising results .... In the last few years, the opportunity of meetings and exchanges with foreign societies (beyond the personal participation of single analysts in international meetings) have been officially structured in regular conferences with the Paris Psychoanalytical Society (SPP) and the American Psychoanalytical Association (APA) .... [W]e consider this opportunity of meeting you not only an important goal, but above all a stimulating starting point for future

collaboration in order to explore and enlarge together our fascinating common scientific ground.

During the first Dialogue held in London, the British colleagues were impressed by the clinical and research interest of the Italian analysts on sensoriality and bodily issues incorporated into their clinical material. Through the specific subject chosen for each dialogue, the group was able to build in a unique way, unlike other international exchanges, upon the broad on-going theme of the relationship between the mind and the body. This linchpin enabled the group to gradually identify and sketch successive working themes on these issues up to the last Dialogue held in Turin in 2013. The body–mind relationship was continuously developed between one Dialogue and another, as it was taken up in the bi-annual meetings of the British-Italian group, and eventually influenced the subject of our book *When The Body Speaks*.

During the course of the Dialogues and under the guidance of the new Italian Scientific Secretary Giuseppe Berti Ceroni and the leadership of Luigi Caparrotta and Mariapina Colazzo Hendriks, a regular working party of eight analysts from each Society called the British-Italian group was formed to meet every six months beginning in November 2005 with the aim of examining in detail their clinical work. The regular frequency of the meetings and the group's persistence over time has allowed everybody to acknowledge the reliability of the setting. The constancy and resilience of Luigi's and Mariapina's leadership enabled the group to thrive in spite of the rotation of the some passengers on the "train" and the deaths in 2011 of Sergio Molinari and Giuseppe Berti Ceroni, two venerable Italian members of the group. There was a notable curiosity about how colleagues worked in the other psychoanalytic societies, especially how they conceived, discussed and recorded clinical material. These aims underpinned and shaped the work of the British-Italian group. While reciprocal clinical contributions and discussions moved forward, it became apparent that it would be helpful to write papers arising from these encounters with a view to publishing them as chapters in a book.

During this time there was an on-going inquiry about the differences between British and Italian psychoanalysis and whether it was possible to talk of an "Italian psychoanalysis" as opposed to a

"British psychoanalysis". Eventually the group came to realise that its way of working was in fact less dissimilar than had been anticipated. While Italian psychoanalysis appeared more diverse perhaps because it was distributed in various Italian Centres, that could not be said for British psychoanalysis. Although in the past decade a Northern Training has been established in the north of England centred around Leeds, at the time the British-Italian groups started meeting the training and scientific life of the BPS was centred around London. However, the international population of British analysts meant that there was always a heterogeneous cultural and ethnic composition in the British Society. Perhaps this multicultural nature of the British Society contributed to the British analysts' enthusiasm and openness to the idea of learning more about Italian psychoanalysis in general and the theme of sensoriality in particular.

The focus of these twice-yearly workshops were verbatim clinical sessions, which were both informed by and contributed to the theoretical base whose evidence was, in turn, to be found in the clinical cases. This way of working facilitated, for example, an accurate scanning of single sessions without initial background history. The group was thus able to focus more on the interaction between analyst and patient. This method could enable the group to dissect in more detail differences and similarities, and consequently enrich the group's clinical repertoire through the pleasure of research and cross-fertilisation. The clinical material in *When the Body Speaks* is derived from the methodology developed in the British-Italian group. The conceptualisation of the clinical work emerged from the dialogues between British and Italian analysts who met twice a year for 14 years prior to publishing this book.

Appreciation

Access to a book is often through it Index. We think that the inquiring reader will be as grateful as we are for Klara King's keen eye and thorough indexing.

We also want to thank Philip Stirups, Senior Production Editor at the Taylor & Francis, for patiently bringing editorial unity and consistency to *When the Body Speaks*, a book that represents many nationalities and psychoanalytic cultures.

Donald Campbell and Ronny Jaffè

About the authors

Giuseppina Antinucci is a Fellow of the British Psychoanalytical Society (BPAS) and a Full Member of the International Psychoanalytical Association. She trained and worked in London, in private practice and at the Anna Freud Centre, where she ran a mother and toddler group for many years. She taught an MSc course on Psychoanalytic Theories of Child Development at University College London. She worked as an honorary consultant on the Directorate at the London Clinic of Psychoanalysis. She has a private practice in Milan and teaches on a variety of subjects on the online courses of the BPAS. She is on the Editorial Board of the *International Journal of Psychoanalysis*. Her latest publications are: "Poetics in the shadow of the other's language: the melancholic discourse of the trilingual poet Amelia Rosselli" (2016), *Int. J. Psychoanal.* 97 (5): 1321–1342. "Beating phantasies: mourned and unmourned" (2016), *Int. J. Psychoanal.* 93: 615–639.

Benedetta Guerrini Degl'Innocenti is a Psychiatrist, PhD in Psychodynamic and Neurophysiology and Training and Supervising Analyst of the Italian Psychoanalytic Society (SPI) and of the International Psychoanalytic Association (IPA). During the last ten years she has been consultant and supervisor for Artemisia, a non-governmental organisation working in the field of combating violence against women and children in Florence and she is now Honorary Judge in Juvenile Court. She was on the editorial board of *Psyche*, the SPI magazine of psychoanalytic culture, she is editor of the psychoanalytic series of Giovanni Fioriti Publisher and she is now Chief of the Editorial Board of *Rivista di Psicoanalisi*. She has been Scientific Secretary of the Psychoanalytic Institute in Florence, where she lives and works in private practice as an adult and adolescent psychoanalyst. She has published papers on mother–infant attachment, perverse relationships and unrepresented states of mind.

Donald Campbell is a Training and Supervising Analyst, Distinguished Fellow of the British Psychoanalytical Society and Full Member of the International Psychoanalytical Association. He is qualified to work analytically with children, adolescents and adults. He served as President of the British Psychoanalytical Society and as Secretary General of the International Psychoanalytical Association. He worked for over 30 years and served as Chairman at the Portman Clinic, an outpatient National Health Service facility in London that provides assessment and psychoanalytic psychotherapy for violent and delinquent individuals and those suffering from a perversion. He has written papers on violence, perversion, child sexual abuse, adolescence, and horror film monsters. His most recent book, written with Rob Hale, is *Working in the Dark: Understanding the pre-suicide state of mind*. He is a founding member of the British-Italian group.

Luigi Caparrotta, MD, MPhil is a Consultant Psychiatrist in Medical Psychotherapy and a Fellow of the British Psychoanalytical Society. He is an NHS Consultant in the Psychodynamic Psychotherapy Service for Camden and Islington Foundation Trust and works in private practice. He is a founding member of the British-Italian Psychoanalytical Dialogue. He has lectured in Italy and has published a number of papers on clinical issues and chapters in various books including: Ghaffari, K. & Caparrotta, L. (2004) *The Function of Assessment within Psychological Therapies*. London: Karnac [also published in Italian (2007), Borla Editore)]; Caparrotta, P, & Cuniberti, P. (Eds) (2012) *Psicoanalisi in Trincea (Psychoanalysis in the Trenches)*. Franco Angeli, Milano Lemma, A. & Caparrotta, L. (2014) *Psychoanalysis in the Technoculture Era*. London: Routledge, Caparrotta, L. (2016) Chapter 6 and 7, in *Medical Psychotherapy*, Yakeley, J. et al. (Eds). Oxford University Press.

Mariapina Colazzo Hendriks, MD, a Psychiatrist and Full Member of the IPA and SPI (Italian Psychoanalytical Society), trained at the Tavistock Clinic, London in Adolescent Psychiatry and worked in various psychiatric services in Ferrara and Bologna. She also has a Master in Nutrition from Bologna University. She is a founding member of the British-Italian Dialogue. She works in private practice, was a lecturer in Psychotherapy in the Psychiatric Section of Ferrara Medical School and was a reviewer for the Italian *Rivista di Psicoanalisi*. She has published a number of papers on clinical issues.

Patricia Grieve did her psychoanalytic training at the Institute of Psychoanalysis, London, and also trained as a child psychotherapist at the Tavistock Clinic. She is a Member of the British Psychoanalytical Society and a Training Analyst of the Madrid Psychoanalytic Association. She works in private practice in Madrid and teaches and lectures on various psychoanalytic subjects. She has presented and published papers on child and adolescent psychoanalysis, the history of psychoanalytic concepts and other subjects. She is a chair of the Forum on Adolescence of the European Psycho-Analytic Federation.

Ronny Jaffè is a Psychologist and member of the IPA and SPI, Training Analyst of the Italian Psychoanalytical Society and responsible for the Local Committee of the Training Analysts in Milan (2013–2016). He has been President of the Milanese Centre of Psychoanalysis since 2017, and Co-Chair of the IPA Ethical Committee since 2012. Jaffè was Vice President of the European Psychoanalytical Federation from 2009 to 2013. As a member of the EPF Working Party on Initiating Psychoanalysis, he was among the authors of *Beginning Analysis* (Routledge, 2018). Jaffè worked for several years in the Psychiatric and Infantile Neuropsychiatric Service as an individual and group psychotherapist. He has written on such subjects as first interviews, the body–mind relationship, individual and group links, and sibling complex, and was co-editor of the book *Caos, labirinto, villaggio*, which deals with the theory and technique of child group psychoanalysis.

Barbara Piovano, Full Member of SPI and IPA and Child/Adolescent Psychoanalyst, was born in Turin and studied Medicine and specialised in Child Neuropsychiatry in Genoa. She was awarded a Fulbright Scholarship (1989) to attend the adolescent treatment programme at the Northwestern Memorial Hospital in Chicago. She was Professor of Child Psychiatry at Chieti University and conducted a Child Guidance Centre for children and adolescents in Rome where she lives and has a private practice.

Her publications reflect her interest in pre-symbolic levels of the mind and include: *Parallel Psychotherapy with Children and Parents*, Aronson (1998), "The function of the analyst's boundaries in the psychoanalytic relationship" presented at the British-Italian Dialogue in Rome (2003) and published in the *Bulletin of the British Psychoanalytical Society* (2005), "Acting, dreaming, thinking in adolescence" (2010) *Int. Forum Psychoan.* and "Creative adaptation to iatrogenic trauma" presented in Bologna in 2018 (which will be published in Italian).

Bernard Roberts is a Teaching and Supervising Analyst and a Child Analyst of the British Psychoanalytical Society. He is Head of The London Clinic of Psychoanalysis Child and Adolescent Clinic. He is an Honorary Consultant Psychiatrist in Psychotherapy at Central North West London Foundation NHS Trust where he was Lead Psychotherapist and led the Parental Mental Health Service in Kensington and Chelsea. He trained at The Cassel Hospital and Tavistock Clinic.

Cristiano Rocchi is an Italian SPI–IPA Psychoanalyst, native of Pisa, who lives in Florence where he carries out his clinical and research activity and teaches in Rome as a Training Analyst. He has been dealing for many years with the functioning of the analyst's mind in the analytic session and with countertransference (even somatic) in particular; on these topics he has published several articles in international and Italian journals. He has always been interested in Ferenczian and relational psychoanalysis and on these subjects he has held many seminars in Italy and abroad (Russia, Bulgaria, Portugal) and recently has participated in the publication of a collective volume entitled *Rileggere Ferenczi oggi. Contributi italiani* (Borla, 2016). He is currently focusing his attention and his writings on psychoanalytic training and in particular on supervision.

Joan Schächter trained in medicine and psychiatry before qualifying as a Psychoanalyst in 1983. She is a Training and Supervising Analyst for the British Psychoanalytical Society. Whilst training in psychoanalysis, she worked at the Cassel Hospital (an in-patient psychotherapy hospital for adolescents, adults and families) and at the Brent Adolescent Centre. She worked as a consultant psychotherapist in the NHS for 24 years until 2007, since when she has been in full time private practice. She was a member of a research project at the Anne Freud Centre, which offered subsidised analysis to young adults who had suffered a breakdown. Schachter has a longstanding interest in the body–mind relationship and taught psychosomatics at the Institute of Psychoanalysis. She has been a member of the British-Italian study group since its inception in 2002. She has published chapters in *A Psychoanalytic Understanding of Violence and Suicide* (1998), and *Female Experience: Four Generations of British Female Psychoanalysts on Work with Women Patients* (2008) edited by Rosine Perelberg and Joan Raphael-Leff. She co-wrote a book on *The Late Teenage Years: From Seventeen to Adulthood with Luis Rodriguez de la Sierra* (2013 Routledge), and edited with Prof Ken Robinson a book on *The Contemporary Freudian Tradition: Past and Present* (2020 Routledge).

Sarantis Thanopulos is a Psychiatrist and Training Analyst of the Italian Psychoanalytical Society and was on the Board of the Italian Society from 2005 to 2009. His articles on various psychoanalytic subjects are published regularly in the Italian newspaper *Il Manifesto*. Thanopulos has published numerous papers in *Rivista di Psicoanalisi* and many books including: *The Legacy of Tragedy* (with A. Giannakoulas (2006), *Hypothesis Gay* with O. Pozzi (2006), *The Space of Interpretation* (2009), *Psychoanalysis of Psychosis: Today's perspectives* (with R. Lombardi and L. Rinaldi (2016), *Desire and Law* (2016), *The Devil Wears Isis: The stranger of our home* (2018), *Hidden Truths* (2018), and *The Solitude of the Woman* (2018).

Introduction

Donald Campbell and Ronny Jaffè

THE ITALIAN CONTRIBUTIONS

Giuseppe Berti Ceroni, together with Donald Campbell, Luigi Caparrotta, Sheilagh Davies and Mariapina Colazzo Hendriks, launched the British–Italian group in 2003, and inspired the birth of this volume. Yet, sadly, Ceroni's unexpected death in 2011 did not allow him to see it published.

The British–Italian group[1] met twice a year to study the link between body and mind in the analytical couple. The group's method was to present and discuss clinical cases where the body featured. The aim was to use the clinical discussion as the basis for formulating some provisional theoretical hypothesis and theories of technique. *When the Body Speaks*, which is the result of that study, was made possible by the group process, a fruitful melting pot where lots of ideas crossed one with the other.

In 15 years of meetings between the British and the Italian analysts the clinical cases were studied with different viewpoints clearly illustrated. Barbara Piovano's chapter illuminates common ground, convergences and differences between the British and Italian psychoanalytical cultures. What is interesting about the group process during this time is that each analyst, equipped with their personal background, could listen and contribute to a creative group mind. Italian and British colleagues came to share the idea that the body–mind relationship could be understood in a relational perspective where the analytical dyad "becomes the place where a dialectic movement between body and mind and between subject and object can be realized and articulated" (Piovano, this volume, p. 163).

Italian and British analysts also shared the view that there is a paradox between the fact that psychoanalysis has focused its attention on sexuality, aggressiveness and drives while leaving in the shadow the centrality of the body. These analysts believe that the world of drives lives in the body and cannot be disconnected from it.

Benedetta Guerrini Degl'Innocenti in her chapter thinks of the body "as both the *Körper* 'the body I have', a prerequisite to the psyche, according Laplanche's (1987) definition, as well as *Leib* –'the body I am'". These theoretical footsteps remained as traces of thoughts, which were developed by Freud's heirs.

In recent decades psychoanalysis has considered the centrality of the body in its entirety. The authors in *When the Body Speaks* believe that the "psyche is rooted in the bodily matrix of the self ... since the child's matrix is located from the moment of conception in the mother–child relationship, this means that we need always to take in account the mother–child dyad" (Thanopulos).

The moment of conception is supposed to be a lively and creative bodily exchange. This means that the centrality of the body is not the equivalent of the psycho-somatic, but is related to how the mother makes the infant feel in his or her body. From there, during the process of growth, the subject feels its body, with its body, with pleasure in movement, speaking, eating, dressing, doing sport, or, on the contrary, with an unpleasant physical sensation when he or she sweats, feels cold or hot and so on. In contrast many theoretical paradigms relate the topic of the body when it's connected to psychic pain or to a psycho-somatic illness instead of considering the body also in its wellness and integrity "as a way of being" (Thanopulos), which can meet the way of being of the other. This can create a first link before creating an inter-psychic link. So, the body of the subject relates immediately to the otherness of the mother. This, of course, occurs also in the analytical relationship. So, in the consulting room, it is important to consider vital expressive bodily communications when these occur.

Besides the focus on the wellness/illness of the body, another element that links the authors of the book, though with different perspectives, is the focus on the psychosomatic unit. In this respect it's interesting to quote the different viewpoints mentioned by Bronstein when she writes that whereas Grotstein proposes that the

mind–body constitutes a single holistic unity and mind–body are always inseparable ... André Green argues that a monistic approach does not necessarily entail a homogenous unity and that somatic and psychic organizations differ in their structures ... and that while the body refers to the libidinal body (erotic, aggressive, narcissistic), the soma refers to the biological organisation.
(Bronstein 2011, p. 174)

Gaddini, referring to the initial stages of mental development and mental differentiation, states that "one ought to distinguish not the mind from the body, but rather from a mind/body continuum and a virtual area in which these two continua are connected" (Gaddini 1985, p. 732). Several authors believe that this statement pertains to the patient as well as the analyst.

In *When the Body Speaks* many authors present clinical cases that illustrate their way of being in touch with their own body–mind unit when listening to, thinking of and interpreting the patient. They show what can happen in an analytical relationship when there is a disconnection, break or split in the analyst's link between his body and his mind.

This can happen especially when there is a hyper-presence of the patient's body which can be very invasive in the analytical process as in the case presented by Cristiano Rocchi. Or when the patient touches, unconsciously, pre-consciously or consciously some blind spots, scars or fragments of the analyst's body as in the cases presented by Mariapina Colazzo Hendriks and Ronny Jaffè. If the analyst manages to listen to his bodily reactions and countertransference, this can open additional pathways to get in touch with the patient's suffering and disturbed body–mind unit.

In Chapter 1 Giuseppina Antinucci illustrates the changes and invariants in the body–mind relationship from Freud's topographic model to his economic model. Antinucci investigates the traces of the early relationship, the primary maternal object and the pre-symbolic order by following "Freud's intuition concerning a continuous and cohesive way of sensations, feelings and thoughts within a subject–object relationship" (Antinucci, this volume). Freud thinks that the infant is a "helpless living organism as yet un-orientated in the world, which is receiving stimuli in its nervous substance" (Freud 1915, p. 119). However, there is no reference to who offers these stimuli. Antinucci believes that there is a "shadow" who offers the stimuli meaning. The metaphor of shadow enables Freud to anticipate future developments without still defining a theoretical construction. Twenty years later Freud will say that the figure who offers stimuli will be embodied by the mother. This is a fundamental change in Freud's theoretical development because he opens up the world of the mother with her care and tenderness, but also with her drives, sexuality and seduction. Antinucci maintains that: "In psychoanalysis no maternal care or tender attachment and love can be disarticulated from the eroticism of the body, for both baby and mother" (Antinucci, this volume).

The shadows became clearer when Freud recognized in Femininity (1933) that his patients' "seductive phantasies had in reality originally been connected with their mother" (p. 13). Following the separation between infant and mother Freud immerses himself in the origin of psychosomatic states, which are not only "the realm of pure psychology (but also) the borderland of physiology" (Freud 1926, p. 93, from Antinucci, this volume).

In Chapter 2 Sarantis Thanopulos illustrates the connections between drive, psychic area and body. He views the epistemological foundation of psychoanalysis as a psychic body, a body of drives which "connects somatic excitement with psychic activity" (Thanopulos, this volume), and where the drive is a borderline concept between the psyche and the body. The body of drives is a prime body because drives start from the beginning of life: the baby "who doesn't yet realize the difference between himself and the object of care creates a mark of his mother's body in his own body which is a pre-inscription of a relationship not yet recognized" (ibid.) and for the author this "pre-inscription becomes the area from which the organization of the psycho-bodily experience sets off" (ibid.).

Thanopulos emphasizes how the baby is active and full of desire incarnated in bodily sensations from the start, but of course the mother also has to long for the contact with her child. A relationship of this kind creates, through different stages, the "essential structure of the baby's subjectivity". A relationship with the mother, mediated by the mother's body and the baby's body, creates the source of life.

So, the infant's first stage is marked by a living, desiring and spontaneous body which also naturally incorporates the mother's body; this stage precedes the forming of the function of a psychic representation; in fact only in a second stage does psyche develop and create a psychic image of the corporeal self.

The spontaneous bodily gestures, through the growth of the mind, become an intentional body in search of the mother and the highest expression of this intention will be the use of words. Speech and bodily movements will interweave one with the other giving birth in what is called body language. Speech will be also the basis for an abstract thought and when this event happens, there is a definitive differentiation between mind and body and between baby and mother, which coincides with "a lessening of the availability of mother's body" (ibid.). But, before arriving at the world of words, we need to consider that a baby can express a desperate aim to possess the mother's body, a ruthless love (Winnicott 1945), but also a hate towards the mother for not possessing her.

It is also through hate that the baby realizes the subjectivity of the mother and from there he discovers that the mother's body has its own subjectivity that is different from the baby's body. The baby wishes to take possession of the mother, but as a separate object. We are here in the area of an hysterical body, "the body that speaks in its own way, without using words".

In the analytical relationship the analyst can get in touch with this area by observing "the corporeal manifestations and expressions when the body is able to represent, by using hysterical and proto-symbolic language, what words cannot, when the body is unable to symbolize, or when it lacks spontaneity and vitality" (Thanopulos, this volume). Thanopulos illustrates different situations where the body is obstructed in its expressiveness and vitality. Where there is a complete lack of expressiveness by the body we are in touch with psychosis, "the silence of the body". So, the analyst has to be equipped with a great capacity for reverie in order to restore the patient's bodily expressiveness, trying to give life first to a relational body, and then trying to move towards the symbolic body.

In Chapter 3 Ronny Jaffè focuses his attention on the "bodily fragments" (Gaddini), "body scars" (Hautmann), "spots of the bodily self" (Spira) that in their different facets correspond to the bodily "eye of a needle", which transmit sensorial communications in the analytical field. Jaffè's hypothesis is, if the analyst is able to listen, to work through and metabolize his own bodily states that are aroused by the bodily and sensory fragments of the patient, the analyst's body and senses can then become "the instrument and the heart of the core" (Ferraro 2010, p. 32). In this way the analyst can actually feel and be in unison with the aching and distressed patient's body. The analyst, through a deep understanding on a bodily level, can give an interpretation "that can be heard, seen, touched, and smelled" (Bion 1963, p. 20) and shared by patient and analyst.

Through the presentation of two cases the author illustrates his way of using the sensory and bodily dimensions and focuses attention on how to interpret these levels. The first case focuses on the question of the smell in the analytical process and how the transmission of the stench and an olfactory memory enable the analyst and patient to get in touch with a tangle of sexual and aggressive drives that leads back to the relationship between the patient and his mother.

The second case centres its attention on an illness of the skin in a patient affected by very primitive identifications within symbiotic mechanisms. Jaffè refers to the skin as a container of "a body for two" (McDougall 1989), and a "skin fusion" (Anzieu 1985, p. 58) where one can have the phantasy to be infected by the other, and this, of course, can also happen in the consulting room. As in the first case, the analyst also worked through the encounter of the patient's bodily spots that resonated in the analyst's bodily scars. This allowed both patient and analyst to face the pain and discomfort of all these fragments, scars and spots, which could infect the analytical dyad. Working through the archaic somatic transmission and the bodily countertransference allowed the patient and analyst to get in touch with painful and split off somatic areas and try to restore them in the body–mind unit thus supporting an integrative process.

In Chapter 4 Mariapina Colazzo Hendriks faces, with great courage, a difficult issue with a patient suffering from different bodily symptoms and, in particular, with compulsory trichotillomania (pulling out hair) since she was very young. The patient explains that trichotillomania started from the age of ten because she "was curious to see the roots of her hair" (Colazzo Hendriks, this volume), but then it became a compulsive action. As a result the scalp sometimes had various open spaces, which created a sense of desperation, isolation and shame.

During the analysis the patient expanded the meaning of ripping out her hair and said that "the hair leaves the scalp ... and I smell it" (ibid.). In a narrative and evocative way, the patient explained all her pleasure and pain in playing, touching, smelling, ripping out her hair. The patient also strewed the analyst's private practice with scents and discourses on perfumes and flavors that the analyst cannot smell, but only remember. Several years before starting this analysis, the analyst suffered an injury to some of her sensorial functions and, in specific, a complete loss of the sense of smell. These olfactory communications raised in the analyst a very intense bodily countertransference and archaic identifications.

Colazzo Hendriks' sensibility in moving through her countertransference and bodily memories of far-off active sensorial functions came together with the patient's transference wish to penetrate inside the entrails of the analyst's body. The analytical couple was infused by a sensorial tangle through a deep, ancestral transmission from one unconscious to the other. Sensorality and the necessity of the analyst to think about her own body are crucial in order to be in touch with "the double-register of the injured body and the body which feels an invisible wound with and for the other" (ibid.). The analyst shows how the possibility to be in touch and think about her own damaged body can be a tool for understanding deep and archaic psychic layers of the patient.

Colazzo Hendriks uses her memories of her previously functioning sensory channels to elaborate within herself the trauma of a loss and accept what she calls "a sensorial minus" (ibid.). This allowed her to feel what the patient was communicating through smell and scent and get in touch with the roots of the patient's problematic bodily identity that was strongly linked to a very tangled, ancestral and conflictual relationship with her mother, her grandmother, and many other females including, of course, the analyst, thereby creating a primitive and symbiotic identification that was repeated in the transference.

In Chapter 5 Benedetta Guerrini Degl'Innocenti describes the importance of the use of metaphor in connection with bodily states in the presentation of a very detailed clinical case. She states that "the body is the metaphorical source of all the metaphors" (Degl'Innocenti, this volume). Following Campbell and Enckell (2005) she draws attention to the existence of a psychoanalytical metaphor "which elaborates non-verbal representational meanings as perceptions, feelings, thoughts, memories" (Degl'Innocenti, this volume) but also in reveries, dreams and sometimes symptoms.

In the most severe pathologies, as the patient with a bony and tragic body illustrated in this chapter, the body is affected by the loss of metaphor, it's simply a "thing" linked to a mind that is aimless and unable to transform concrete experiences in a metaphorical direction. The author refers to the theory of the reflective function and thinks that when there is a lack of this function a subject does not have a sense of being and feeling. "There is the body I have, but not the body I am" (ibid.).

In considering the early stages of human development, Guerrini Degl'Innocenti believes that the capacity of the reflective function and the self-fulfilment of subjectivity is possible when the child's caregiver is able to tune in effectively with the child (Stern 1985). A caregiver, who is capable of mirroring, in its various facets, allows the transformation from body sensations into subjective states. This means that the acquisition of subjectivity, the sense of being a body, takes place specifically in the inter-subjective space of the child–caregiver and of the patient–analyst.

Guerrini degl'Innocenti's patient Giulia, who lived in a family environment marked by "physical and empathic absence, inconsistency and failing mirroring" (Degl'Innocenti, this volume) was affected by "the intrusion of unprocessed traumatic parental aspects" (ibid.). She looked "not human" in the consultation room, which created a sense of fear in the analyst who had to see and work with a starving and bony body. In this state of fear, the analyst remembered the film *Alien* (1979) and through this image she came in touch with a destructive, intrusive and un-symbolized *Alien* located in the patient's mind and embodied in her body. The analyst was ready to live a frightening experience and to find through the reverie of *Alien* a transformation during the analytical process that allowed the patient to be in touch with her feelings and affects and to activate step-by-step "a metaphorical and symbolizing function in the analytic field" (Degl'Innocenti, this volume).

In Chapter 6 Cristiano Rocchi affirms that "important elements concerning psychic events of the two members of the couple cross over the bodily countertransference" ... and if the body of the analyst loses its container–connector function so does the analytic function" (Rocchi, this volume). These considerations are in connection with a monistic position and in opposition with the Cartesian body–mind dualism. The author affirms that "the body is the original matrix of the mental function" (ibid.) and refers to Freud's last writings where he affirms that "psychic phenomena depend largely on bodily influences, powerfully affecting in turn the somatic processes" (1938, p. 7).

Besides this monistic viewpoint Rocchi affirms that the corporeal states can be understandable only within an interaction matrix; this means that in the analytical relationship the analyst can acknowledge what's happening in the interaction if he includes, besides his "emotions, thoughts and images, also all his somatic events"

(Rocchi, this volume). Through a very moving account of a patient with terminal cancer at the end of her life, Rocchi shows how the loss of the analytic function was provoked by the patient's absence from several sessions due to her illness. The concrete absence of the patient was felt, contrary to expectation, like a sort of " hyper-presence" (ibid.) of the patient's ill body.

The absent hyper-presence which foreshadowed forthcoming death affected the analyst in such a way that his thought collapsed and his body was useless. Rocchi explained his simultaneous breakdown as a consequence of extreme psychic pressure on a mind–body unit that constitutes a single holistic unity that is always inseparable.

In Chapter 7 Barbara Piovano gives a clear description of the underlying common ground and diversity due to different cultures and different psychoanalytical traditions within the British-Italian group. Piovano also emphasizes a strong willingness and curiosity in the group to understand and listen to each other thereby fostering a creative exchange of ideas and perspectives, which could converse one with the other.

The description of the group is accompanied by a detailed reference to authors who focused attention on the body–mind relationship. Winnicott, Bion, Ferrari, Isaacs, Gaddini, from different perspectives, underlined "how much the psyche is rooted in the bodily matrix of the self" (Piovano, this volume), and that this element "is located from the moment of conception in the inter-subjective context of the mother child relationship" (ibid.). In addition, Piovano points out some key aspects of the analyst's technique that are used to work with the issue of the body–mind relationship beginning with the analyst's body that can become "the instrument and the heart of the cure" (Ferraro 2010). Many patients affected by a psychic disorder that affects their body are very sensitive to the analyst's body.

Piovano draws on her experience as a child analyst, and focuses her paper on the body in child analysis in a way that underlines how important the inter-body dialogue and communication between patient and analyst can be. In the last decades analysis of children and adolescents has made very important clinical and theoretical contributions to the treatment of adults by: (1) going through the inter-bodily communications between an analyst and adult patients, and (2) trying "to distinguish between unconscious nuclei composed of somatic-sensory sediments that are un-transformable and irreducible to meaningfulness, and considering contents relative to sensorial experiences and somatic-sensory ones that can be transformed into thoughts" (Piovano, this volume).

In the analytical relationship the analyst can get in touch with this area by observing "the corporeal manifestations and expressions when the body is able to represent, by using hysterical and proto-symbolic language, what words cannot when the body is unable to symbolize, or when it lacks spontaneity and vitality" (ibid.).

THE BRITISH CONTRIBUTIONS

In Chapter 8 Luigi Caparrotta's chapter *When the Body Speaks*, which inspired the title for this book, Caparrotta's patients Justin and Hayley repeat in the present their experience of not being heard in the past. There was an absence of an experience of the use of language to communicate affects, especially anger, inhibited relationships. The translation of sensory registration of affects in the body into symbols relies on the development of language. This chapter raises many questions that Caparrotta addresses from a developmental perspective and follows Gaddini's (1969) view of the role of imitation in the acquisition of the bodily self. However, Caparrotta reminds us that imitation alone will not lead to identification unless the affective interaction between mother and infant reflects an appropriate degree of affect attunement (Stern 1985).

For Justin, a middle-aged man and Caparrotta's first patient, the impact of puberty had long-term consequences. In Justin's case having a body that became more masculine proved to be too threatening for him and precipitated a regression. Justin sought refuge in a pre-Oedipal erotic attachment to a boy.

Justin projected unacceptable feminine identifications onto his nipples, and in a delusional state, cut off the tips of his nipples, which he thought were the source of his shame and feminized body. Caparrotta reflects on the use that Justin makes of the severe split between his sexual body and his affective states to the extent that initially he lacked a capacity to symbolize feeling or, indeed, recognize affects when they were "spoken" through his body.

Hayley, a 34-year-old woman, was also frightened of the way her emerging adult sexuality in puberty had aroused her identification with her ambivalently cathected mother. Early in her analysis Hayley confessed to a secret solution to her need to keep herself cut off from the outside world, which was to use illicit drugs to create a "bubble" that she lived within. Gradually, she relinquished her "bubble solution". However, Hayley's dependence on an artificial stimulus (drugs) to create pleasurable feelings in her body had acted to suppress angry and aggressive feelings, which were now expressed through her body in hives, sinusitis, and amenorrhoea, a genital condition that required surgery. Hayley did not use these somatic "messages" to reflect upon as part of a dialogue with her body or her analyst. Instead, these symptoms discharged disturbing affects and disappeared before they were thought about or interpreted. Hayley created a split between her mind and her body. She did not use her mind to reflect on her physical symptoms. Rather, as she said, "My body speaks for me".

Hayley suffered from separation anxieties related to earlier absences by her mother, which were revived in the transference by her analyst's holidays. Hayley's anxiety about her sexual body led her to suppress her sexual desires, while she unconsciously preserved and attacked her sexual body by inhibiting its sexual function. Her body seemed to speak to this anxiety with heavy periods, which would "announce" the absence of a living being in her womb.

From a development perspective, was Justin and Hayley's experience of their bodies speaking to them an expression of later unconscious projections onto their bodies, which are registered as somatic sensations? From this later perspective the body is not the originator of the affect, but the screen or canvas upon which the projected unconscious is registered. As a consequence of the projection, the ego has an awareness of an affect or sensation that is reintrojected, but experienced as originating not from the ego, but from the body.

In Chapter 9 Patricia Grieve identifies the role of projections, particularly from the mother, in the ego's experience of the body. Grieve explores Freud's observation that the ego is derived from bodily sensations, chiefly from those springing from the surface of the body, through her analysis of a young female patient called Cristina. Grieve is able to trace the vicissitudes of the transition from the skin as a physical medium for the earliest somatic and sensorial experiences to the development of the skin as a psychic apparatus, particularly as manifest in Cristina's dreams.

In considering the function of the skin as a boundary between and mediator of the mother's early holding and containing, Grieve refers to Winnicott (1945, 1963, and 1969), Gaddini (1987) and

Anzieu (1985). Grieve emphasizes that what is communicated from the mother's body to her child's body is mother's love of her child, her love of her own body, her love of her child's body, or lack of love, or anxiety about loving her own and/or her child's body. The introjection of these projections will influence the child's cathexis of their own body.

When the mother is able, in Winnicott's phrase, to provide a holding environment that the child can cathect, there is the basis for an early organization of the body ego, which Anzieu (1985) conceptualized as a "skin ego". Grieve, following Anzieu, identifies several perceptual achievements that follow on the establishment of the representation of the surface of the body as boundary and as container, such as me–not-me, inside outside, body–psyche.

Given the nature of the object relation and the anxieties involved, interpretations may have, for long periods of time, the paradoxical status of being uttered from a position of a subjective object, that is, of an object not fully recognized as external to the subject, but which is also the carrier of ego functioning. In Cristina's case her mother's intrusion of high anxiety, critical and demanding behaviour, and father's violence, threatened to overwhelm her and prevented the establishment of a skin–ego that could perform a protective function and restore ruptures in the holding environment. Eventually, Cristina was able to have free and satisfying intercourse with her boyfriend. This was followed by a dream of her hymen being perforated, which led to further understanding of the Sellotape dream and the underlying anxieties about passivity, penetration and loss of anal mastery enacted during a session of silent retention following explosions of anger expressed in excessive weeping.

In Chapter 10 Joan Schächter shares Grieve's starting point that "the ego is first and foremost a bodily ego" (Freud 1923). Although Grieve's 16-year-old female patient's symptom of vaginismus was enacted in interaction with her boyfriend's body, it was the body of Schächter's 22-year-old borderline patient Conrad that became "a battlefield". While the conflict for Cristina occurred in an interpersonal dimension, Conrad's conflict was between a split-off aspect of himself and his body. He attacked his body in three suicide attempts, was hospitalized after one attempt and again before a holiday break from analysis. Prior to his first suicide attempt Conrad felt acutely self-conscious and could only silence the voices of his parents who he thought were living inside his head by killing his mind.

Introduction

In his analysis there was a strong regressive pull into the mother, which led to anxieties in the transference of being taken over by his analyst and need for physical reassurance regarding his castration fears by visiting the toilet before and after each session. Schächter represented this dynamic in her mind by thinking of Heine's poem "The Lorelei" about a small boatman who is so transfixed by a beautiful golden-haired woman singing a siren song high on a cliff that his boat crashes on the rocks below and he drowns. In Conrad's case he is aware that sexual excitement for his analyst, the incestuous object, would lead to a deadly entrapment. Schächter's countertransference attunement to the physical danger Conrad felt himself to be in led her to fantasize that he had brought a knife to the session to stab her. Conrad had talked about his fantasies of knifing his parents as a justifiable homicide of a mother who had murdered his liveliness and masculinity.

The analysts' body may be vulnerable with patients whose severe anxieties leave them feeling that their lives are at risk with a threatening transference object. The analyst's physical vulnerability with their patients featured in the analyses reported by Caparrotta, who was drawn into a hypnotic–somnolent state of mind, Campbell, who felt physically threatened when his patient hit his fist into the palm of his hand in front of Campbell's face, and Schächter who felt physically vulnerable to her patient's homicidal impulses, when she thought he was going to stab her. All three analysts understood their physical reactions as the result of projections of their patient's aggressive states of mind. Specifically, Schächter's use of her physical reaction was crucial to understanding Conrad's response to leaving her a telephone message on a Thursday evening that Schächter did not respond to. She had a sense that Conrad would be enraged. When he went to the toilet as usual before his session on Friday, she heard a click and thought he had brought a knife to stab her. This may have been a communication between the patient's unconscious and the analyst's unconscious.

Each analyst refers to the impact that puberty has on their patients' anxieties about their sexuality. Schächter's patient Conrad suffered from pre-Oedipal anxieties about engulfment by his mother, which were aroused by his growing genitality and the revival of Oedipal identifications and an increasingly eroticized transference. These anxieties were projected into the patient's body. Campbell's patient Stan, Caparrotta's patient Justin, and Conrad entertained and/or enacted suicidal fantasies in which the body was experienced as a split-off bad object that should be got rid of.

While Schächter's patient Conrad physically threatened others and himself, in Chapter 11 Donald Campbell's adolescent patient Stan actually assaulted another boy causing grievous bodily harm. This case study of a violent male adolescent traces the transformation of the defensive use of the body in violent acts to the use of the body to *illustrate* violence.

Bodies featured in Stan's growing up. His mother found it difficult to hold him. Stan's next youngest brother died shortly after his birth and his third brother was born with Down's Syndrome. Stan's father was physically violent and Stan fought him until his mid-adolescence. Stan's body was rejected and assaulted and used by Stan to defend against threats to his self-esteem and masculinity. Stan's violence was supported by his identifications with a concretely violent object, his father, and fictional destructive and omnipotent monsters, androids, and superheroes.

Stan felt that he had a special, intimate, intuitive relationship with his mother. However, there were consequences.

Stan's severe anxiety about being engulfed by women and castrated by men motivated Stan's violent behaviour. He developed the musculature to do damage to others with his aggression. He had a reputation as a "hard man" and was feared for his violence at school. On one occasion he beat another boy over the head with a hammer and served six months in prison.

Through the use of his therapy Stan was able to redirect his aggressive instincts and fantasies from self-preservative, ruthless violence to illustration, a socially acceptable sublimation of his aggression. Campbell draws attention to the integrating function of sublimation (Muller 1999), which is apparent in Stan's illustrations of violent assaults. Campbell refers to another source of sublimation that arises from what Meltzer (1987) describes as the aesthetic reciprocity between the mother and her child, which is the mutual impact of the interior quality of the mother's motherliness and the interiority of the child's babyness. In one drawing of blood and gore, severed limbs and slashed bodies, Stan drew a little boy who is integrated and self-contained, curious, untouched and not frightened. Stan's drawing of the calm observing little boy depicted his own capacity to use sublimation to process aggressive internal mayhem.

Sublimation may also serve to process disparate aspects of sexuality. In another set of drawings that were inspired by William Burroughs' *Naked Lunch* (1959) Stan drew a female phallus injecting a man's arm, which depicts his confusion about his psychic bisexuality.

Stan's sublimatory activity facilitated therapeutic work. As Campbell explains, work in Stan's psychotherapy "enabled enough lifting of the repression of incestuous phantasies and enough resolution of castration anxieties for the repressed infantile energy to be available to drive his graphic representation of his phantasies and anxieties. This is not to say that the sublimatory process of drawing was therapeutic in and of itself for Stan, but that his illustrations exposed unconscious preoccupations that could be interpreted and worked through, particularly those related to his mother's rejection of his body and his father's assaults on his body (p. 246).

A body that was damaged from birth features in Chapter 12. A congenital body defect dominated the life of Bernard Roberts' patient Peter since his birth. Roberts explores the consequences for ego development of a boy who was born with an enlarged tongue, a congenital non-malignant lymphatic tissue tumour of the tongue. The disfigurement was both internal and externally visible until surgery at age four. The disfigurement of the tongue continues to require surgery from time to time. During the seven-year analysis reported by Roberts, Peter continually expressed his lifelong grievance about his deformity, which, he believes, entitled him to hurt envied normal people who are in debt to him forever.

Roberts builds on the philosopher Brian O'Shaughnessy's observation that the ego cannot fully retreat into the mental realm devoid of contact with the physical body. "The mind looks to be irremediably infected with the body" (1980). Rene Spitz (1955) views the body ego as originating from sensory experiences inside the oral cavity. Like no other organ in the body the mouth is both an internal and external preceptor. Bonnard (1960) describes the tongue as the primal organizer of the self. The tongue's exquisite sensitivity and muscular control enables it to become the "rudder" of spatial awareness in the mouth, the explorer of internal and external objects, and the shaping of words.

The five times a week seven-year analysis was dominated by Roberts struggle with the countertransference. Roberts was traumatized and invaded by Peter's material. Roberts' mind often felt paralysed, confused, disgusted and full of pity. Peter's anger and helplessness about the intrusion into his body (surgeries on his tongue, suppositories inserted into his anus to reduce pain) was enacted with Roberts. Likewise, the chronic disappointment in the mother's eyes when she looked at her baby's disfigured face, and the father's rejection of Peter after the birth of his healthy brother when Peter was four years old was evoked in the sessions.

During his analysis and just before his twenty-first birthday Peter's brother was offered a place at university that had eluded Peter. Peter fled the pain of his depression and disability into a drug-fuelled manic, paranoid and delusional state reporting to Roberts that his HIV-positive girl friend injected him with her needle in the tongue and anus. Peter wandered the streets unkempt and smelly. He was admitted to hospital for ten days, and followed by an Early Intervention in Psychosis Service for three years.

Peter has made remarkable progress with Roberts during the seven years of analysis. For the first time he has a steady girlfriend, an active sex life, and a regular job. However, the traumas of his disfigured tongue and surgical interventions, which are on-going, have not been fully symbolized and continue to "inject the mind". As Roberts continues to work through the transference, Peter is increasingly able to use his analysis to repair his damaged ego.

Although the body of the patient and the analyst features in the 12 clinical studies described in *When the Body Speaks*, each patient and analyst is different. The reader will learn that these differences contribute to how the analyst understands what the body of the patient is trying to say.

Note

1 This group of British and Italian psychoanalysts also included over the intervening years Italian colleagues Giuseppina Antinucci, Benedetta Guerrini Degl'Innocenti, Riccardo Lombardi, Sergio Molinari (now deceased), Barbara Piovano, Cristiano Rocchi, Sarantis Thanopulos and recently welcomed Marco Monari, Cristina Saottini, Andrea Scardovi and Massimo Vigna Taglianti. British analysts who participated in the group included Sira Dermen, Giovanna Di Ceglie, Carlos Fishman, Patricia Grieve, Brian O'Neill, Bernard Roberts and Joan Schächter. Heather Wood and Deyra Courtney recently joined the group.

References

Anzieu, D. (1985) *The Skin Ego*. New Haven, CT: Yale University Press.

Bion, W.R. (1963) Gli elementi della psicoanalisi. Rome: Armando, 1983.

Bonnard, A. (1960) The primal significance of the tongue in normal and aberrant conditions. *The International Journal of Psychoanalysis*, 41: 301–307.

Bronstein, C. (2011) On psychosomatics: The search for meaning. *International Journal of Psychoanalysis*, 92 (1): 173–195.

Burroughs, W. (1959) *Naked Lunch*. London: Penguin Modern Classics (2015).

Campbell, D., Enckell, H. (2005) Metaphor and the violent act. *The International Journal of Psychoanalysis*, 86: 801–823.

Ferraro, F. (2010) Ascoltare il corpo. In *Esplorazioni dell'incoscio*. Volume della SPI Taormina.

Freud, S. (1915) Instincts and their vicissitudes. *S.E.*, 14.

Freud, S. (1923) The ego and the id. *S.E.*, 14.

Freud, S. (1926[1925]) Inhibition symptoms and anxiety. *S.E.*, 20.

Freud, S. (1933) Femininity. New introductory lectures on psychoanalysis. *S.E.*, 22 (pp. 112–135).

Freud, S. (1938) Some elementary lessons in psychoanalysis. *S.E.*, 23: 281–286. London: Hogarth Press, 1959.

Gaddini, E. (1969) On imitation. *The International Journal of Psychoanalysis*, 50: 475–484.

Gaddini E. (1985) La maschera e il cerchio. In *Scritti*. Milan: Cortina.

Gaddini, E. (1987) Notes on the mind–body question. *The International Journal of Psychoanalysis*, 68: 315–329.

Laplanche, J. (1987) *New Foundations for Psychoanalysis*. Cambridge, MA Oxford Blackwell, 1989.

McDougall, J. (1989) Teatri del corpo. Milan: Cortina, 1990.

Meltzer, D. (1987) On aesthetic reciprocity. *Journal of Child Psychotherapy*, 13 (2): 3–14.

Muller, J.P. (1999) Modes and functions of sublimation. *Annual of Psychoanalysis*, 26: 103–125.

O'Shaughnessy, B. (1980) *The Will*. Cambridge, UK: Cambridge University Press.

Spitz, R. (1955) The primal cavity: A contribution to the genesis of perception and its role for psychoanalytic theory. *The Psychoanalytic Study of the Child*, 10: 215–240.

Stern, D.N. (1985) *The Interpersonal World of the Infant: A View from Psychoanalysis and Developmental Psychology.* New York: Basic Books.

Winnicott, D.W. (1945) Primitive emotional development. *International Journal of Psychoanalysis*, 26: 137–143.

Winnicott, D.W. (1963) Case work and mental illness. . In *The Family and Individual Development* (1965). London: Hogarth Press.

Winnicott, D. W. (1969) Additional note on psycho-somatic illness. In Winnicott, C., Shepard, R., Davis, M. (eds), *Psychoanalytic Explorations.* Cambridge, MA: Harvard University Press, 1989.

1
TRACES OF THE EARLY RELATIONSHIP IN THE CORPUS OF FREUD'S WORK

A re-reading

Giuseppina Antinucci

INTRODUCTION

In my endeavour to elucidate the contemporary polarization between metapsychological and relational psychoanalysis, I think it expedient to re-read Freud's oeuvre, to seek evidence of the complexity of his theory of subjectivity, which encompasses the psyche-soma – drive vicissitudes – and extends to the domain of relationships and culture. I relate selected passages which articulate the infant's experience before words, when the modalities of early care are registered somatically. On close reading, the early object relationship that leaves traces on the psyche-soma appears to be there from the start in Freud's work: it is an object whose presence is a shadow that constitutes the flesh and blood of the theory. I define *work of re-reading* my search for the shadowy presences and anticipations of that object relationship.

This chapter introduces a publication that addresses the infant's early relational vicissitudes, as they are inscribed and leave permanent traces in the body, re-emerge in many aspects of life and are semantically reconstructed in the consulting room. I follow closely Freud's endeavour to find models to articulate the process of subjectivation in its somatic, intra-psychic and interpersonal dimensions. The focus is on the body, locus of the drives and borderland where the encounter with the other occurs.

A theory that addresses the subject, as s/he grapples with the meaning of their intra-psychic and interpersonal experiences, relies on multiple observational vertexes, only one of which can be employed at any one time, but this should not result in fragmentation or reification of the entire theoretical scaffolding (Semi, 2001). Freud himself takes pains to critique the objectifying medical discourse, its taxonomy and categorization of normalcy and degeneracy. Giving words to the speaking psyche-soma of the hysteric, Freud sets out to recover the polysemy of human expressions, which he turns into psychoanalytical discourse, and extends to anthropology, as he does in footnote 2 to the *Three Essays* (1905a, p. 139), where he quotes Bloch's studies of *inversion* in classical Greece, emphasizing the cultural meaning of homosexuality, previously classed as psychopathology. From *Studies on Hysteria* (1893) onward, Freud consistently exposed the philosophically and ethically questionable medical category of *degeneracy*, founded on a binary with sanity. Conversely, his interrogation concerned the double consciousness – *conscience second* – of the hysterical patients' presentation as body phenomena, which clamoured to be signified as semantics of human suffering, and translated into psychoanalytic discourse, relevant to think about the divided, de-centred subject, whose unconscious uncannily breaks the continuity of the self.

The choice of one observational vertex at any one time – the drives, external and/or internal object relationship, phylogenesis or culture – is inevitably partial, albeit a necessary expedient to throw light on one specific aspect of the subject's complexity. The metaphor of the shadow – I argue – is suggestive for its capacity to anticipate future developments whilst, at the same time, indicating the traces that demand further development. The word 'shadow' is rooted etymologically in the Latin *umbra* and recurs in the verb *adumbrate*, whose meanings are: to express in an indirect or veiled manner, to represent, to outline, to anticipate, at a temporal crossroad between past and future. Such *umbra* cannot be disarticulated from the image it is fused with, and which constitutes the flesh and blood of the body of theories. From the observation of the shadow, slowly emerges a form that catches the eye, the form of an object, and object-relationship; an object that has come and gone within the Freudian corpus, and whose arrival has been anticipated and foreshadowed since the early days of psychoanalysis. As an object of investigation it appears only intermittently in the manifest text, whilst also constituting a *fil rouge* running through Freud's thought, even when it signals only the implicit level of theory formation. My exposition will eschew conclusions, and will be limited to gathering fragments and suggestions from Freud's work, which need to be interrogated and inquired further.

EARLY PSYCHOANALYTIC DISCOURSE

I will begin with an early Freudian text to argue for the continuity of the remote past with the present of psychoanalysis, where tradition intersects innovative enquiry.

A passage from the section 'Thought and reality' of the posthumously published *Project* states:

> As regards judging, there is further to be remarked that its basis is obviously the presence of bodily experiences, sensations and motor images of one's own. So long as these are absent, the variable portion of the perceptual complex remains un-understood – that is, it can be reproduced but does not point a direction for further paths of thought. [...] The perception may correspond to an object–nucleus + a motor image. While one is perceiving the perception, one copies the movement oneself – that is, one innervates so strongly the motor image of one's own which is aroused towards coinciding [with the perception], that the movement is carried out. Hence one can speak of a perception having an *imitation-value*. Or the perception may arouse the mnemic image of a sensation of pain of one's own, so that one feels the corresponding unpleasure and repeats the appropriate defensive movement. Here we have the *sympathy-value* of a perception.
>
> (Freud, 1950[1895], p. 333)

Not an easy read, this cumbersome extract; the prose is convoluted, perhaps confusing, as it is written in an obsolete scientific language; nonetheless, it conveys Freud's intuition of the formation and encoding of primordial nuclei of experience through the coming together of sensations, feelings and thought within the context of a subject–object relationship, mediated by the perception of a form, reproduced through imitation. The modernity of the image of two entities whose relationship occurs at the borderland where to imitate the form of the other is to (ap) perceive the self, sympathetically (from the Greek sun-pathos: or suffering, or *feeling together with the other*), recalls Gaddini's (1969) concept of imitation, or Joseph Sandler's (1987) view of primary identification, not to mention the neuro-scientific discovery of mirror-neurons – which I can only mention, it being beyond the scope of this introduction. Freud's image is striking for its syncretism, which the later scientific investigation methodologically breaks apart, bringing into relief some strands at any one time, whilst others are momentarily overshadowed. One such strand points to free associations that re-establish the links in the chains of affect-laden memories.

Texts belonging to later models of the mind provide further traces of the early relationship, in places where the theory does not hold tightly, leaving gaps and openings for the work of re-reading to take place. I will remain focused on the object – of the relationship – which is intermittently glimpsed at, until it is finally revealed by a theory – as the writing of *Mourning and Melancholia* (1917) testifies. The closer the focus, the more the object reveals its being an aggregate of unconscious phantasies. The enigmatic maternal object is first external and only partially internally represented, whilst uncannily felt as fused with our flesh and bones. The object of libidinal, aggressive, and epistemological desires, if considered internal, is somewhat more knowable than any external object could possibly be; nevertheless it remains elusive and frustrating, by virtue of its fundamental otherness. Resorting to our metaphorizing capacities, we may imaginatively come closer to the elusive object that lives like an uncanny stranger in our internal world, and only occasionally emerges in the unconscious epiphanies of the signifying subject.

The reward of re-reading Freud is further evidenced by the contemporary research into the absence of registration of early traumatic experiences, which demands of our technique to provide the conditions to initiate the process of subjectivation, through the psychic work of figurability (Cesar and Sara Botella, 2001), or re-presentation (Scarfone, 2006). Other psychoanalytic thinkers inquire into the origin of psychic life, at the border between the somatic and the psychic, around the empty space where experiences have never reached representation, and drives and affects are in excess of the binding function of thought, or, when psychic registration has occurred, this is at the level of the body and the opaqueness of the somatic presentation. This is the pre-symbolic register – where words are close to thing-presentation, affects and imagery – which emerges in the analytic space as the psychic domain where transference and countertransference function together to activate a mode of thinking close to dreaming.

The enigmatic presence of the body in today's clinic takes us back to pre-psychoanalytic practice, when it was excessively visible, as shown in the theatre of the hysteric, photo-graphically inscribed in the history of the Salpêtrière, while Charcot demonstrated the mental malaise ensconced within. The hysteric's body was there to be seen by all, touched by doctors who applied the pressure technique on the contracture of the paralyzed limb, to bring about a hysterogenic attack.[1] Likewise Freud experimented with the pressure technique to relax the patient and enlist her cooperation, so as to access the unconscious conflict underlying her illness. These historical references legitimize the hypothesis that the hysteric induced in the physician's psycho-somatic subjectivity multi-sensorial excitations which were progressively deposited, and contained, to finally coalesce into the provision of the psychoanalytic setting.

The view that unconscious conflicts underlie somatic symptomatology and the body preserves the memory of the (seductive) relationship, where sexuality functions as the marker of the difference between organic illness and psychological malaise, was there from the start, to demand clinical and theoretical listening, and the framing metapsychological apparatus was to follow. However, the relationship between the seducer and the analysed remains theoretically off-screen, leaving centre stage the body and its pathological excesses, in quest of signification. This is the madness of the origin of the human subject, expressed in the language of passion (Green, 1980). The archaic subject–object relationship, affectively overcharged, will gain momentum on the theatre of the transference and countertransference, where the patient's intra-psychic structures are played out in the inter-subjective encounter with the analyst.

Likewise Freud's trauma model advocates an excess of the real body of the seducer, which subsequently gives way to the imaginary of the infantile internal world, oedipal and pre-oedipal wishes, phantasies and objects. But the shadow of the original seducer haunts the theory, so much so that the place of that incestuous relationship is never quite settled, although Freud regards the body only as the location of the drives in his metapsychology, whilst in the consulting room the sensorial contact between patient and analyst recedes towards the symbolic domain – and that of the theory of transference and countertransference.

DORA: THE BODY OF THE TOPOGRAPHICAL MODEL

In the back and forth movements across time and frames of reference in Freud's corpus, one enigmatic character seems to compound the nurturing and the sexual relationship to the breast, epitome of the maternal erotics: this is Dora's governess. Freud's narrative is replete with sick bodies and their vicissitudes, which struggle to find systematization within the topographical model, between the conceptualization of infantile sexuality and that of the transference repetition. He acknowledges his predicament, when he writes in *An Autobiographical Study*:

> [T]he impressions of that early period of life, though they were for the most part buried in amnesia, left ineradicable traces upon the individual's growth ... but, since these experiences of childhood were always concerned with sexual excitations and the reaction against them, I found myself faced by the fact of *infantile sexuality*. [...] Under the influence of the technical procedure which I used at that time, the majority of my patients reproduced from their childhood scenes in which they were sexually seduced by some grown-up person. With female patients the part of the seducer was almost always assigned to their father. [...] When I was at last obliged to recognize that these scenes of seduction had never taken place, and that they were only phantasies which my patients had made up or which *I myself had perhaps forced upon them* (my italics), I was for sometime completely at a loss.
>
> (1925, pp. 33–34)

Freud's self-analytical *a posteriori* signification shows the psychoanalyst ill at ease with the impressions and the ineradicable traces of the "dark continent" of the original matrix, resorting to forceful interventions: he forces himself and his theory onto the patient, to validate his theory of infantile sexuality, posited as a *scientific fact*. The reader witnesses the unobjectionable scientific fact – and mind

– at work, obscuring the *objectionable* therapeutic pressure technique waived into the transference–countertransference *seduction*.

Freud does not listen with open mind to what Dora says about the governess, an important character who makes but sporadic and tantalizing appearances in the text. This is remarkable, especially as Freud identifies with her, when Dora breaks off the analysis, giving two weeks' notice, which was customary with a servant. To draw the clinical picture of Dora, who presents with a list of somatic complaints, such as *tussis nervosa*, sensations of disgust and loss of appetite – all inscribed in the semantics of orality – Freud seems to search for theoretical coordinates. Yet he appears disingenuous when, in his autobiography, he acknowledges how he straddles between two models: no longer believing in the trauma theory, he had not fully discarded it, for the topographical model. 'If the trauma theory is not to be abandoned, we must go back to her childhood and look about there for any influences or impressions which might have had an effect analogous to that of a trauma' (1905b, p. 27). But he can only go back to Dora's adolescence and consider traumatogenic the event in Herr K.'s office, when the man pressed his lips forcefully against hers. However, eluding the theoretical constraints, early experiences surreptitiously appear in the references to the persistence of sensual sucking, residual oral fixation. Dora recalls scenes from her childhood, when she sat on the floor in a corner, sucking her left thumb, and tugging at her brother's earlobe with her right hand. This evokes a vivid sensory memory of the baby holding between her lips the nipple of the nurse's right breast, while exploring another part of her body with her free hand! Freud does not hesitate to define this autoerotic activity as a 'complete form of self-gratification by sucking' and, to further his argument, he mentions another case that 'could shed a clear light on the origin of this curious habit' (p. 52). The patient is a young woman who could not renounce thumb-sucking, and reported a memory from the first half of her second year, in which 'she saw herself sucking at her nurse's breast and at the same time pulling rhythmically at the lobe of her nurse's ear' (p. 52).

There are shadows of early objects and sensual nursing relationships that leave somatic traces everywhere, in this poignant narrative. Freud, however, repeatedly distances himself from this crucial point, when he adheres to a pre-ordained theory, or quotes in Latin the Early Christian Fathers' description of the origin of life: '*inter urinas et faeces nascimur*', and these products of a woman's body, the mother's body, in fact, 'cling to sexual life and cannot be detached from it, in spite of every effort at idealization' (1905b, p. 31). Freud's effort to elevate the affect of disgust to the status of a concept (idealization) appears strenuous, whereas what sticks to his writing is the shadow of a carnal relationship that, at this stage, is tantamount to getting too close to the vertiginous site of the real (thing-presentation), with its horror, and excesses of incestuous passions, which are scotomized by abstract thought.

Freud catches himself oscillating between theoretical frameworks, whilst Dora oscillates between different objects of desire – male and female, mother and father – but he seems unable to see that she is perturbed by her governess to the point of wanting her dismissal. The reader learns that the governess used to read sexual books to Dora, binding the little girl to her, in a secretive relationship that excluded the father. Freud does not heed this, but the clinical account succeeds only partially in scotomizing the forbidden sexuality of the relationship with the nurse; in another passage he focuses on the autoerotic traces of early sucking, disjoining it from the relationship with the nurse's body. The theory cannot embrace the quality of the maternal handling of the infant's body, whilst this archaic embrace leaves traces that Freud disputes, when Dora articulates them. He dismissively states that the girl must have recalled her governess' seduction, when she was barely a nursling. Not the infant, retorts Freud, but her father, was the object of the governess' desire, thereby denying the sensuous pleasures the early relationship entails for both members of the couple. Excess of pleasure, which eludes the incest prohibition, as the governess was not the mother! Dora's mother is hastily dismissed as an obsessional, frigid, denying and self-denying housewife. Conversely, the sensual aspects are preserved, but under the heading of autoeroticism, a pivotal if ambiguous concept: in this work it obliterates the object-other-than-the-self, whilst also indicating psychic phenomena belonging to experiences prior to self-object differentiation.

AUTOEROTICISM: *FIL ROUGE*

An attentive examination of autoeroticism reveals its essential link with the unconscious phantasy of the early bond: autoeroticism – claims Freud – needs the addition of some psychic work to exit the domain of pure self-captivation and become narcissism. But who, if not the mother, with her loving care, can provide the additional psychic work, initially aimed at supporting the immature ego? As Freud remarks in *On Narcissism* (1914), treating one's body as the object of someone else's desire, unconsciously recalls the archaic relationship with the mother, where the unconscious phantasy – constitutive of the subject's desire – is adumbrated as the container of a secret passion ensconced within the self. The unconscious phantasy will be conceptualized later; at this stage infantile autoeroticism, coupled with the omnipotent phantasy of being a self-sufficient nutritional entity, contains the anticipation of the theoretical object, whose amorous gaze marks the libidinal body.

The Freudian primacy of the oedipal structure was to last until 1933, when the publication of *Femininity* initiated the inquiry into the pre-oedipal attachments and passions – which he compared to the Mycenean civilization underlying the Greek – with the momentous acknowledgement that his patients' seduction phantasies concerned their mothers, who were the original seducers. The ambience of maternal potency is conveyed almost like an emotional and theoretical surrender by the father of psychoanalysis, whose recommendation is to turn to the poets' greater understanding, in order to fill the gap beyond the reach of theory, and language.

Let's return to Dora: Freud's impasse with his hysterics had led to the emphasis on psychical reality, its unconscious determinants and repression, to arrive at the momentous formulation of the topographical model and the instituting of free associations. Yet the original seduction theory leaves enduring traces which are the marker of the construction of the subject's desire. These traces sowed the seeds of further developments: it suffices to mention Ferenczi's seminal 'Confusion of tongues between adults and child' (1933) and Laplanche's theory of general seduction that proposes the enigmatic sexual message as foundational: an anthropological ontology (1997). Furthermore, the passage of Freud's autobiography might spur *après coup* reflection on his unconscious contribution in staging a technical seduction in the analytic room, through the pressure technique, consisting in applying hand pressure on the patient's forehead, while asking penetrating questions. Could this be an enactment of the primal phantasy of seduction, with the attendant hypothesis that the analysand developed the transference disturbance to psychically comply with the countertransference disturbance of the analyst?

The erotic charge of the scene is more thinkable if the seducer is the father, carrier of the symbolic relationship, rather than the omnipotent mother, representative of the carnal bond, with echoes of fusional, homosexual phantasies for patients of both sexes, whose bodies reclining on the couch the analyst touches. Free association and abstinence institute the fundamental rule and the ethics of prohibition of eroticized touch. Are these some of the ineradicable traces which Freud intuited, but diverted towards the path of infantile sexuality, which provided a paternal, phallic handling of symbolic matters, far removed from the excesses of passions and original body matters that cling to the sexual body in too concrete a manner, like the urine and faeces in which we are born (Freud, 1905b). This is the realm of the maternal that Freud, identifying with Goethe, qualifies as dark and mysteriously beyond the representational register.

THE TOPOGRAPHICAL MODEL

If differentiating self-preservative instincts from sexual drives provides a provisional answer to the metapsychological questions posed by the drive theory, especially if narcissism is considered, what remains unanswered is how primary care, inscribed in the somatic sensations constituting the sensorial envelope, forms the core of the subject's erotic idiom. The de-sexualized object of the self-preservative instincts features merely as the object of the drives, at the time when the infant's primitive anxiety has already been transformed by the mother, who is now well represented and libidinally invested. Focusing, however, on the rich texture of this object, its contours and presence are strikingly connoted by the calm sensuousness that characterizes the psycho-somatic narcissistic well-being and is foundational for the advent of sexuality. The pre-oedipal mother clamours to be embodied in the theory, whereas what Freud proposes is the *constancy principle*, borrowed from Fechner, but employed defensively to scotomize the woman who guarantees that very narcissistic homeostasis.

Instincts and their Vicissitudes distinguishes an external stimulus from an instinct, which, unlike the former, is perceived as a constant internal impingement: a need demanding 'adequate satisfaction'. Freud invites the reader to imagine a 'helpless living organism as yet un-orientated in the world, which is receiving stimuli in its nervous substance' (1915, p. 119), but swiftly the evocation of a mother holding, gazing and satisfying the needs of the *helpless organism* gives way to the language of muscular activity, which permits the elated infant to move away from the object s/he so utterly depends on. This theoretically ambiguous position could well betray the underlying slow shift from the seductive Oedipal father of the trauma model to the – not less traumatizing – pre-oedipal mother of the papers on femininity, written between 1931 and 1933. After all, the sexual adult – mother or father – always carries a traumatizing potential for the *helpless organism* and the infantile psyche.

Freud now chooses the perspective of the infant, described from within his illusion, which he ascribes to omnipotent nutritional self-sufficiency, in an extraordinary imaginative rendering of the infantile subjective world. The discourse of the drive model addresses the infant's experiences – both intrapsychic and interpersonal – where the other of the relationship has a definite presence, albeit lacking a conceptual status. But this is not the whole story. The self-preservative instincts, in fact, also known as ego-instincts, together with the ego, the body and its surface, are brought into the picture, and situated at the border between inside and outside, between the subject and the object. Thus the sensory remnants of the skin-to-skin delights, echoing the sensuous sucking of Dora's account, *adumbrate* the object, in the location of the registration of the early relationship.

Another passage of the text reads: 'There is nothing to prevent our supposing that the instincts themselves are, at least in part, precipitates of the effects of external stimulation' (1915, p. 120), revealing again the shadow of the primary relationship that stimulates sensuous responses to body care, thereby claiming the infant to instinctual life and leaving traces, or *precipitates*. In spite of his fascination with origins, Freud recoils from investigating the pre-symbolic registration of maternal care, attributing it rather to a mythical phylogenesis – a concept that belongs to the complemental series, alongside ontogenesis – but in this context provides a speculative solution to the question of the baby's helpless subjection to the (m)other, merged with nature. Interspersed here and there in the text, lurk the infant's physical pain that does not settle, her hunger that is not satiated, so the object returns as the object of the self-preservative instincts. What has been said so far solicits the question as to whether the primary relationship provides tender care, and/or a seduction to life and pleasure, intermingled with terrors and enigmas. Nurturing carries additional value at a price, and infants are exposed to a (m)other who reverses love and hatred onto them, when they inhabit her body and then her psyche. Mother and infant are merged in an intimate relationship which is – Winnicott (1951) maintains – paradoxically entirely physical and entirely psychological: a body within a body, preserved in the psyche within the psychic vicissitudes of the internal world. Body and mind appear once again embedded in the earliest relationship, which must be renounced and mourned but always leaves traces and shadows. At the heart of the Freudian opus is the complex struggle of the subject – and the theory – to find and re-find the primary object, whose demise is never complete.

MOURNING THE LOSS

Published between 1914 and 1917, the seminal metapsychological papers systematize the topographical model, whose evident inconsistencies and aporias will eventually strain it. Amongst the themes addressed are the dialectics of the body-of-needs, and the body-of-desire, equally demanding an object of satisfaction. Arousal of need, construction of desire, and object–relation follow a trajectory with its specific characteristics and destiny, examined in the construction of the internal world of *Mourning and Melancholia* (1917). This work marks a transition towards the darker structural model: the metaphorical underworld of a descriptively vaster domain of unconscious phenomena and conflicts between psychic agencies.

Strachey helpfully suggests we read *Mourning and Melancholia* as a companion piece and extension of the work *On Narcissism*, which aids our search for the object in the folds of the self. Freud writes:

> The patient knows *whom* he has lost, but not *what* he has lost in him. This would suggest that melancholia is in some way related to an object-loss which is withdrawn from consciousness, in contradiction to mourning, in which there is nothing about the loss that is unconscious.
> (*Mourning and Melancholia*, 1917, p. 245)

This loss is felt to be a narcissistic injury, so much so that it can compromise the integrity of the body-self, identified with the lost object, and unconsciously affecting the somatic continuity – a shadow falling upon the body-ego.

Going further back, we find an underlying *fil rouge* in *Draft G* on melancholia of the Fliess papers:

> a) the affect corresponding to melancholia is that of mourning – that is longing for something lost. Thus in melancholia it must be a question of a loss – a loss in *instinctua*l life. b) the nutritional neurosis parallel to melancholia is anorexia. The famous *anorexia nervosa* of young girls seems to me (on careful observation) to be a melancholia where sexuality is undeveloped. The patient asserted that she had not eaten, simply because she had *no appetite*, and for no other reason. Loss of appetite – in sexual terms, loss of libido.
> (Draft G, 1895, p. 200)

This lucid passage adumbrates the effects and affects which account for the failure of sexuality to intervene and reclaim the body to the instinctual life of the subject, owing to their entrapment in the encrypted identification with the lost object.

In note 4 to *Two principles of mental functioning* where Freud writes about the 'nutritional autism' contained in the narcissistic enclosure organized to be enslaved to the pleasure principle, he employs the metaphor of 'a bird's egg with its food supply enclosed in its shell' (1911, p. 220). This organization is a judicious theoretical fiction, 'justified when one considers that the infant – provided one includes with it the care it receives from its mother – does almost realize a psychical system of this kind' (ibid.). Thus the object makes its appearance, captured in its developmental *function* of providing support to the infant's illusion of self-sufficiency: nutritional and erotic object at once, it is there from the start, and is destined to be lost before it can find a theoretical place as the object of the drives.

In development – and in the theory – the object acquires autonomous status when it reveals the workings of the drives, whilst the self-captivation of the 'autistic nutritional organization' preserves its secrets, until the manifestations of the derivatives of the unconscious phantasy can emerge. However, if the unconscious phantasy is at work even in apparently objectless states, and permeates the autoerotic domain, it is at the point of autoerotic activation that the secret shadowy object can be located. This object has been woven into the texture of the subject's body-self, its flesh, bones, and blood. Autoeroticism thus becomes the screen and the boundary where the subject unconsciously appropriates that very infantile body which was the object of the mother's loving care, what Helen Parat calls maternal erotics (1999).

OBJECT OF NEEDS, OBJECT OF DRIVES

In the concept of *nutritional autism*, the object of the self-preservative drives vanishes anew. Following the appearance and disappearance of the object in its function of providing narcissistic well-being, food, stimuli and sensuous experiences, we can see the problematic issues it carries, because it can no longer be desexualized and held to be subservient to sheer survival, hence the nutritional autistic illusion comes close to autoeroticism, with its shadow of the object. Could we then hypothetically regard this disarticulation of the object as a theoretically defensive disassembling of an all-providing early object, which persists as a set of somatic sensations and memories that flow into the unconscious phantasy of the autoerotic (re)finding of the object fused within the self, its flesh and bones? In other words, in psychoanalysis maternal love cannot be disjoined from the erotics of corporeality, as Freud will finally acknowledge in *An Outline of Psychoanalysis*:

> This first object is later completed into the person of the child's mother, who not only nourishes it but also looks after it, thus arousing in it a number of other sensations, pleasurable and unpleasurable. By her care of the child's body, she becomes its first seducer.
>
> (1938, p. 198)

Traversing times and models, in search of the shadow of the object, I suggest pausing on the incipit of *On Narcissism*:

> The term narcissism is derived from clinical description and was chosen by Paul Nacke in 1899 to denote the attitude of a person who treats his own body in the same way in which the body of a sexual object is ordinarily treated.
>
> (1914, p. 73)

Manifestly these narratives regard the self: but if the self-love is situated within the autistic shell, we find a subject fused with the shadow of the object, and the body-as-object becomes the locus of the incorporation of the (m)other, and her loving gaze. Necessary corollary of this affirmation is the interrogation of the differentiation of narcissistic from anaclitic object choice: after all, the subject who 'treats his own body in the same way in which the body of a sexual object is treated', does not know whether his unconscious phantasy might reveal incestuous passions. The triangular structure is maintained, yet the father of the theory of narcissism is external to the mother–infant couple, leaving the early, pre-oedipal predicaments to the paradox of the highly charged body melancholically full of the incestuous scent and touch of the (m)other. It is a predicament to be worked through by the theory and by the subject, if s/he is to find an object to love.

Tracking down the ineradicable traces of the object to signal its intermittent presence and disappearance, one is immersed in a foggy world, where the object's contours are blurred. Only when we arrive at the structural model can we finally see the ego as a metaphorical underworld, the precipitate of object relationships, identifications, feelings, sensations and perceptions, which are all in particles, and fragments. Those primordial, 'elementary sensations [...] are multilocular, like external perceptions; [...] may come from different places simultaneously and may thus have different or even opposite qualities' (1923, p. 22). It is a world of confusion and discord, of shadows, revenants, mystery; it resembles the Faustian world of mothers, who reclaim their due, whilst Freud the man of the Enlightenment had previously tried to conquer chaos by his penetrating scientific logos, and attempted to put into words the mysteries of the unconscious and its manifestation through the sufferings of the psyche-soma.

ASSOCIATIONS TO THE CENSOR'S CUTS

In a footnote to Freud's often-quoted statement: 'There is much more continuity between intra-uterine life and earliest infancy than the impressive caesura of the act of birth would have us believe' (1926, p. 138), Strachey makes the following suggestively intriguing remark: ['*Caesur*'. In the 1926 German edition only, this was misprinted '*Censur* (censorship)'. The word 'caesura' is a term derived from classical prosody, and indicates a particular kind of break in a line of verse.] (p. 138). Freely associating around the semantic area of the pre-oedipal traces in language, evinced by its prosody and poetic components, such plenitude is at variance with the acquisition of language: another loss or caesura which, like birth, introduces the infant to the paternal, symbolic cultural world. Likewise the structural model represents a break with the first topography, partly prompted by the necessity to adequately formulate the concept of the internal censor – which had been a feature since the early days of the *Studies* – now formalized as superego. In the structural model, inaugurated by *The Ego and the Id* (1923), together with the new formulation of anxiety – as outlined in *Inhibition Symptoms and Anxiety* (1926) and whose main function, is to signal a danger – a new theoretical position is also allocated to affects, and to the body. It is perhaps the same sensuous body that underlays a mode of functioning where the word has a carnal resonance, and that reappears in the prosodic aspects of language as the embodied word. This sonorous halo of language is the domain accessed by the poet, who can tear away the symbolic level, to delve into the depth of language, in close contact with the sensorial ambience created by words. Even though the *censor* demands a symbolic scientific language, the text of *Inhibition, Symptoms and Anxiety* preserves its capacity to evoke a maternal ambience, while also spelling out the primacy of object relationships. Nonetheless, the drives are still there, with the corollary of needing to find and re-find a theoretical systematization that is never completely satisfactory and is forever shifting. All the same, what remains rooted and embodied in the theory is that from now on, *drives* and *affects* are conceptualized as *psycho-somatic states* aiming at communicating with the mother. The father – and censor – is contained within the scientific language and, momentarily leaving aside the symbolic domain, Freud can now concentrate on the most archaic levels of experience, whilst also signalling the difficulties of holding in mind and representing the scientific primal scene with all its characters on stage simultaneously. One of the characters is always missing from the theoretical scene.

Aware of the shortcomings of the earlier model which viewed anxiety as a creation of repression, hence a by-product of the conflict with the external reality, Freud now puts forward a new frame of reference which opens up the question of the internal sources of anxiety. He writes:

> If we go further and inquire into the origin of that anxiety – and of affects in general – we shall be leaving the realm of pure psychology and entering the borderland of physiology.

> Affective states have become incorporated (in other words, have been located in the *mental configuration of the body* [my italics]) in the mind as precipitates of primaeval traumatic experiences, and when a similar situation occurs they are revived like mnemic symbols.
>
> (1926, p. 93)

The term mnemic symbols – as Strachey emphasizes in a footnote – recurs in *Studies on Hysteria* (1893), to explain hysterical symptoms (see note 1). This passage may be regarded as a tentative indication of the permanence of early relational vicissitudes as affective memories *in* and *on* the body. Together with the somatic mnemic traces, the shadow of the traumatizing object returns to the theoretical stage, as a seducer, who no longer appears to be the father, but the mother. The primary object of *Inhibitions, Symptoms and Anxiety* is, in fact, a mother who gives birth, provides early care and containment. She is connoted by words like 'innate hysterical attacks', 'objective', 'phylogenetic', words signifying the emergence of a substratum, a bedrock, construed as the domain beyond representation, hence within the realm of the not-yet-represented, psycho-somatic contents not reached by images or word-presentation. Between the two domains there is a hiatus.

In *Inhibition* Freud proposes that birth is the baby's first exposure to anxiety, and becomes the prototype of all life experiences and events that we anticipate and construe as dangers, which arouse the signal of anxiety: '*objectively* (my italics) speaking, birth is a separation from the mother. It could be compared to a castration of the mother' (1926, p. 130). What is implied, here, is Freud's reference to the psychosexual development of the woman, based on the equation of the baby with the penis, hence birth represents castration: a multilayered loss the mother experiences narcissistically and somatically, as well as the loss of the baby inside. But separation is a relational event which involves a loss for both parties, at whatever level that loss and the ensuing anxiety might be experienced. Could the idea that exclusively the mother feels the pain contain the awareness that the chaotic experience of the infant still lacks a theoretical discourse at this stage? It will fall to Freud's successors to develop a theory of primitive infantile states and maternal functions. Here, however, Freud intuits it, but his recourse to the adverb *objectively* seems to serve the function of silencing all scientific objections, while also silencing the screams and primitive agonies of infants in arms who need loving holding, together with the life-preservative feeding.

A dual perspective points to the baby's narcissistic enclosure, on one hand and, on the other, to the mother's vital function of lending her own containing and transformational capacity to the infant to support the illusion of narcissistic completeness. The mother is there to give the timely, welcome, warm milk and the additional pleasure and reassurance of somato-psychic fulfilment, to support the omnipotent illusion to be enjoyed together with her baby. Freud oscillates between the infant's subjective perspective and the objective scientific one and opts for the former when he maintains that the baby only experiences affects arising from the *negative economy of the drives*, because the object lacks psychic existence. This problematic statement concerns solely the object of *representation*, whereas, initially, the object is libidinally invested, *known* through sensations and the perception of touch and sight, namely *infantile bodily events* involving skin and eyes that capture a form to be perceived while being imitated. Freud himself contradictorily demonstrates that

> A person's own body, and above all its surface, is a place from which both external and internal perceptions may spring. It is *seen* like any other objects, but to the *touch* it yields two kinds of sensations, one of which may be equivalent to an internal perception.
> (1923, p. 25)

Anxiety and loss are felt by the mature maternal ego – Freud posits – nonetheless, the concept of anxiety, as a response to danger, is unsettled by internal questions, as the following passages indicate. 'But what is a "danger"? In the act of birth there is a real danger to life. We know what it means objectively; but in a psychological sense it says nothing at all to us. The danger of birth has as yet no psychical content' (1926, p. 135), because the helpless infant is affected only by a disturbance in the narcissistic homeostasis, the regulation of which is but another maternal function! Freud-the-scientist laments the scarce knowledge of the mental make-up of the newborn; therefore his hypothesis that all later anxieties recall that primary object loss appears tentative and inadequately grounded. However, just a few lines above, he describes in economic terms the incremental acquisition of libidinal significance of a certain bodily part, seemingly the mouth, because that organ, by virtue of augmented libidinal investment, *foreshadows* object cathexis. Thus the mouth becomes the prototypical organ that organizes the mouth/breast relationship, and registers the opening and closing of the self to the object world; hence a body part is construed as the specific locus of psychic transformation: from sensory perception to the organization of representation. In this instance the shadow anticipates, that is, adumbrates the object-to-come.

The shadow of the object comes and goes. I would argue that what appears and disappears from *Inhibitions, Symptoms and Anxiety* – and the entire Freudian corpus – is the object relationship at the origin of life, which is implicitly there from the start, in the theory, but can be put in sharp focus only intermittently, when it becomes the object of representation. Otherwise the early object fades into the various givens of biology, objective reality or phylogenesis, i.e., the structural invariants, or the domain of the unthinkable, where even the all too present affect of anxiety becomes meaningless, when it is defined as a *universal, innate, hysterical attack*, which brings back the mnestic residue of the hysterical body of the woman/mother of the origin. This is a figure of the unconscious that condenses biological and psychological bedrocks.

The caesura of birth is compensated by the psychological extrauterine symbiosis, and bodily intimacy returns in breast-feeding, whose sensual intensity is reciprocal and, from the baby's vertex, it is halfway between foetal absorption of food through the umbilical cord and mastication. The philosopher Nancy (2011) observes that the infant's mouth adheres to the breast and, by actively exerting pressure on the nipple, makes the milk flow; mouth and breast are indistinguishably foundational to the psycho-somatic infantile phantasy 'I am the breast', as a quintessentially carnal experience which leaves marks on the body. A complex task – Nancy adds – to try and know, or imagine, how from that original symbiosis the ego slowly emerges, in what he calls *disbiosis*, a process whereby

> I begin to exist apart from the other body – this is how I myself am a body – and this progressive detachment makes itself felt as such. My own existence is separate, but I am separate inasmuch as I am bonded and related to an external world from which I find myself severed.
>
> (Nancy, 2011, p. 25, my translation from Italian)

Corollary of disbiosis is disidentification, but the former articulates specifically the somatic and its exquisite sensoriality. Likewise Freud employs the language of sensoriality in the footnote to the famous statement 'the ego is first and foremost a bodily ego' (1923, p. 26), which appears only in the English translation of 1927 and reads:

> [the ego is ultimately derived from bodily sensations, chiefly from those springing from the surface of the body. It may thus be regarded as a mental projection of the surface of the body, besides, as we have seen above, representing the superficies of the mental apparatus]
>
> (p. 26)

This passage addresses the psychic work involved in the same constitutive experiences Nancy describes with his subjective, impressionistic language. Complementary languages and complementary perspectives are required for the paradoxical relationship of the infant with the mother, wholly physical and wholly psychological.

FEMININITY: THE UNDERWORLD

Finally, I propose re-reading *Femininity* (1933), a descent to the Underworld of mothers, predicated on Freud's dialogue with Goethe, who epitomizes the poets called upon – like Perseus' armour – to confront Mother-Medusa's awesome head. In the lecture's closing remarks, Freud candidly acknowledges feeling out of his depth, conscious of having made fragmentary observations about femininity, and of sounding quite unfriendly at that! The sword he had employed to assail the fortress of femininity had been the theoretical reduction of women to nature, due to their sexual function. This weapon now proves to be unserviceable and Freud surrenders: 'If you want to know more about femininity, enquire from your own experiences of life, or turn to the poets, or wait until science can give you deeper and more coherent information' (1933, p. 135).

Doesn't one's own 'experience of life' imply the return to the indelible traces of mystery and the unknown, bearing uncertainty and emptiness, rather than anxiously reaching for theoretical conclusions, or needing to confirm infantile sexual theories, as with Dora? Another serviceable tool might be the recourse to poets, identifying with their use of language, close to its sensory aspects, which recreate a sound envelope. Poetic language and the prosodic aspects of words capture and re-find the body-as-thing: words are imbued with somatically affective memories, on the way to being transformed into metaphors and symbolic structures.

Disarmed of his *idée fixe* of the primacy of the phallus, Freud feels of course defenceless, defeated by the ensnaring and alluring Medusa-like woman. He laments the impotence of his theoretical logos, and his own infantile helplessness in the face of a powerful incestuous mother, interwoven with the earliest anxieties defined as 'innate hysterical attacks', beyond the reach of theory and representation.

Another passage of *Femininity* shows Freud's intuition of the importance of the pre-oedipal phase. Recalling the transition from the trauma model to the topographical model, he writes:

> It was only later that I was able to recognize in this phantasy of being seduced by the father the expression of the typical Oedipus complex in women. And now we find the phantasy of seduction once more in the pre-Oedipus prehistory of girls; but the seducer is regularly the mother. Here, however, the phantasy touches the ground of reality, for it was really the mother who by her activities over the child's bodily hygiene inevitably stimulated, and perhaps even roused for the first time, pleasurable sensations in her genitals.
>
> (Freud, 1933, p. 120)

If this shift of object conveys an extraordinary intuition, an extraordinary blindness is manifest in his confining the importance of the prehistory inscribed in bodily care solely to girls, as though, after the demise of the phallus, a real penis should preserve the boy, the male, Freud-the-theoretician from the re-emerging of incestuous shadows, which will fall on other thinkers to investigate.

Note

1 All throughout his changing theoretical frameworks, Freud holds on to the notion of 'hysteric attack', a rather opaque concept, which – as I will show later – in the structural model will indicate the primitive anxiety that cannot be represented and signified as signal anxiety, but persists as a residue in the body, hysterically identified with the mother's body.

References

Botella, C., Botella, S. (2001) *The Work of Figurability*. London: The New Library of Psychoanalysis, 2005.

Ferenczi, S. (1933) Confusion of tongues between adults and the child. In *Final Contributions to the Problems and Methods of Psycho-Analysis*. London: Karnac Classics, 1994 (156–167).

Freud, S. (1950[1895]) Project for a scientific psychology. *S.E.*, 1.

Freud, S. (1893–1899) Studies on hysteria. *S.E.*, 2.

Freud, S. (1895) Draft G: Melancholia. Extracts from the Fliess Papers. *S.E.*, I, 202–206.

Freud, S. (1905a) Three essays on the theory of sexuality. *S.E.*, 7.

Freud, S. (1905b) Fragment of an analysis of a case of hysteria. *S.E.*, 7.

Freud, S. (1911) Formulations on the two principles of mental functioning. *S.E.*, 12 (213–226).

Freud, S. (1914) On narcissism. *S.E.*, 14.

Freud, S. (1915) Instincts and their vicissitudes. *S.E.*, 14.

Freud, S. (1917) Mourning and melancholia. *S.E.*, 14.

Freud, S. (1923) The ego and the id. *S.E.*, 19.

Freud, S. (1925[1924]) An autobiographical study. *S.E.*, 20.

Freud, S. (1926[1925]) Inhibition symptoms and anxiety. *S.E.*, 20.

Freud, S. (1933) Femininity. New introductory lectures on psycho-analysis. *S.E.*, 22 (112–135).

Freud, S. (1938) An outline of psycho-analysis. *S.E.*, 23.

Gaddini, E. (1969) On imitation. *International Journal of Psychoanalysis*, 50: 457–484.

Green, A. (1980) Passions and their vicissitudes. In *On Private Madness*. London: The Hogarth Press, 1986 (214–253).

Laplanche, J. (1997) The theory of seduction and the problem of the other. *International Journal of Psychoanalysis*, 78 (4): 653–666.

Nancy, J-L. (2011) *DHEL – la Nascita della Felicità*. Brescia: Massetti Rodelli.

Parat, H. (1999) *L'Erotico Materno*. Rome: Borla, 2000.

Sandler, J. (1987) *From Safety to Super-ego*. London: Karnac.

Scarfone, D. (2006) A matter of time. Actual time and the production of the past. *Psychoanalytic Quarterly*, 75 (3): 807–834.

Semi, A.A. (2001) *Introduzione alla Metapsicologia*. Milan: Raffaello Cortina.

Winnicott, D.W. (1951) Transitional objects and transitional phenomena. In *Through Paediatrics to Psycho-Analysis*. London: The Hogarth Press, 1982 (229–242).

2
THE "PSYCHOANALYTICAL" BODY AND ITS CLINICAL IMPLICATIONS

Sarantis Thanopulos

THE BODY OF DRIVES, AS THE SPONTANEOUS, SILENT BODY

What body is psychoanalysis speaking about?

Any attempt to relate the body, as natural science conceives it, to the psyche, as psychoanalysis conceives it (activity of representation of inner and external reality in terms of ideation plus affects), involves great difficulty. As much as these two dimensions are interconnected and we can imagine the existence of a continuity between them, the presence of an insurmountable discrepancy in cognitive terms is an unquestionable fact of the human condition.

Psychoanalysis is not exactly a humanist science: it cannot disembody or dematerialize its study object like philosophy, history and sociology can (within certain limits). Psychoanalysis, much more than anthropology, radicates the subjective experience in an a-social body (which is also a-philosophical and a-historical), free from any cultural and normative conditionings (notoriously based on the subjugating power of speech). The psychoanalytical body is neither the body studied by medicine or biology nor the body analysed by socio-cultural disciplines. An unquestionable fact in psychoanalysis is the hysterical body, the body that "speaks" in its own way. But the evidence of a "speaking" body leads to the following question: where does this body spring from?

To answer this question, Freud uses an elegant, simple epistemological device. The axiomatic assumption is the following: the primary source of every psychically fulfilling experience is a process of excitement that takes place in the body and that can be explained by medical physiology.[1] The bond between the psyche and the body (unknowable as it may be) lets somatic excitation act on the psyche, forcing it to meet the body demands in ways that medical physiology ignores. This specific *constraint* of the psyche is what Freud calls *drive*. It belongs to the psyche, because conforming the psychic activity to the somatic excitement it constitutes itself as an "innervation" of the psychic movement, but it also comes from the body – it actually represents the body's interests in the psychical field. In Freud's words (1915) it is the *psychical representative* of body stimuli:

> If now we apply ourselves to considering mental life from a biological point of view, a drive [trieb] appears to us as a *concept on the frontier between the psychic and the somatic*, as the psychical representative of the stimuli originating from *within the organism* and reaching the psyche as *a measure of the demand* made upon the psyche for work in consequence of its connection with the body.
> (pp. 121–122)

Drive is an epistemological concept, instrumental to the construction of a new scientific field – it is not an object for natural sciences to investigate. It is a borderline concept between the psychic and the somatic that makes it possible to move from the concept of nervous energy (excitation of nervous terminations that is transmitted to the whole nervous system) to the concept of psychic energy. Hence psychical energy can be derived from the energy of the body and at the same time its dynamics can be studied by a specific theory independent from medical physiology. L. Kahn (2003) underlines how drive, as a borderline concept, allows to cross the frontier between the body and the psyche without saying anything about the crossing itself:

> This concept is not a solution, it is a solution of continuity" that recognizes the existence of a knowledge gap: the passing to the other part of the frontier allows to abandon the language of neurophysiology and use a psychoanalytical language.
> (p. 75)

The epistemological legitimization of psychoanalytical research comes from its being deployed *in correspondence* with a precise solution of continuity[2] with respect to the medical research, without annulling it. Psychoanalysis establishes a cognitive discontinuity that is valid because at the same time it is also a continuity: the psychoanalytical discourse starts where the medical one ends and not anywhere else. Thanks to the notion of drive and its relevant concepts (energy, excitation, cathexis, discharge, tension–detente, pleasure–unpleasure), psychoanalysis crosses the knowledge hiatus between the bio-medical body and the psychic space without expecting to unify them.

The epistemological foundation of psychoanalysis is a psychic body, a *body of drives*, a prime body that comes before the hysterical body. The body of drives in which somatic excitement is connected with psychic activity, connects the body studied by physicians with the hysterically expressive body.

Wish (desire) is not exactly what Freud meant

Wishes animate the body of drives but the meaning of the *wish* (*wunsch* in German) must be clarified. In *The Interpretation of Dreams* (1899) Freud defines it as follows:

> A hungry baby screams or kicks helplessly. [...] A change can only come about if in some way or another (in the case of the baby, through outside help) an "experience of satisfaction" can be achieved which puts an end to the internal stimulus. An essential component of this experience of satisfaction is a particular perception (that of nourishment, in our example) the mnemic image of which remains associated thenceforward with the memory trace of the excitation produced by this. As a result of the link that is thus established, next time this need arises a psychical impulse will at once emerge which will seek to re-cathect the mnemic image of the perception and to re-evoke the perception itself, that is to say, to reestablish the situation of the original satisfaction. An impulse of this kind is what we call a wish; the reappearance of the perception is the fulfillment of the wish; and the shortest path to the fulfillment of the wish is a path leading direct from the excitation produced by the need to a complete cathexis of the perception.
>
> (pp. 565–566)

It seems evident that Freud defines wish as a direct psychic derivative of the drive (as the point of a direct hold of the drive on the psyche). It is presented as the psychical impulse that seeks to re-cathect a mnemic image.[3] Its fulfilment would be this image coming to coincide with the very act of fulfilment. Hence, wish aims at *the identity of perception, up to it being realized as a hallucination* (that is typical of the original psychic activity) as Freud adds after the quoted passage. Freud knows that the prolonged non-coincidence between perception with the actual achievement of the ceasing of bodily tension would undermine the fulfilment of wish. What he wants to underline is that in its essence the wish ignores the objective, physical conditions of its fulfilment. This original form of wish, that owes its existence to motherly care, is the engine of an all-mighty psyche.

In the passage quoted above Freud does not mention sexuality. Later, in *Three Essays on the Theory of Sexuality* (1905) he will explain that in the fulfilment obtained through nutrition, beside the pleasure of being relieved from hunger stimuli there is also a sexual, erotic satisfaction deriving from the child's oral mucosa rubbing his mother's breast. However in his concept sexuality originates like the rib of physical fulfilment for support and becomes autonomous only later, when the need of repeating sexual satisfaction is separated from the need for food. This initial overdetermination of the erotic pleasure on behalf of the pleasure derived from fulfilling a need appears to be problematic, especially if we consider that Freud subordinates the birth of wish only to the annulment of excitation. A psychic apparatus based on such a defined wish would be static, constantly aimed at recovering its initial condition, lacking from the start any explorative or creative skill.

The experience of physical relief plays a key role in protecting the psychic apparatus from excessive turbulences and infringements. In this way the developing psyche keeps its feeling of omnipotence thus avoiding any early adaptive development which would deprive it of motivation and creativity. Nevertheless what should be more properly defined as wish is the psychic movement that goes not from a physical excitation to the mnemic image of a previous relief, but towards pleasure associated with a persistent excitation, towards complex pleasant sensual stimulation. If it is true that the baby tends to extend (with the help of motherly care) intrauterine life by mainly investing stimuli cessation, it is also true that *from the start there is a motion in the opposite direction, orientated towards all sorts of pleasant sensations* that soon prevails. This motion immerses baby's life into a sort of creative dance which combines pleasant excitation and relaxation, thus giving a profound waving progress to the experience of pleasure and prolonging it,[4] and deeply *involves* the whole psycho-bodily structure. Here the erotic sensory experience plays an hegemonic, leading role for two reasons:

a) it entails a psycho-bodily involvement and consequently also a psychic one, more intense and profound.
b) it takes place at the point where the baby's meeting with his mother's body is the most felt for both of them bringing the baby into contact with something that is made of his own "substance" of feelings and bodily sensations and experiences. This other part of himself, because the baby doesn't yet recognize the otherness of his mother, allows him to extend the area of his psycho-bodily experience beyond his own corporeal borders.

The drive baby, who does not yet realize the difference between himself and the object of care,[5] and moves exclusively under the affect of the drive spur, creates a "mark" of his mother's body in his own body which is a pre-inscription of a relationship not yet recognized and subjectively assumed. This pre-inscription, a complex changing surface of a moving contact that includes sight and hearing, becomes the area from which the organization of the baby's psycho-bodily experience sets off.[6] The centre of gravity of this organization is the sensual sensory experience of the baby with his mother's body.

Under the drive's influence the baby tends to search not only a representation of a fulfilling experience (whose utmost expression is sensual) but also for a physical, engaging *contact* with the mother. More than *wish* it is *desire* (*begierde* or *lust* in German) that pushes the baby into his first steps in life. *In the initial stage of life, the bodily dimension of psychic activity is very intense, because the body influence does not only come from the psyche being connected with somatic excitation but also from the tight and straightforward bond between desire and body motion.*

The very existence of a baby cannot be conceived as he being passive and static vis-à-vis the mother who feeds and takes care of him. Mother and child move each towards the other, searching for an optimal level of reciprocal stimulation. The baby's desire cannot be fully satisfied unless the mother's desire is satisfied, too. If the mother is not desirous and satisfied in her desire, she will not be sufficiently desirable or satisfying.

The spontaneous, silent body

By adjusting his movements with his mother's, the baby builds — with her indispensable help — the conditions for getting in touch with her breast exactly when and where he is ready for it. He then falls under the illusion that he himself has created the breast (as Winnicott suitably says) but in creating illusorily the breast, the child also creates the essential structure of his subjectivity, the core of his way of being.

The movements by which the baby is weaving his encounter with his mother are spontaneous manifestations of an existence driven by desire, a non intentional and non "socialized" existence that deploys with no other aim but that of letting experience flow freely and smoothly. The existence of a baby at the beginning of his life, with all his body motions and gestures, can be compared to a flow of water going down a slope, under the effect of gravity, trickling and dribbling on its way down, with the only "aim" of continuing to flow.

Movement, breathing, heartbeat, look, gestures, facial expressions and vocalizations of the baby are, in this initial phase of life, spontaneous manifestations of his being desirous and alive when meeting the mother. This meeting is so much more intense and true the more the separateness of the mother is unknown. These manifestations, that can also be defined as *spontaneous gestures*[7] (Winnicott 1965a), allow the baby to enter, by means of his body, a type of communication with his mother that Winnicott calls (1965b) "silent". "Silent communication" is not a proper communication because the communicating subject is "isolated and not communicating" and he perceives his counterpart as an extension of his body and his subjectivity (*subjective object*). Nevertheless, silent communication is meaningful: mother and child communicate with one another not by means of codes having a semantic meaning, typical of intentional communication, but by mutual transmission, mediated by their bodies, of *experiential data deeply rooted in the sense of being* which cannot be thought (in the sense of proper thinking, articulated according to a verbal or preverbal language and intentionally communicated).

The spontaneous body of drives is a silent body which doesn't serve any mental activity and does not want to express, explain any experience or thought. Its silence is the silence of the life that animates it. This silence, the silence of a desire that flows ignoring education, the existence of its own object and the influence of material reality is the lymph nourishing the expressive gesture of intentional communication, and speech as well. Like invisible forces keep Kandinsky's colourful micro-organisms in harmony in space (*Bleu de ciel*, Sky blue Paris 1940), also the silence of a spontaneous gesture sustains invisibly the equilibrium of intentional communication. Where gesture spontaneity is interrupted, equilibrium is broken and the silence of death descends (death of desire, of emotion, of expression).

Even if it does not communicate intentionally, the spontaneous body "represents" by moving (forms a way of being). In the spontaneous gesture, the *form* (representation) cannot be dissociated from the *content* (what is represented).[8] Furthermore, in this phase the body has not yet become an object of the mind nor is its activity of representation subject to the activity of mental representation. The supremacy of mental representation does not start very early in life. E. Gaddini (1980) criticizes those who consider *right from the start* the mind as subject and the body as object: it is only in a *second* moment that the mind, differentiating from the body, is able to create a mental image of the corporeal self. It is only in a second moment, we might add, that the activity of body representation ends up being subordinate to mental activity and aimed, under its guidance, at expressive, intentional communication.

Before the infant is able to perceive his body as separated from that of his mother, the mental (ideational) representation of the encounter between the two bodies coincides with the spontaneous movement of the infant who represents the encounter by putting it into practice. In the spontaneous baby mental representation and representation through the body, bodily movement and psychic movement overlap.[9] While a more mentally evolved subject acts according to his representation of the world, the spontaneous child represents (himself) by acting.[10]

The silent, spontaneous body is a *bio-psychic* entity, that cannot be reduced to the biological body. It is the *essential material* of human subjectivity.[11] At the beginning the psychic body is indissociable from its concrete movement in space. At the moment of the separation from the mother the body movement differentiates from the psycho-bodily entity it belongs to and becomes an *instrument* of its expression and communication which is no longer spontaneous but intentional.[12] Here bodily movements are *expressive gestures* intentionally created by the baby in order to inform the mother on his emotional and mental states.

THE HYSTERICAL IDENTIFICATION AND THE EXPRESSIVE INTENTIONALLY COMMUNICATING BODY

Human life is based on the continuity of spontaneous gesture, expressive gesture and speech. This continuum crosses the space of the *constitutive antinomy* of the subjectivity, the space of the co-presence of two opposite modes of being. One mode is the silent, spontaneous existence that ignores the presence of the other in a feeling of omnipotence with nothing to express, nothing to communicate. The other mode, instead, is based on the very differentiated relationship with the other; and it must deal with the objective conditions of survival and accept the mediation of a communication means that affects and socializes subjectivity: the speech (communication by words). Here mind is capable of an abstract thought totally differentiated from the body, although not disconnected from it, and is also able to think the emotion.

The expressive, intentionally communicating body represents the bridge between these two antithetic modes, it is the hinge of their antinomy. When the baby begins to realize that his mother is gradually separating from him (since her attachment to him is decreasing) it is the lessening of the availability of her body that he first experiences in a concrete way. His body movements reveal to him all their impotence to seize the mother's body whenever he wants in order to satisfy his desire. Psyche (mind, desire and emotions/affect) cannot insist on its omnipotence without risking being dissociated from the body and it reacts by a transformation of the omnipotent desire that follows two opposite ways. In the first moment the baby addresses the mother with passionate love, which corresponds to what Winnicott calls *ruthless love*. This love recognizes its object's difference but rejects its subjectivity and the only aim it has, when the baby meets the mother, is her possession without limitations or preoccupation. He hates her every time he realizes that she is escaping his possessive demand and the hate is part of the love. It is the hate that allows the baby to gradually recognize that his mother has her own subjectivity (her own desire and will) that he can affect but without being able to possess as he wants. Gradually he understands that his mother's hated subjectivity is what makes her alive and desirable. He discovers *that he hates his mother for the same reason he loves her* and realizes the importance of protecting her from his excess of possession.

This is the moment when the baby can fully assume a position he has already moved to and which, in my perspective, corresponds to the *primary masochism* in human beings: the pleasure to be possessed by his mother's desire, effacing himself in her during their encounter, in order to lose the sense of confines and cancel the painful perception of her separateness, of her otherness. Submitting to the object he desires, making himself possessed by it, becomes for the baby a means to catch the subjectivity (the original way of being) that moves it, that breathes life into it.

Ruthless love and primary masochism integrate each other in a reciprocal balancing: the former pushes the body to sustain a certain degree of psychic omnipotence (seizing and manipulating the separate mother's body as an object deprived of will, that one can shape according to his desire). The latter brings the psyche to comply with the impotence of a body deprived of a continuous maternal support accepting to be shaped along with the body by the mother's desire, in order not to succumb to her (dying in her hands) but to get possession of her way of being (Thanopulos 2012).

Ruthless love and primary masochism gradually converge on the configuration of a *hysterical identification* of the baby with the mother. Hysterical identification is clearly and elegantly defined by Freud (1908) on a pathological level: it is a relationship which is also, and at the same time, identification with the object the subject is relating with. This kind of identification is also a physiological dimension of the human psyche that is a fundamental function in dreams. Identifying with the other, keeping our difference from him and relating with him on the basis of this difference, occupying two different positions at the same time, is a very important part of our life rooted in the phase when the baby has to deal with his separation from the mother. The difference between pathological and physiological hysterical identification consists in the fact that in the first the identification tends *to retain* the relationship because of the invasive nature of the object (which is perceived as the aggressor).

The hysterical identification allows the baby to bridge the distance with his mother seen, at the same time, as a separate object and as the "other" part of himself. The identification with the mother helps him to comprehend her and to better relate with her difference, but he has to use intentional communication able to affect and attract her. This communication is made by the baby's body movements and gestures that become an instrument of expression of his desires, emotion and intentions.

Baby's ability to mentally represent his body and the mother's body in terms of separateness is unattainable without the co-presence of an intentional communication that takes into account the diversity of the intentions that reside in two separate bodies and makes the negotiation of the times and of the modalities of the their joining, separation and rejoining, possible. The development of the intentional communication begins when the mother learns that she has to wait for a manifestation by her baby (through which he communicates his desire or need) instead of anticipating this manifestation with her own intervention. A mother reduces the rhythms of her initial engagement with her baby not only because of her need to get back to the normal course and to the other pleasures of her life, but also on the basis of her perception that the progressive growing up of the baby rends more difficult the comprehension of his needs and desires. She realizes that she has to give him the time to manifest them, if she wants to manage them without misunderstanding them.[13] Once a mutual understanding on the care of primary and elementary desires and needs is established the negotiation between mother and baby shifts to more complex desires that the mother cannot satisfy in an immediate rapid way by empathy. For the baby joining the mother through the space of their separation implies an effort of expression and communication that brings him over the spontaneous, natural existence towards the "socialization" of his experience.

At the beginning the baby doesn't distinguish between his emotional states (moods) and their bodily correlates. When separating from the mother he succeeds in realizing that she pays attention to these correlates, if they reach an external manifestation, and she intervenes according to them; he begins to intentionally anticipate their externalization before they happen in a spontaneous, not intentional way. Here the baby's emotional state begins to dissociate from its bodily correlate which is transformed into an instrument for the expression of the emotion in the contest of an intentional communication. In a successive moment when the hysterical identification with the mother arises, and one relationship with her subjectivity is established, the baby becomes aware that his mother's interest is for his emotional states and not for their bodily correlates. At this point he can use the *imitation* of the external bodily correlates of his emotional states in the communication with her in order to express his own desires and emotions independently on a pressing state of need or desire. In this way the baby reaches a full dimension of the *expressive gesture* (heir of the spontaneous gesture) and enters the world of the imitative gestures and of a body language made by the metaphorical use of gestures, so increasing in an exponential way his possibilities of relating his feelings and communicating them.

The expressive gesture structures a deeply *hysterical* body by which the baby speaks to the other addressing himself and speaks to himself addressing the other. This body makes the capability of thinking one's own experiences possible. The development of this thinking leads to a mental activity able to go over the initial elementary organization of the representations of the sensorial impressions and to relate these representations in a first system of representation both of the baby himself and of the surrounding environment. This allows the baby to get over the discontinuities of the maternal adaption developing his capability both to comprehend their temporariness and to negotiate new conditions of encounter. He can now think his actions, anticipating their organization in an experimental way, and uses his body to express, to communicate his desire not only in order to satisfy it. In this way the mental activity offers to the desire a concrete way out from the illusion of his omnipotent satisfaction and, at the same time, reconnects the psyche to the body anchoring the psychic movement (the trajectory of the desire) to the expressive, hysterical gesture.

The hysterical identification allows the baby to avoid the risk of a dissociation between his psyche and his body, caused by the separation between his body and his mother's body, in two modes. On one side the baby acts on the separateness of his mother's body, getting it closer to him by identifying hysterically with her and engaging her in a close bodily, gestural communication. On the other side he reduces directly the distance between his psyche and his body because hysterical identification facilitates the development of the first proper form of thought, which is able to reflect the psychic movement, representing it, in a specialized part of the body's movement finalized to the intentional communication).

PSYCHOANALYSIS AND THE CLINICAL USE OF THE BODY

In clinical psychoanalysis the body is traditionally confined to the field of psychopathology: the body affected and concretely transformed by a psychic disease (psychosomatic diseases, anorexia) and the body as semiotic field of a psychic disease (hysterical conversion). What psychoanalysis risks missing is the presence or absence of the body as an important tool of (intentional or not) communication in the analytical relationship. This body has nothing to do with the disease but with the direct, spontaneous manifestation or the indirect expression of a way of being.[14]

What is emotion?

The power of the spontaneous and the expressive gesture lies in their bond with the emotions they are impregnated with. Psychoanalysts sometimes overlap *emotion* and *affect* (as Freud defined it). Matte Blanco (1975) deals with the question in an original perspective. He defines emotion as a compound of *sensation – feeling* and of *thought*. "Thought" here doesn't mean logical thought but includes all the conscious mental activity with its important not logical aspects. Sensation–feeling is the basic, psycho-bodily in nature, pleasant or unpleasant affective experience from which emotion originates: a vague, fleeting sensation, impossible to seize. In my opinion it is strictly related, even if not the same thing, to what Freud means when he describes affect as the qualitative expression of a quantity of drive energy (quota of affect). Emotion, Matte Blanco says, born as a sensation–feeling immediately "puts thought on" and becomes something that one is gradually aware of with the increase of the thinking component. Following him we can conceive emotion as a two-way transition between two poles. On one side, where logical thought prevails on the conscious mental activity as a whole and on sensation–feeling, thought is not as much a component of emotion as an instrument for its representation (however, even the most abstract thinking has always an emotional dimension which cannot be eliminated). On the other side, where sensation–feeling prevails on thought, one might speak of an "emotional" thought.[15]

Sensation–feeling has to be integrated by conscious representations in order to become emotion and persist. Nevertheless it rises from the spontaneous psychic body and its becoming emotion passes through the connection to expressive gestures before reaching a thinkable and expressible in words state. The expressive body which is impregnated and moved by emotion corresponds to the greatest proximity between unconscious and conscious representations. The closer to body gesture the more emotional and intense the discourse of our patients is, the closer to their unconscious desires.

The bodily language in the analytical relationship

Dealing with expressive body in their clinical work prevents analysts from focusing too much on representation and neglecting emotions. This work can be carried out:

1) Through a direct observation of the corporeal manifestations and expressions when the body is able to represent by using hysterical, proto-symbolic language what words cannot, when the body is unable to symbolize (inexpressive body) or when it lacks spontaneity and vitality.
2) Indirectly, by analysing discontinuity, contradictions or inconsistencies that may be found in the patient's speech. The analyst can realize when this speech is disembodied or not, by perceiving the lack of proper emotional support. I am not referring here so much to the tone of the voice or to other preverbal signs, but to the formal content. When the speech is not embodied, the formal content is not personalized: or it appears to be too well constructed or it lacks perspective, not having a point of convergence.
3) By analysing dreams. The hysterical body animates the dream. If, following Winnicott (1953), we place the transitional object "at the roots of the symbolism in time", we can grasp the primary meaning of the symbolic function: the realization of a transition from "the purely subjective to the objectivity". The function of symbolism in dream is not limited to designate an object; in a more meaningful way it also assures the transition

from a subjective quality of the object (which is present in the psychic world of the dreamer) to one of its objective qualities (that belongs to its being "other" with respect to the dreamer). This symbolic function repeats the bodily expressive gesture of the child (which is subjective and objective, at the same time) and it is similarly founded on the hysterical bond between *identification* and *relationship* with the other. Every character in the dream represents the dreamer and contemporarily a direct or indirect object of his desire. The expressive movement of the body, suspended in its concreteness and remaining at the potential state inspires and nourishes on the stage of the dream the movement of the oneiric figures and scenes. Thanks to this peculiarity the dream is the best tool:

a. to identify the spaces of body silence in the interruptions of the oneiric plot and to understand their meaning by comparing them with the areas where the symbolic speech of the body survives;
b. to recognize the areas where the body starts expressing itself for the first time.

The silent body of psychotic patients

The body of a psychotic patient is variably but significantly *deadly silent*. I use this term to distinguish the *silence of death* from the *silence of life* present in the spontaneous body of drives. The psychotic body is structured around *reactive* needs interrupting the continuity of its existence (Winnicott 1949).

Working with psychotic patients I take into account some theoretical elements:

- The initial representation of the body focus on the area of dynamic interaction between two bodies: baby's body and mother's body. Body is from the beginning a "relational" body (strongly related to other bodies) and never an isolated entity.
- It is mother's reverie (her capability to contain the emotional and sensorial pressure on him) that allows the baby initially to keep his psycho-bodily experience spontaneous and then to use the body in order to hysterically communicate with her. The baby's capability to represent his body as a separate entity comes subsequently as a physiological consequence of the successful

achievement of the two first steps. When his body lacks spontaneity or expressiveness the baby is not able to realize an adequate representation of it.

With a psychotic patient the analyst has to address his reverie to the patient's ability to restore his body's spontaneity and expressiveness, becoming gradually able to organize and manage a relational body for the first time. Life can arise from death within the analytical relationship when what is dead as an *achieved* experience, because it has been interrupted just at the moment it was achieving existence, and remains alive in a *potential* state waiting for a form. In this case the spontaneous manifestations that had been nipped in the bud and kept, as undefined tension, in a potential state, tend periodically to re-expand and revive. The re-expansion is a dangerous "temptation" at the same time: if not recognized and mirrored by the analyst it can renew an intolerable feeling of death.

The patient tends, from time to time, to set in the middle between withdrawal and spontaneous manifestation, hopeful of going ahead but also ready to step back at the smallest uncertainty. If the analyst is able to tolerate the tension, without forcing the patient to go ahead, a spontaneous manifestation comes out at the end. When the analyst succeeds in reflecting it in his emotions and his mind and, finally, in his speech, the potential of spontaneity and expressiveness is released and it can find a form in the patient's body movements, dreams and speech.

As far as I am concerned, I pay special attention to the erotic body, to its silence, to its coming back to life, because we cannot dissociate spontaneity and expressiveness from desire. Mother is not purely *reverie* (Bion) or *environment* (Winnicott). Mother is above all a body that the baby enjoys establishing a profound contact with – an alive erotic body that the baby's body matches, a place of creative encounter. It is very important that the mother's body is sensually involved (not simply excited or, conversely, depressed in its liveliness), that her body satisfies the baby, making him feel alive, not merely relieving him.

DISTRACTION

Eugenia is a young psychotic woman who is periodically treated with neuroleptics. She was hospitalized in a psychiatric hospital in the past but the healthy part of her personality is functioning sufficiently.

She has just graduated from university and is looking for a job. Eugenia was conceived as an "understudy" in order to repair her mother when she was depressed after the death of her first son, who died soon after birth because of a respiratory crisis. Another brother was born when Eugenia was three years old. During her childhood she used to say she was one year older than her age. The age of her elder brother if he hadn't died.

One day she tells me a dream: *She is in a car with her friend C., who is driving. They have to get out of a parking lot in reverse motion and while doing so the car falls off a cliff towards the sea.*

I comment: "Your dream reminds me of *Thelma and Louise*. Did you see the movie?"

"Yes, I did, some time ago. I had rented a DVD. I watched it with C."

"This falling down in your dream, did it look like a suicide?"

"Neither suicide nor a mistaken manoeuvre. It could have been a mistake. Actually it was out of *distraction*."

I think about suicide, a theme indirectly present in the dream, as the fear inside her to mortally stumble when walking on the risky grounds of sexual pleasure. To lose herself falling with no possibility of climbing back up. I tell her: "I think *distraction* is describing something that is taking shape in you, something other than your fear of making mistakes and that has to do with the desire of living and not with the wish of dying."

In the following session she says: "I had sex with L. two weeks ago, but he came straight away. He said, 'I've come', very quietly, as he had done six months ago. I felt a little empty inside."

I say: "To feel, to inhabit your woman body, you have to distract yourself from what's around you, losing yourself in the experience. But you can't do it without the presence of another person. You can feel your body alive only in a relationship with another living body."

Although the meaning of *distraction* seems quite clear in the hysterical part of her experience, I sense the presence of an uncertain area, where openness to new emotions and meanings and fear of falling down are mixed. In the next session she tells me another dream:

I'm sleeping and I'm trembling. My mother reassures me and tells me everything is ok, nothing is going to happen and tries to wake me up. But I can't. *I want to continue sleeping. I only want to be reassured that nothing is going to happen.*

I tell her anything about her fear of orgasm. My interpretation could go faster than her emotional and sensorial states as it happened with the precocious ejaculation that L. had with her leaving her empty inside. I decide to say: "You want your mother to tell you it is ok to sleep (let your self go) despite the trembling. That you can accept emotional involvement without sensing an earthquake. But your mother tells you exactly the opposite: 'Nothing will happen to you if you wake up (if you interrupt yourself)'."

A few sessions later she tells me a new dream with C.: *She is again in a car and C. is driving. C. has to park in reverse motion and she does it perfectly.*

She says that this dream is far more reassuring with respect to the one of falling down into the sea but is also disappointing. She prefers distraction. I realize that we share the same worry: dwelling on the hysterical field, is limiting the semantic and emotional field of "distraction".

Around this time Eugenia tells me that she learnt about her brother's death when she was eight years old. She began to think she was supposed to embody the dead baby and make him come to life again.

Some weeks later she tells me a dream: *There is a baby in a bath. His mom wants him to learn how to breathe under water. The baby swims under water and air bubbles can be seen. His mother is looking at him.*

An "amphibian child", I tell her.

She says: "Maybe I'm that child". She goes on: "The bubbles remind me that when you dive in sea water you have to breathe out. The bubbles are the air you breathe out in water".
I tell her: "You *breathe in before* diving into water."
She says: "Yeah, but you breathe out once you're under water. It's logical. You do like this (she makes the movement of exhaling). You blow air out so that water can't get in."

The association by the patient goes beyond the configuration of an amphibian being: air bubbles bring the patient's speech into senseless, delirious space, though staying at a level of phantasmal representations (amphibian, hermaphrodite). The analyst may create meanings in his mind (the autistic, autarchic breathing in an undifferentiated, suffocating relationship; the child–fish being the phallus of the mother) but at a certain point he realizes that the patient remains alone.

What Eugenia describes is an impossible situation where her anguish is only partially contained by the representation of an amphibian being. This anguish can be described as follows: "If I breathe out, I suffocate" (preclusion of exhaling). As she cannot tune her breathing with that of her mother's, she must *keep* her own breath in the hand-to-hand fight with her.

You cannot tell your patient "You're holding your breath". You can only say: "Your dream is about your desire to breathe freely." Remembering her dream of "distraction" I tell her: "You need to get distracted in order to breathe freely."

Not much time later she tells me another dream:

She is in a swimming pool, she has touched the bottom, but she can't go back up. She must hold her breath and she is breathless. On waking up she feels the same breathlessness as if she was still trying to resist under water.

She associates saying she does not want to be an amphibian who can also breathe under water. I think of her dead brother who could only live in the amniotic fluid in his mother's womb, and who couldn't survive outside it, and I think of her as an amphibian–hermaphrodite.

I interpret it in this way: "You are starting to recognize that if you identify with your dead brother, who cannot differentiate from your mother, the relationship with her can become so suffocating that you are breathless." In the space of a few days she tells me two dreams.

In the first *she is falling down from a great height but she is transformed into a boy and she is safe.*

In the second *she is swimming in the sea when a huge wave arrives and is about to submerge her but a boy appears out of the blue. She catches hold of him and the wave passes without carrying them away.*

I tell her: "In the extent that you are reducing identification with your dead brother you are discovering your alive brother. On the one hand you persist with the identification with the lost son of your mother, in this way saving yourself and her from the involvement (in terms of emotion and desire) that you both live as falling down. On the other hand, you are discovering a body other than yours which lets you get involved without feeling as if you are drowning in undifferentiation."

I can describe, *a posteriori*, the movement that occurred in my analytical relationship with Eugenia in the following way:

- At a certain point appeared both a spontaneous and expressive "gesture" which arose in the field of hysterical language: *distraction*. It was something that by giving space to a spontaneous movement, went, at the same time, towards the expressive communication (drawing the attention to an obstacle to spontaneity).
- A adjustment in the semantic field of hysterical origin followed.
- At the end a proto-expressive gesture (not yet fully developed hysterically) appeared which was based on an inconsistency: by giving shape to the apparently senseless act of exhaling, when under water, the patient drew my attention to the existence of an incomprehension inside our understanding at the level of hysterical communication.

Substantially what Eugenia communicated to me was: "I want to breathe freely. That is why I have to exhale." If I had told her she was holding her breath I would have replaced her desire with defence. Once she recognized her desire to get distracted in order to breathe freely, it was she herself who realized and communicated that she needed to keep her breath because of a suffocating mother.

"Distraction" led the patient out of the area of identification with the phallic mother (identification represented by C. in her dreams) and shifted, at the same time, the perspective of our work out of the hysterical plot of the dream towards a spontaneous experience.[16] This experience was previously frozen in her psychic space and remained cut out of (foreclosed) from the dream.

Notes

1 In the original psychic apparatus (dominated by drives) frustration cannot be represented: it creates psychic deficiencies that only fulfilment may compensate for. It is only at a later stage that the psyche becomes able to represent frustration.
2 This solution of continuity corresponds to the gap between dream images and the bodily regulation of sleep and, pathologically, between hysterical conversion and brain lesions.

3 Wish would be the movement the psyche is forced to make, because of a direct hold of the drive, to re-cathect the mnestic image making it a representation.
4 In this up-and-down pattern where excitation fades away the sensation "persists", then inurement brings about satiety. Sensory pleasure is not like orgasmic eroticism where excitation going up and down, organized around an acme and a fall has a much more complex structure.
5 Even if the baby can vaguely perceive this difference he is not able to conceive it.
6 This is my interpretation of what Freud (1922) said: "The ego is a body ego, it is not merely a surface entity but it is itself the projection of a surface" (The Ego and the Id, p. 488).
7 A gesture that periodically expresses a spontaneous impulse associated to sensory and motor states.
8 Furthermore the representative subject here coincides with the beneficiary of the representation.
9 Ideative (mental) representation is not the brain recording of sensory data. Many might wonder: how can you consider two things like the living configuration of the movement of a part of the body (e.g. a limb) and the ideative representation based on the mnestic trace present in the brain that recorded this very movement as if they were not separate, even if in an early stage of life? Actually this question is misleading because it stems from an improper overlap between anatomic differentiation and psychic differentiation.
10 At the beginning of life the sensorimotor component dominates experience and thus ideative representation, affection and body movement are perceived by the child as if they overlapped.
11 It is in this material that the original core of the unconscious is found (the unconscious located before the "navel of dreams").
12 When body movements are used intentionally (whether consciously or not) to communicate a desire – which is not like a spontaneous body manifestation of desire (in this case, nothing is communicated but one's own existence) – the mental representation of desire and the body movement representing it differentiate from one another though remaining closely connected. When one gets to express and communicate a thought to one's own body the difference between a thought and a gesture is clearly recognizable. For the spontaneous child or for the spontaneous part of an intentionally communication subject this difference does not exist.

13 This is an important aspect of the maternal function because the mother has two opposite attitudes: on the one side she longs to have her freedom again and on the other side she maintains a strong desire for possession addressed to her baby.
14 I refer not to the body per se but to its spontaneous and expressive physical movement (including facial movements and tiny non pathological alterations of body functions such as voice tone, incarnate, breathing, etc.).
15 If we consider emotion, as Matte Blanco conceived it, not as constituted permanent structure of the psycho-bodily functioning but on the diachronical level of its constitution, we can say that at first ideative representation, affection (sensation–feeling) and spontaneous body movement overlap in the child. Later the psychic apparatus (affection and ideative representation) starts differentiating from the basic biopsychic, psycho-bodily entity, the psychic body. At the same time in the psychic apparatus mental activity (the production of ideative representations) starts differentiating from the affective dimension. Mental activity, organized according to the rules of intentional communication, becomes a targeted thought, a true thinking that dresses affection up, giving shape to emotion. When speech comes into being, thought can think emotions; but it can do so properly only ex post. If it does it when emotions are being deployed, it inevitably stops their flow (to a variable degree).
16 As I said before, a patient's spontaneous experience reflected in the analytical relationship is not the spontaneous gesture of the child (the patient is not psychically a new-born, not anymore). The perception of a spontaneous use of different materials (dreams or speech), in contrast with a previous vacuum, is what really counts.

References

Freud, S. (1899) The interpretation of dreams. *S.E.*, 3.
Freud, S. (1905) Three essays on sexuality. *S.E.*, 4.
Freud, S. (1908) Some general remarks on hysterical attacks. *S.E.*, 9.
Freud, S. (1915) Papers on metapsychology. *S.E.*, 8.
Freud, S. (1922) The ego and the id. *S.E.*, 9.
Gaddini, E. (1980) *Note sul problema mente–corpo*, in *Scritti 1953–1985*. Milan: Raffaello Cortina, 1989.
Kahn, L. (2003) *Far Parlar il Destino*. Rome: Borla, 2007.
Matte Blanco, I. (1975) L'Inconscio *Come Sistemi Infiniti*. Turin: Einaudi, 1981.

Thanopulos, S. (2012) Identificazione isterica. *Rivista di Psicoanalisi*, 58 (1): 47–66.

Winnicott, D.W. (1949) Mind and its relation to the psyche-soma. In *Through Paediatrics to Psychoanalysis*. London: Routledge, 1975.

Winnicott, D.W. (1953) Transitional objects and transitional phenomena. In *Playing and Reality*. London: Routledge, 1991.

Winnicott, D.W. (1965a) Ego distortion in terms of true and false self. In *The Maturational Processes and the Facilitating Environment*. London: Hogarth Press and The Institute of Psychoanalysis.

Winnicott, D.W. (1965b) Communicating and not communicating: Leading to a study of certain opposites. In *The Maturational Processes and the Facilitating Environment*. London: Hogarth Press and The Institute of Psychoanalysis.

3

TRANSMISSION OF SOMATIC AND SENSORY STATES IN THE PSYCHOANALYTIC RELATIONSHIP

Ronny Jaffè

Psycho-analysis ... explains the supposedly somatic concomitant phenomena as being what is truly psychical, and thus in the first instance disregards the quality of consciousness"

(Freud 1938, vol. 11, p. 639)

BRIEF THEORETICAL FRAMEWORK

We have long known that the concepts of countertransference, mental attitude of the analyst, analytical function of the mind, container/contained relation have become basic instruments of our daily work with our patients.

These concepts are imbricated with the function of thinking not only in relation with the patient's emotions and affects, but also with the emotional and affective states which the patient's discourse can produce in the analyst. In line with Bion's container/contained model, I am referring to affects, emotions, feelings that have to be listened to, received, metabolized, deciphered and finally given back to the patient once they have been transformed and decontaminated.

Furthermore, we know that some of these affects and these emotions go through and travel also in the analyst's senses and body areas, i.e., they are embodied in that intra-psychic/somatic area of which Freud sketched the first theoretical outline.

In this work I am going to discuss the bodily and sensory, primitive and basic resonances that a patient can create in the analyst and argue that a silent and intimate reflection on these resonances can later become a useful vehicle in understanding the patient's disharmonies and somatic illnesses and I like to keep in mind Bion's words:

> The embryologist speaks about "optic pits" and "auditory pits". Is it possible for us, as psycho-analysts, to think that there may still be vestiges in the human being which would suggest a survival in the human mind, analogous to that in the human body, of evidence in the field of optics that once there were optic pits, or in the field of hearing that once there were auditory pits? Is there any part of the human mind which still betrays signs of an "embryological intuition, either visual or auditory"?
>
> (Bion 1977)

I shall therefore refer in particular to three authors: Eugenio Gaddini, Marcelle Spira and Giovanni Hautmann, who have greatly contributed to this topic with their work.

By referring here to the container-contained model developed by Bion in "Learning from Experience", where he explains how an object, "the contained", can be projected into the container (Bion 1962, p. 154), I mean to indicate the movement that can follow this projection; as a matter of fact the contained can be worked through by the container, which makes the following re-introjection of the modified contained possible. This means that "in the container-contained relation what is being re-introjected is not only the contained modified by the container's working-through, but the working-through function itself (alpha function)" (Nicolosi 1987, p. 88). Therefore, we are not dealing only with an exchange between mouth and breast, from which the container-contained model stems, but with an exchange between introjected mouth and introjected breast.

These three authors have not only provided a general, exhaustive and structured framework regarding bodily and sensory aspects as well as the mind/body relation, but, through a very delicate and sophisticated theoretical and technical work, they have also focused their attention on the listening to and the working-through of "bodily fragments" (Gaddini), "body scars" (Hautmann), "spots of the bodily Self" (Spira) to be used as narrow passages to reach and get involved with the complex and sometimes chaotic mind/body relation.

Now, referring also to the concepts of projective identification and primary and basic identifications, I would like to point out how useful it can be to listen to and work through the fragments, the spots, the scars which belong to and resonate in the patient's as well as in the analyst's body in connection with the patient's expression; as a matter of fact, being able to pause, listen and hence reflect upon the primary and archaic bodily sensations the analyst can experience in connection with a patient can be a useful guidance in getting in touch with some awkward feelings and disharmonies in the somatic and mental life of a patient.

FRAGMENTS, SCARS, BODY SPOTS

Giovanni Hautmann and body scars

According to Hautmann, body scars and mental scars belong to a specific theoretical–clinical axis beginning with Freud's meta-psychology and reaching as far as Bion, with particular reference to the notions of alpha function and beta elements.

Hautmann argues that one area of interest of meta-psychology is "explaining the passage from a-symbolic to symbolic and vice versa, both inside the universe of drives and on the borderline between drives and biology, as well as, therefore, the formation of the self" (Hautmann 2003, p. 156); the a-symbolic–symbolic oscillation, while remaining in the background of Freud's theory, becomes central in Bion's through the notions of alpha function and beta elements.

I would like to point out that beta elements indicate pure sensory impressions, the things per se, pre-symbolic as well as a-symbolic things and this a-symbolic register belongs to the "psychosomatic" order (ibid., p. 160); the alpha function operates in the direction of symbolizing such beta elements and therefore promotes the symbolization and mentalization of the somatic schema.

As we know, the individual can show gaps and failures in the schema of transformations, proceeding from the a-symbolic to the symbolic, and they can produce scars replacing the psychosomatic symbolic configuration meant as the subject's capacity to mentally represent one's functions of body: the presence and existence of these scars "can determine the physical expressions we traditionally call psychosomatic symptoms, that is, in a sense, body scars, no longer mental scars only" (ibid., p. 165).

One of the functions of analysis, through the encounter of the two minds that work analytically "is that of recovering the meaning that these mental scars had or should have, i.e., starting the symbolization process again" (ibid., p. 166) in order to loosen, to smooth down, to undo body injuries.

Gaddini and the bodily fragments

Gaddini argues that "in the process of individual growth, the development of the mind is a gradual process proceeding from the body to the mind, a sort of emergence from the body, which coincides with the gradual mental acquisition of the bodily self" (1980, p. 472). On the other hand, always according to Gaddini, the psychoanalytic knowledge develops "in the opposite direction, from the mind towards the body ... towards the initial stages of the mental differentiation starting from the functioning of the body" (ibid.). Therefore Gaddini thinks that "one ought to distinguish not the mind from the body, but rather a body/mind continuum from a mind/body continuum and a virtual area in which these two continua somehow imbricate" (Gaddini 1986, p. 732).

The mental acquisition of the body is not a global process, but it takes place "through the aggregation of sensory fragmentary experiences" (Gaddini 1986, p. 480); I think that being able to pay attention to these fragmentary experiences is very important in creating bonds and meanings between body areas and mental areas and in creating pieces of meaning between oneself and the other, between the past, the present and the future, between different areas and stages of the mind. The fragment becomes therefore an important element in these transformation processes, since, "as regards the incessant flow of the body functioning" (Gaddini 1986, p. 479), it can be a tiny guiding light in the world of the bodily nebulae.

Furthermore I believe that as the mother and the child communicate with each other through a communication "mediated by their bodies" (Thanopulos 2010, p. 52), there is a communication made of bodily as well as sensory fragments and elements which are transmitted between the patient and the analyst; this implies that the analyst has to intimately listen to his own private bodily states aroused by the bodily and sensory fragments of the patient; then the analyst's body and senses can become the "instrument and the heart of the cure" (Ferraro 2010, p. 32), however only if they are carefully and closely listened to, worked through, represented inside oneself and hence metabolized.

Marcelle Spira and the spots of the bodily self

Whereas Gaddini identifies the continuity connection between body and mind in the notion of fragment, Marcelle Spira, a Kleinian analyst, tells us how important it can be to put together, to bind, to collect the unused fragments: in her work she asks herself how the analytic function of the mind can mentally represent such sensory and bodily fragments. My assumption is that Marcelle Spira mainly refers to the latest Klein when she for instance argues that "valuable elements of one's personality and fantasy life can be found in the split parts of the self and of the impulses" (Klein 1958, p. 550), a topic that is addressed with great attention also by Hanna Segal (1972) in connection with creativity.

Listening to bodily fragments

I would now like to focus my attention on those patients showing bodily as well as sensory fragments and carriers which are the expression of a "lack of continuity" (Spira 2005, p. 105), i.e., "in whom the unconscious bond between what is situated in the body and what is situated in the mind has been broken" (ibid., 24); such break leaves "an emptiness trying to find a way to fill it … suffering" (p. 105), suffering which, in the infant, is expressed through the somatic channels as a desperate signal of the search for a contact between oneself and the object.

Marcelle Spira refers to a body that becomes aching and distressed because it has not been able to make itself understood in its psychic and physical needs while demanding care from a maternal function. Failing such function, the infant responds with a splitting or encystation and, in the most severe cases, with a fragmentation of his own partial and internal objects with responses and reactions of the body: such event will be the basis of "a point of fixation hampering the evolutive dynamics" (Spira 2005, p. 20) because the child will feel psychically obstructed and invaded by non-integrated somatic precipitates. All this brings about a state of anxiety which grows and expands also because there is "a feeling of being unable to control them" (ibid., p. 19) since the break of the bond between oneself and one's own split internal objects makes the latter inaccessible and incomprehensible. Such objects are full of basic emotions and of "tactile, auditive, gustative, visual, olfactory sensations" (Spira 1993, p. 123) which turn out to be dissonant, split, not perceived, confused.

The interpretation ... becomes embodied

Of course this passage by Spira harks back to what Bion writes in "Elements of Psycho-analysis":

> [W]hat is interpreted must have, among other features, that of being an object of the senses ... in other words when the analyst offers an interpretation, it must be possible for the analyst and the analysand to see that what he is talking about can be heard, seen, touched or smelled in that moment.
> (Spira 1993, p. 20)

Therefore the interpretation must be situated in the relevant spot of the bodily self and one of the tasks of the analyst is to go or rather to expand his own containment functions towards the patient's elsewhere, consisting in the split and fragmented bodily part or in those chaotic sensations in which it might be expedient to identify "the sensual reference point having the function of coordinating the other sensations ... such reference point is defined as 'psychic coordinator'" (Ferrari 2004, p. 38).

I believe that in order to formulate an interpretation situated in such painful, split, non-integrated parts of the body, the analyst cannot just listen to the bodily and sensory aspects of the patient, but needs to dwell silently upon his own bodily and sensory states, allowing for a particular communication value within a close relationship" (Franchi, Castriota and Chiarelli 2006, p. 167); in line with the thought of Bion, the Barangers, Nino Ferro and many others, we know how much the primitive, pre-verbal, sensory and bodily areas of the mind of the one (the infant, the child, the patient) are imbued, infiltrated, transmitted into the other (the mother, the parent, the analyst) and that it is up to the latter to feel, to experience and therefore to understand and decipher these basic and bodily emotional states which are present in oneself, in the other, in the relationship.

Now I am going to introduce the cases of Federico and Giulia, both in their fifth year of analysis, since I believe that around the last year the analytic relationship was able to operate functions of symbolization and thinkability on the "body scars" imbricated in the "mental scars" (Hautmann 2003, p. 165), scars which have taken the "place of a psychosomatic symbolic configuration" (ibid.).

FEDERICO

Federico began his analysis five years ago due to a serious affective and emotional crisis. In his forties, self-employed, married, with small children, he comes from a quite religious and rigid family, especially on the side of his mother, who died of cancer when the patient was about 20 years old. The father, an elderly man, lives an independent life and Federico reports having a good relationship with him.

He asked for an analysis because he had long been feeling no passion for his wife, whereas he was living a secret affair with another woman he was desperately in love with, but who made him suffer with continuous excesses and instability. After about one year of analysis, he separated from his wife in an apparently conciliatory way, while the relationship with his lover ended stormily.

One year after the separation – in his second year of analysis – he began a significant affair with a woman who had suffered various family traumas "a childhood full of turbulence, sufferings and tragedies, very different", the patient said, "from mine, which was instead peaceful, serene, full of games, in a solid and warm family". And, a bit between the lines, with an emotional detachment that sounded suspect to me, he added, "although my mother was a little gloomy and introvert".

From here on the patient begins to get in touch with a dark and depressive side, his mother's, which until then had remained hidden, revealing in the analysis, besides a paternal transference, a maternal transference as well.

In the first period of the analysis, the patient put off an identification with a father who was independent, serene, satisfied, but also self-satisfied and rather absorbed in himself, and very fond of his interests; between father and son there are significant elective affinities: however, on the other hand, Federico has silently suffered a certain detachment of his father from his mother's world. In the paternal eclipse, he had felt gently drifting towards the minefield of his mother's universe, which at a certain point in the analysis appears through a primitive and upsetting dimension of idealization. If from the paternal figure we move on to make contact with the maternal world, then an unprecedented hidden and secret transference relationship is revealed in the transference, as in a sort of suitcase with a false bottom; a very peculiar style of idealization of the analysis is inaugurated, strongly reminding me of Green's words: "the patient has an idealization of the analyst's image, which is supposed to be kept intact and at the same time to be seduced, in order to arouse his interest and his admiration" (Green 1980, p. 273), but also in order to keep him stiff and mummified in a velvety and soft atmosphere. It is therefore at this point that I recalled another important quote by Green, i.e.: "the complex of the dead mother is a revelation of the transference" (ibid.).

These theoretical assumptions became clear in my mind when the patient recently began to touch on the mother figure with sketchy memories and dreams, and above all from the moment when, in the patient's discourse, some of his women assumed the features of some maternal areas, especially those with a depressive character. However, what really struck me, was the fact that I was feeling somehow stiff and mummified while listening to the lengthy patient's monologues, almost without being able to say a word, not because the patient was consciously preventing me from doing so, but because it was as if I felt my voice stifled in my throat.

THE OLFACTORY MEMORY OF THE ANALYST

However, on one of these sessions, and in particular when I felt like reactivating myself and commenting on a dream, I suddenly recalled an olfactory sensation connected to the bad smell emanating from the patient's perspiration in every session of the first two years of the analysis, a smell that later had suddenly disappeared and has not appeared again so far. Naturally, I asked myself what use I was supposed to make inside myself of the re-emergence of such olfactory memory in a stage in which I was experiencing a sort of paralysis of the words, i.e., when, in my relationship with Federico, my preverbal and sensory areas were getting the upper hand over the verbal area. Besides, it was not Federico's armpits that were smelling bad, but my mind that was suddenly recalling the memory of a past stench. It was my nose that was smelling the stench, not the patient that was being smelly. I was in touch with an "emotion that could either smell good or stink" (Bruno 1997, vol. 1, p. 11) and what could the meaning of this sudden olfactory flash be?

I am going to relate two of the patient's dreams and my countertransference perceptions, which got me closer to giving an answer to this enigma.

The two dreams

First dream

"*Marta* – his present partner – *and I are in a magnificent medieval village and there is a business meeting; I don't know anybody, however they invite me to participate and the situation is very pleasant and relaxed: I feel at ease. The problem is that when the meeting ends everybody is supposed to reach his own room. I feel embarrassed at going to my room with Marta, as if this could actually confirm our affair, because I am afraid of other people's judgement.*

The medieval place makes me think of a gathering of friends at the seaside, at which Marta felt uncomfortable with them and this made her look ugly to me.

I understand that Marta is not Marta, but an ugly 'twin-self of mine' I am attributing to her: I think that the dream has to do with the pleasure I feel when I withdraw to my room and masturbate, but I also think that to lock myself up and masturbate distracts me from my relationship with my partner", i.e., here Marta is felt not only as a part of oneself but also as a real object, that can invade the internal masturbatory areas of the patient.

The patient, feeling guilty, often tells me that perhaps Marta actually is "ugly", meaning that she is a far cry from his ideal of beauty and from a certain ideal model of femininity of his; on the other hand, he feels for this woman an intense eroticism and a strong passion.

Me: "*I also think that Marta is not Marta, but I have the impression that right now, as in a masturbatory situation, you must make and say everything yourself, maybe because you think that I might build myself a bad image of Marta. Instead, we can try and see together who is there behind this female figure.*"

And it is right in the moment when I am saying this, that the so-called "ugliness" of Marta brings back the memory of the bad smell emanating from the patient's armpits in the first period of the analysis, a smell which was totally ego-dystonic compared to the extreme care he took over his appearance.

At that time I thought that this stench was indicating an element the patient experienced as dark and dirty in connection with his masturbatory sexuality, while I had doubts about the fact that it "meant to transmit repressed hatred and fury" (Ferenczi, 1985[1988], p. 156); certainly it was a means to make one smell "the scent of feelings" (ibid., p. 157) and I thought that, in that case, I could only limit myself to sniff those feelings without giving too hasty answers.

I had deposited all this in my olfactory sense and from there in my mind, without translating it into words, also because I was afraid of being intrusive and indelicate, maybe "violent": besides I thought that talking about it – in step with what Bruno writes – I could "easily offend the feelings of the patient" (1997, vol. 1, p. 15).

And now, about two years after this smell had spontaneously disappeared, this sensory memory was coming up again and obviously inducing me to wonder what was hiding behind the emergence of this mnemonic flash.

The working-through process of sensory memories

Second dream

Patient: "*I had a dream I dubbed 'the bra dream', in which the topic was a crime to be discovered.*

It's a dream that feels like a thriller. I am sitting in a car with a detective and a fat black woman, his assistant, and we are about to drive to a place where a misdeed, maybe a crime, has been perpetrated. While we are in the car, this woman turns into my ex-wife, who says: 'women use this bra to receive kicks better ... certainly the idea of a crime makes me think of Hitchcock' (he mentions a number of films in which the victim is a woman killed by a man)."

Here the figure of the analyst, at first connected with an unreal, ineffable, ideal Dr Freud, later becomes something closer to a detective who accompanies him, allowing him to get close to the crime scene where the woman, instead of having a receiving and comforting breast, wears a defensive and repelling bra.

Me: "*You feel urged to give a name to this dream, the bra dream, because you understand that a child – your childlike part – can cry and get angry if, instead of a soft and comforting breast, he finds a hard and repelling bra.*"

Contrary to his usual behaviour, the patient stays silent for a long time and in the last few minutes of the session says: *"My eyes were shut ... the only image that comes to my mind is a top hat ... for me the top hat is something magic ... I was watching this top hat moving around the room ... so I thought of hypnosis ... and I must say that every now and then I think that hypnosis could help me remember things that I cannot remember with the analysis."*

"A magic spell!" I cry.

At this point it is useful to report my memories, appearing immediately after the image of the top hat: I recalled a dream by Federico, dating back to a few years earlier, in which he would walk down a wide road and see two columns topped by the sculpted heads of his mother, that had made him think of a tomb. In some sessions of that period he had talked, with an emotionally detached tone, about the illness and death of his mother, adding a detail that at that time had greatly impressed me: when his mother had got worse and found it difficult to move, Federico had taken care of dressing, undressing, changing, washing her and he recalled in particular that he had found it physically very demanding to carry her to the bathtub to bathe her. At that time I was impressed by this fact, also thinking that Federico used to tell me that he had had very few physical contacts with his mother during his childhood, because of her "repelling" character and the severity of her morals.

Naturally I began to reflect on the meaning of incestuously making contact – at a later time, during adolescence – with the mother's body, and more specifically with a sick and deteriorated maternal body. So, I reformulated in my mind the question regarding the patient's bad smell, not only as something pertaining to instinctual aspects mixed with a masturbatory and aggressive nucleus, but also as a relational residue of a sick maternal body – possibly emanating bad smells – and the patient's body that was toiling and sweating while washing his mother.

So, I began to understand that that bad smell from the armpits was "a way of venting something, i.e., feelings, emotions that had remained locked in him as in a coffin ... but also an insulator, since it was able to keep the others at a distance" (Bruno 1997).

It actually took me two years before I could recall his perspiration, which at that time had given me a slight feeling of disgust: smelly perspiration/disgust were obviously becoming an insulating barrier in some area of the analytic field, such as to make it impossible to utter suitable and usable words.

However, it was in a condition of countertransferential *après-coup* – the emergence of my olfactory memory – that I could work through the bad smell that was circulating in my nose, recalling bad smells which were no longer present, which embodied the sick and smelly maternal body the patient had been continuously in contact with. Most probably the patient was emanating bad smells during the sessions because, at a certain point, I had evoked in him a mother emanating bad smells.

Re-activating this sensory memory later in time allowed me to feel at ease, to find the words again and to use with the patient expressions like "to sweat blood", a metaphor as natural and simple as apparently inaccessible to my mind at that time.

A VITAL TRANSFORMATION

From a rotten cave ... to an airy room

I will conclude by reporting two dreams that Federico recently brought in a session and which made me think that, when we have the possibility of dwelling on mummified and deadly areas emanating bad smells, as in this case, then, however, there can also be a change leading to a working-through and to a vital process.

Federico: *"In the first dream there is a beautiful house and I dream my mother's mother whom I think I have hardly ever dreamed of. She is very old, much older than the age at which she died: then I was 18. I am supposed to take her into her room, but her room is made of rock, a sort of cave, and I realize it is full of cobwebs that have to be swept away ... My grandmother reminds me of the old musician in the movie* Un Coeur en Hiver, *so from here on I thought of myself, since for years I have felt identified with the young, cold protagonist, who was a regular visitor at the musician's house; the young musician would freeze all affections and feelings, and only in the last few years I have been able to distance myself from this figure. It must also be said that the film was set in an atmosphere as cold and dark as my grandmother's gloomy and shadowy house with its luxury and magnificence."*

In the second dream there is again a magnificent house: *I can see it in the distance because it is lit. When I get there, there is a stranger, then I understand he is the boyfriend of my daughter, who is a grown up in the dream; this boy tells me that my daughter is taking a bath in a bathroom beneath the house, in a wonderful secluded place, that reminds me of something I designed long ago when I was a boy. In the dream, I am not my daughter's father but her mother and everything seems to be projected in the future ... I don't know why I dream myself as a mother – he adds – maybe to replace my ex-wife, because I don't feel her to be ready when my daughter will be grown up, because I think she is a woman who cannot transmit a sense of femininity."*

The first thing that has come to my mind in connection with these dreams is a sort of oneiric space geometry: in the passage from a house almost symmetrical with the other there is the transformation from a place full of cobwebs, where the grandmother lives, to a bathroom where a young adult daughter gets washed and takes care of herself. However, my memory of Federico accompanying and washing his mother's sick body was also inevitable.

Through the contact with the representation of a grandmother/mother/spider and of his own defensive freezing in which bad smells are set free – a signal of serious distress in the sessions – Federico can afford to dwell on a developmental and maturative identification with a mother who can at last go beyond the darkness and make herself available to think of the coupling of her children according to an adequate Oedipal configuration.

The old grandmother, taken into the cave full of cobwebs, becomes a vital and "enlightened" figure: "the distant, dull, almost inanimate (p. 265) ... eternally mummified (p. 290) figure" (Green 1980) can be buried at last in order to give birth to and liberate a maternal function or more generally a parental function that might be a source of vitality and creativity, perhaps based on the first sensory pleasure represented by the sense of smell.

GIULIA

> We encounter a number of skin layers that once were superficial or conscious and now are free associations.
>
> (Bion 1974, p. 89)

"The skin, which should guarantee one's boundaries and well-being, sometimes becomes the object of extreme care and apparently senseless attacks, which however sometimes express the ultimate attempt at securing a boundary" (Badoni, 2000, p. 38); therefore the skin can become the place of an emotional and instinctual over-cathexis, a place of idealization and persecution, a "coat of arms" (Anzieu

1985, p. 161) and a crown of thorns where often ambiguous and confused anxieties, affects, tensions travel, coagulate, become real.

Through Giulia's case I would like discuss what seems to be the presentation and representation of a persecutory and idealized phantasm of "a fusional union in one body" (McDougall 1989, p. 40) between mother and daughter, which can find new expression in remarkable bodily elements, which, according to a keen expression by J. McDougall, can be described by the words "a body for two ..." (ibid.); in Giulia's story this archaic and primitive level has found *"as a trick of fortune"* its displacement and realization in a "skin fusion" (Anzieu, p. 58) with the father "which can be portrayed as a tactile image in which the two bodies have a common surface ... are glued together" (Anzieu, p. 58); as a result, beside the phantasm of a fusion with the mother, there is a sliding down from the aspiration to an ideal encounter with the Oedipal and separative father to a boundary violation of archaic and primitive nature between one skin and the other; this has caused a breakdown in the already troubled Oedipal process.

Taking care of, treating and thinking about these primitive areas of the mind, which expressed themselves also through a skin phantasm connected to a real skin ailment, was, in my view, an important function of this analysis, in order to have Giulia go beyond those extreme, obstinate and senseless treatments she had had for years. These treatments made of her skin a split and fragmented object which not only could not be integrated in the more extended mind/body apparatus, but would instead trigger inevitable psychic dysfunctions due to the contact with the apparatus itself.

The skin and the infection fantasies

"I would like to feel well in my skin, but this saying does not apply to my case", Giulia said in a recent session.

Giulia is a young woman, who began the analysis with me five years ago. Giulia's parents separated when she was very small and she has seen her father only occasionally, living in a thoroughly maternal universe. After adolescence the contacts with her father increased, however at the same time she began to develop frequent and acute anxiety for fear of contracting sexually transmitted diseases following occasional intercourse.

A year after the onset of her anxieties, Giulia began to show red blotches in different areas of her body; naturally this made her think that she had been indeed infected with a serious disease, and later she was diagnosed with a form of nettle-rash. A year after the onset of this disease, characterized by itchy red swellings, her father got the same disease too and this made the patient think of *"having magically infected him"*. In Giulia, there was the fantasy that one could get this disease through a more direct, more overtly physical contact, and there also was the idea that nettle-rash could as magically disappear.

Throughout the first three years of analysis, I dealt with a deep feeling of mistrust by the patient: Giulia was afraid of being completely dependent on an analysis that evoked the fusional bond with her mother and that, besides, in the long run, would prove to be useless, ineffective and interminable in solving this problem, which, according to various doctors, had psychosomatic origins. However, in these three years, important processes took place, increasing the patient's trust: an almost complete disappearance of the irrational fear of diseases, the decision – later realized – to go and live on her own, a significant reconciliation with her father, major satisfactions in her work, when she started to manage the family store, and, finally, an intense relationship with a boyfriend *"who had an angioma on his face"*.

Giulia experienced the encounter with this boy as an *"extreme relationship, the kind of man I could have never thought of having an affair with, because of his looks, completely different from my standards of beauty; I don't know if it is a coincidence, but when I met him the nettle-rash increased ... I don't know what this stuff is."*

The patient creates a real, magical, persecutory connection between him and her fantasies regarding her body. I don't think it is an accident that at a certain stage of the analysis there has been this relationship between Giulia, who was suffering from nettle-rash, and her partner who had an angioma.

Her meeting with this young man and a progressive reconciliation with her father made me also revise Giulia's theory, according to which she had infected him: it could have been a cover-up of the anxiety and the anger for the reverse being true. In fact, around the third year of analysis, getting in touch with her hard feelings, the patient dared to say *"my father infected me"*, and she said so during a longer talk in which she went as far as saying that *"the infection and its transmission is a chain that can never be stopped ... it seems everybody has nettle-rash."*

As if I were also influenced by Giulia's theory of infection, I thought that Giulia had got in contact with a *"a trick of fortune"*: now a grown up, after having lived for many years in a fusional maternal claustrum full of anger and hatred, she had got closer to a father who had been strongly longed for and idealized during his absence, however, in her fantasy, in this reconciliation they had both become carriers of an *"infecting gene"*.

Listening to the patient as well as following my theoretical paradigms have led me to consider her chances of being eventually able to work through the Oedipal issue in connection with what she believed to be an unhealthy and genetic father/daughter skin bond. Therefore, following the theory of transpersonal infection (Kaës, Neri), I focused my attention on the somatic and sensory movements circulating between us: for example, how much my physical presence and my words, if perceived and understood in terms of an organ language as has sometimes been the case, could be, in the patient's fantasy, evil carriers of infection at the risk of provoking something bad in the patient's body/mind.

For instance, towards the end of the third year of analysis, Giulia had come to the conclusion that I might be affected by nettle-rash as well because of a permanent red blotch I had on my skin: this fact would scare her a lot. However, as I pointed out during a session, when in the early interviews we were facing each other and almost certainly she had glimpsed this blotch on my skin – she had chosen to begin the analysis with me perhaps because she was thinking, among other things, that the affinity between some areas of our skins would have allowed me to better understand her suffering and anxiety. I had also thought that in her case this resemblance might imply a fantasy regarding the boundary violation between one skin and the other: for her this was heralding a sense of alarming risk and fear.

An infecting sensory transmission in the analytic relationship

I am going to discuss a dream and a session following this dream in which there is an intense circulation of bodily and sensory elements.

Dream

"I find myself in a group of people and I am struck by the fact that they are all followers of a witch-doctor, guru, faith-healer. I am supposed to be a follower

too, but I have the impression of rebelling, in short I feel an outsider. Being very anxious, I run away, and a boy comes to help me. He is black but for the back of his hands and feet that are completely red. He helps me and takes me far away, over the mountains.

Certainly his red feet and hands make me think of my problem, but I don't know why he is black ... maybe it suggests the idea of a servant."

The analyst is transformed from an omnipotent guru and faith-healer, a grand tyrannical figure, into a humbler salvific figure that can take her over the mountains, away from a sectarian and close universe. I believe that this is made possible because these red blotches on the back of his hands and feet are contact areas between two somatic containers needing to find a common area, an area in which they can exchange the communications between the two characters in the analysis: the analyst no longer is a mere flap of reddened skin with which the patient is afraid to be confused, least of all a dark skin, indifferent to the light and the sun, heralding anxiety for the patient, but he has his own red and blind spots, not too extended and disabling, and this can provide an empathic contact.

I found Giulia's answer to my comment quite to the point: *"This reminds me of my boyfriend. Every now and then I wonder if he realizes what he has in hand, as if he didn't deserve me: always overstated and so self-conceited as he is, when I think that I spend hours and hours reading for him because of his poor sight."*

The patient's red blotches, the analyst's blind spots

Talking about sight, the actual red swellings made their forceful appearance a few sessions after this dream: I was totally disconcerted and upset when in the corridor of my private practice I suddenly glimpsed her hands, full of marks, outlined by red swellings and streaks, as if wrapped in bandages, that, in a previous session, the patient had described *"as plaster hands, the hands of a dummy, inanimate hands, hands in which one can see the nettle-rash cracks open ... in short, the nettle-rash creeps on"*.

I associate the nettle-rash leaving its marks on her hands with the trace of a deficit of maternal holding and I begin to ask myself whether I have failed as well in my holding function, since I had not noticed such visible blotches. How come I didn't notice them before? How come I had listened with my ears to the suffering connected with her red swellings, but had not been able to see them with my eyes when she would come into and go out of the room? Obviously, I asked myself whether it was me who had blind spots, scotomas, which until that day had prevented me from seeing her blotches, or whether I had provided myself with blinding pseudo-psychic beams of light which were focused more on the contents rather than the container apparatus.

In a recent session Giulia said: *"Yesterday, when got into the shop, a strange thing happened. In the shop there was a new shop assistant I had not met yet. Contrary to my usual behaviour, I was feeling spontaneous, nice, kind, whereas she was very formal, cold, detached; I introduced myself with my first name, but she asked me my family name. Later the situation became more relaxed, as we talked about the shop organization and materials.*

However during all this I had the distinct impression that she had looked down at my hands; it was just a fleeting impression, actually a fragment of an impression, but in that moment I left my hands where they were, maybe I actually laid them on the table. It was something I would have never done. Maybe the word that is closest to this condition, but cannot thoroughly express the idea, is the word 'challenge'. But it is not possible to say with words what I mean, no word is really close enough .... However, I had the impression of being 'profound'"; this term reminded me of Valéry words in Anzieu's quote "the deepest part of a man is his skin" (Anzieu 1985, p. 80).

In the light of what Giulia said during the session, I think an important movement has occurred between us: on one hand she could "profoundly" show her hands (no longer hidden in her pockets or behind her back), because, thanks to the psychoanalytic work, her psychic vital lymph was able to de-cicatrize and resuscitate parts of the self she felt as dead or diseased. At the same time, the fact that I could eventually catch a glimpse of her hands represented the signal of a new perspective: my scotoma or blind spot, i.e., the death of a visual angle of mine – short-circuited with the patient's hands by taking life out of them in the session. In a separate, split, darkened area of the analytic place the patient had infiltrated and transmitted a deadly and dead fragment that had switched off my gaze; on the other hand I think that, having experienced this blindness as a real emergency of the body, which I realized in *après-coup*, made it possible to recover a light that could bring back psychic life to some dead and deadly fragments of the patient's.

CLOSING REMARKS

In conclusion, I believe that looking at Giulia as a whole as well as smelling Federico's stench by getting into contact with my bodily states and my sensory memories gave me the opportunity of hearing in mind these two individuals as more integrated bodies and minds, accepting their request of taking care of their split, clandestine, dissonant parts in order to restore their right of citizenship; as a citizen it is psychically easier to feel entitled to show, instead of hiding, one's own smelly, injured, wounded parts to oneself and to the other.

Finally, I would like to recall that it was of course Freud who sketched the psychic and somatic processes. In "Inhibition, Symptom and Anxiety" (1925) he wrote:

> We notice that anxiety first theoretical and clinical outline of the relationship between is accompanied by fairly definite physical sensations which can be referred to particular organs of the body ... The clearest and most frequent ones are those connected with the respiratory organs and with the heart.
> (Freud 1925, p. 131)

The last page of this work dealing with the relationship between psychic suffering and physical pain is extremely complex and I find Freud's reference to speech particularly stimulating, when he argues that "it cannot be for nothing that the common usage of speech should have created the notion of internal, mental pain and have treated the feeling of loss of object as equivalent to physical pain" (p. 170): actually, a meeting point remains in the emptying of the Ego connected either with the anxiety for the loss of object or with a psychic – physiological or pathological – over-cathexis of the aching parts of the body.

One of the abilities of the analyst is that of taking upon himself the condition of sad emptiness, and, whenever possible, of tracking down those psychic islands that are thick with meaning but are projected far away. In these islands it is possible to identify "the grain of sand around which an oyster forms its pearl" (Freud 1901, p. 82); with this quote I am naturally referring to Dora and to the deepest layers of the somatic and psychic processes where beside "a real and organically determined irritation of the throat" (ibid.) a "point of psychic fixation" has established itself, and parts of her personal history have developed around it.

Grains of sand, fragments, splinters, hollow spaces, minor deviations, are the places to which the analyst lends his ear and his mind in order to be able to attach a meaning to our patients' histories but also to turn rough grains of sand into pearls of life. And not just because he is driven by the pressure of an idealized professional obstinacy, but because he is inspired by a desire – and why not? – by an ideal tension suited to discover unknown and hidden spots that might open up new passages for thoughts and representations on the mind–body continuum.

References

Anzieu, D. (1985) *L'Lo-Skin*. Rome: Borla, 1994.
Badoni, M. (2000) Se la paura prende corpo. In *Psiche*, 8, p. 1.
Bion, W.R. (1962) *Apprendere dall'esperienza*. Rome: Armando, 1972.
Bion, W.R. (1974) *Caesura*. Turin: Loescher, 1981.
Bion, W.R. (1977) *Two Papers: The Grid and the Caesura*. London: Karnac, 1989.
Bruno, W. (1997) La ferita di Filottete Riflessioni sulla comunicazione olfattiva. *Rivista di Psicoanalisi*, 43 (1).
Ferenczi, S. (1985) *Diario clinico 1932*. Milan: Cortina, 1988.
Ferrari, A. (2004) *L'Eclissi del Corpo*. Rome: Borla.
Ferraro, F. (2010) Ascoltare il corpo. In *Esplorazioni dell'incoscio*. Volume della SPI Taormina.
Franchi, F., Castriota, F., Chiarelli, R. (2006) *Il Corpo Nella Stanza d'Analisi*. Rome: Borla.
Freud, S. (1901) Frammento di un'analisi di isteria (Caso clinico di Dora). *OSF*, vol. 4.
Freud S. (1925) Inibizione, sintomo e angoscia. *OSF*, 10 S.E.
Freud, S. (1938) Compendio di psicoanalisi. *OSF*, 11 S.E.
Gaddini, E. (1980) Note sul problema mente-corpo. In *Scritti (1953–1985)*. Milan: Cortina, 1989.
Gaddini, E. (1986) La maschera e il cerchio. In *Scritti (1953–1985)*. Milan: Cortina, 1989.
Green, A. (1980) La madre morta. In *Narcisismo di Vita Narcisismo di Morte*. Rome: Borla, 1992.
Hautmann, G. (2003) Cicatrici mentali e psicosomatica. In Rinaldi L. (ed.) *Stati Caotici Della Mente*. Milan: Cortina.

Klein, M. (1958) Sullo sviluppo dell'attività psichica. In *Scritti, 1921–1958*. Turin: Boringhieri, 1978.

McDougall, J. (1989) *Teatri del Corpo*. Milan: Cortina, 1990.

Nicolosi, S. (1987) La configurazione contenitore-contenuto. In Neri, C., Correale, A., Fadda, P. (eds), *Letture bioniane*. Rome: Borla.

Segal, H. (1972) *Scritti Psicoanalitici*. Rome: Astrolabio, 1984.

Spira, M. (1993) *Alle Sorgenti dell'Interpretatione*. Rome: Borla.

Spira, M. (2005) *L'Idealizzazione*. Milan: Angeli.

Thanopulos, S. (2010) Il silenzio del corpo. In *Esplorazioni dell'inconscio*. Volume del Congresso della SPI Taormina.

4

PERFUME

Mariapina Colazzo Hendriks

I would like to illustrate the problematics connected to a particular knot in the transference/countertransference (Tr/CTr) dynamic in the analysis of a young woman with pluri-symptomatology regarding her body, conducted by an analyst who had not sufficiently worked through the results of a cranial trauma – in specific, the complete loss of the sense of smell.

The sensoriality of both analyst and patient is the focus of a problematic tangle, of the conscious and unconscious strategies for identifying, elaborating and integrating it into the flow of the analytic work.

The wise, ironic aphorism (attributed to Winnicott) about our patients being our best teachers surely includes master lessons – precious teachings, originating in a complex, destabilizing and, to some extent, painful experience. We can hypothesize that in such interchanges, our vulnerable spots, scars, even the dumb areas of the mind are touched and brought to light, through deep communication from one unconscious to the other. Often it has to do with a major knot in the Tr/CTr dynamic, inducing the effect of unbalancing the necessary asymmetry – even if only slightly and temporarily. The dizziness which comes from uncontrollability marks a passing. Nothing will be like it was before. But, encountering once again the "tiger" of CTr, never totally tamed and quieted, can increase the indispensable awareness which Hanna Segal (1981, p. 86) recommends, "countertransference is the best of servants and the worst of masters," "the pressure to identify with it and act it out in ways either obvious or very subtle and hidden is always powerful".

I will share some lessons I received, trying to transform a *vulnus* into a *logos*. In the clinical experience addressed here, I would like to underline the centrality of sensoriality as a vehicle for and the dimension of a deep exchange: from unexpected involvement to the use of the analyst's body, like a compass, in a double-register of the injured body and the body which feels an invisible wound with- and-for the other.

Not much earlier, the analyst had suffered a serious cranial trauma, resulting in partial loss of her hearing and sense of taste and complete loss of her sense of smell. The young woman spoke through symptoms which referred to the body concretely and/or symbolically, such as the compulsion to suck her thumb, occasional trichotillomania, and compulsive shopping.

I will use a meaningful session, a crossroads, in which a transmitter encounters an out-of-service or, better yet, a closed-for-mourning receiver. I would call that meeting point a star-shaped crossroads so as to highlight its value as an intersection, a passage of transformation in the two parties. It is a transformation which brings to mind that which quantum physics calls "entanglement".

REVIEW OF RELEVANT LITERATURE

Interest in questions about the bodies (both the patient's and the analyst's) within the context of the analyst's room grows steadily. As Marilia Aisenstein (2009) writes: "The body is always present in psychoanalytic treatment [...] I would like to argue that the body must be thought of as a 'means' and 'the heart' of treatment at various levels" (the author's translation from the French).

Even A. Green (as cited by Maccari in Franchi et al. 2006, pp. 11–12) concludes that

> taking root in the body is indispensable in our psychic life; nonetheless it is not sufficient for defining it; it is necessary that the psyche-soma unit be inscribed in an I–You dynamic wherein both the I and the You are experienced in both dimensions – the somatic and the psychic ... If the unconscious meaning inherent to a somatic fact cannot, by definition, access the conscience of the symptom-carrier, it can nonetheless access the conscience of the other, thanks to Tr/CTr phenomena.

When the analyst's body is also considered, it is above all because her/his body is damaged, for the risks of "oxidation" and non-integrity of psychic functions which its new condition brings with it. We speak less systematically of the analyst's body as a professional tool which, remaining within the rules of classical technique, restores a holistic vision of the human subject, transforming a burden into an advantage, when possible. For some years now, we have read testimonies from our colleagues, mostly touching and courageous, almost always showing fidelity and faith in psychoanalysis: a providential third party. Delicate situations in private and work life are recounted and so we read between the lines that, for good or bad, nothing will be as it was before (Schwartz and Silver, 1990; Corsa, 2008).

An examination of the literature reveals persistent themes: the analyst's primitive defence mechanisms such as denial, narcissistic regression, the whole repertoire of guilt, castration anxiety, feelings of humiliation, mortification, unfamiliarity linked to the new body–Ego, anger, fear, loss. Finding a new balance between before and after, known and unknown – too often done in complete solitude – becomes an enormous, laborious task full of snares and dilemmas.

We can see risks and dangers for the analyst–patient (A–P) couple: use of the patient to obtain masochistic or exhibitionist gratification or narcissistic compensation, with the obvious risks of role-inversion, autistic withdrawal, or omnipotence displayed in various forms.[1]

The vast area regarding the sense of smell in specific has only an apparently minor place in psychoanalytic literature. In a letter to Fliess (November 14, 1897), an ear–nose–throat specialist, Freud writes about research on a conceivable organic basis for repression. He addresses the question again in 1909 regarding the Rat Man in the appendix and notes (1907–1908), picked up later in 1929 in *Civilization and Its Discontents* (footnote 1, p. 589 and footnote 2, p. 595).

In his Clinical Diary (1932), Ferenczi offers interesting observations on the sophisticated communicative and directive use of the sense of smell in some forms of mental suffering.

Hermann (1943) indicates the role of the sense of smell as an archaic mode of orientation and research when he illustrates the grasping reflex.

However, in psychoanalytic literature, there is very little specifically about analysts' sensory lesions and about how and to what extent the internal response to listening and elaborative work is altered and, in turn, alters the clinical work. Perhaps the most stimulating author is Anzieu who describes various sensory wrappings in his famous "The Skin Ego" (1985). Not only does he declare his difficulties in perceiving odours, but – a pioneer – he equips himself and us with creative tools for receiving not only the contents and movements of the patient, but also the various aspects of CTr.

MS T, FROM THE INITIAL MEETINGS

Separations, holes, replacements.

Arriving slightly late, a young woman, dressed casually and overtly informal, introduced herself with a handshake and her first name, as a child would do.

She had come to me, she said, to finally do something good for herself, to better herself, to like herself a little more ... really, she didn't even know herself that well. In the past she had seen two or three "psycho-people" and after seeing them once or twice, she had given up.

She used the expression "I broke it off" and I was hit by the sense of a tear, as in torn fabric. These professionals had been consulted by her mother, who was worried about her compulsive trichotillomania at the age of 16 (its onset later back-dated to 11).

It struck me that from all the contact she had had with these professionals in her life, all that remained was the scientific names of her conditions. Without even suffering a great deal, she seemed to tell me – it was everyone else who worried.

Those had been hard times. When the patient was 12 or 13 years old, her mother had separated from her father (an event she considered a watershed moment) and had gone back to her hometown, to her family of origin, taking T and her brother, two years her senior.

T's father was abroad at the time due to his job in show business and his new relationship, from which a third child had been born.

Her elder brother had followed in his father's footprints, professionally speaking. One of her uncles, on her mother's side, well-known in the world of show business, stepped in as a paternal substitute in the years following her parents' separation. She did not mention his name at the first meeting but said, almost embarrassed, that she was an actress.

She had gone back to living in her mother's house with her seven-year-old daughter L, after separating from the girl's father. I thought, "she's following the same script", thinking of her profession and her personal vicissitudes. Following in the footsteps – the maternal and paternal ones.

She had had her daughter when she was 25. The separation took place five years later. She was convinced to have returned home like "an irresponsible girl", as her mother always said. She used vague, dull expressions such as "I don't even know who I am or what I am worth," adding "Maybe that's why I'm always jealous ... always in an obsessive way and then" – after an embarrassed silence – "money just slips through my fingers". Another "symptom" thus emerged, expressed with a reference to a body unable to contain her jealousy and with which she tried to keep everything under control. This reckless spending was an important cause of the breakup with her partner, a level-headed insurance broker. She was ashamed of this unchecked compulsivity. She was even more ashamed of still sucking her thumb as an adult. She concluded by saying that she felt lighter having told me this.

Her compulsive shopping was linked to feeling alright and to her inability to choose: she was used to buying lots of clothes, shoes and other garments – often in pairs when unable to choose one over another, or decide which colour she preferred. "In the end, confused about which style or colour can express and enhance who you are," I commented, "you bleed yourself[2] to adorn yourself."

She smiled at me, pleased with the word-play. Obviously I thought of the many corporeal idioms, beyond the immediate metaphor, at play. I noticed, after the first session, that she had a nice light in her eyes: fresh, sparkling, and yet slyly seductive.

In our second session, she announced that she would like to begin analysis with me but could not afford more than three sessions a week. I said that I too had been thinking about the difficulties of analysis for someone in show business. She answered that yes, she understood, but now this was her priority, her daughter was growing up and it had all become so complicated.

OF MEETING AND SEPARATING

Again separations, holes, replacements.

The problems related to her work schedule turn out to be "peanuts" when compared with the vicissitudes of her "sticking and coming unstuck". These began with the difficulties of moving from face-to-face to the couch after the first sessions, breaking eye contact with me. Was it really work or was it her daughter with her growing girl's needs, which she ritually recounted to herself/me? Or was it in fact the difficulty of going forward with the analytic commitment, if not in a different script/narrative? A reiterated attempt at making me/us stay in a whirlwind of re-updated-memory–desire–fear experiences of union and separation?

It was that she felt "just so good", she once let slip, that she was scared of being judged (badly perhaps, and abandoned?) by me. A few months into analysis, she reported a dream.

"After the last session, I was very tired and I had a dream in two parts. I was speaking to you on the phone but I could see you. You were instructing me '*Segna rosso*[3] *e vai a capo.*[4] Remember that!' Then I went for a walk with my mother and my brother to X Square (where my consulting room is located). In the second part, I was taking my daughter to a doctor's office ... You were there too, watching how I behaved with her ... Look at that ... you help me and I'm afraid of your judgement."

She made the association that my office is in the same area as the office of the colleague to whom she was brought when "the hair story" started. She connected sleep with analysis.

I made an interpretative opening: is sleeping so essential because it serves for escaping? Certainly for dreaming about it. In a kind of trans-modal receptive state, she hears my voice and she sees me, while at times she sleeps swaddled in the acoustic wrapping of my words. Red mark and new paragraph. Did the red marks belong to menstrual blood (hers or her daughter's menarche)? I wondered, given that colloquially one says "mark" to mean small menstrual stains. It was a junction. *Si va a capo* = new paragraph/new chapter. She would have to face idealization and therefore also denigration, envy, rancour, Oedipal competition with the desired mother. Now she is both daughter and mother. The analyst watches her (encouraging her?) becoming a woman and a mother in turn, seeking external help in the absence of a father. In the second part, the "red mark" could in fact mutate into the red mark of corrected homework, of a supervising gaze. Furthermore, in financial language, "to be in the red" ("*segna rosso*") is to have a negative balance.

She idolized her mother, saying that she had done her motherly duty intelligently and selflessly, in contrast to how she herself was doing with her daughter.

Men, on the other hand, inhabited a completely separate, distant universe, in particular her maternal grandfather, the perfect icon, a self-educated, avid reader, much loved by T's mother, who often regretted she had not succeeded in having him meet T, due to his premature and unexpected death shortly before the patient's birth. By contrast, she presented her father as a womanizer who even asked her for advice on his love life and illnesses. She had harrowing memories of her brother: she had had to keep a close eye on him due to his drug addiction, "picked up" when they lived abroad with their father. The uncle on her mother's side, who took on the role of putative father after the collapse of her parents' marriage, was experienced as hard and inflexible.

As an adult woman, her male universe was populated by various other characters, seduced and abandoned, at least in her narrative.

I was made the spectator (and I use this term quite deliberately to highlight the element of a *mise-en-scène*) of brief, almost lightning-fast sequences of these dynamics: flings with men curtailed before the enchantment could disappear. It allowed us to distinguish a pattern of the pressures and forces at play in the overturn of passive into active, "who loves whom", "who abandons whom".

The patient's ex-partner, S, father to her daughter, described as a "grey mouse", could not stand T's uncertain profession and her spendthrift ways. He became the cause of constant disturbance in T's relationship with yet another man, D, which began as mutual love at first sight, one year into the analysis. She described him as a fresh, new love, her strongest ever in terms of depth and intensity of feeling. At first he appeared solid, protective and head-over-heels in love (perfect!). However, this relationship would limp along like the others, up to the point where she abandoned him, this time with greater suffering due to the greater self-awareness she had acquired. The session I report is from this period of disenchantment.

Her life narrative (at times like a homework assignment, what an analyst would want to hear) was broken down into before and after her parent's separation, followed by tales of everyday difficulties, such as her daughter's refusal to do her homework, just as she had done as a child, exasperating her mother who had been determined to make her study. History proceeded in its inexorable cycles: her mother rebuked her about the fact that she rebuked her own daughter, perhaps over the same thing and even using the same expressions. One within the other, or rather, one fused with the other, like a real syncytium. This would turn out to be a recurring theme throughout the analysis.

In relation to her maternal "skills", during a session centred on an argument she had had with her daughter (with her mother as spectator) over a plait which had come out wrongly; she also recounted some painful experiences she had never spoken about. A comment of mine had followed the story of the plait about how difficult it can be to equip oneself with maternal skills in the presence of a gaze which feels cruelly judgemental and, after all, it had to do with hair, and to make a good plait some hair has to get "pulled". At a fast pace, with increasing anxiety and confessional need, she spoke of how she had twice lost pregnancies. I asked her what could have been behind the anger for those "rips". I hinted that, yes, there could have been much more.

During the analysis, it came out that neither the patient nor her brother had been breastfed but she did not know why. She breastfed her daughter only briefly because she could not stand not smoking for such a long time. She would have liked to quit but couldn't: "it's my 'dummy'."

Holes. Tears. Repairs.

The tone of her narration was always in tune with how she presented herself. All the clothing for which she "would bleed herself", feminine and "giving" – her words – were lying at the bottom of a wardrobe, intact and still new. Almost always dressed in a grey or blue tracksuit, hair tied (to cover, I would later learn, the bare patch created at the top of her scalp), with no make-up, she exhibited a simplicity which hinted both at a very sophisticated elegance and at her really being a young girl, with a body always disciplined in dance and sport. A body of stone, sculptured, a kind of muscular shell, a "second skin". In any case, *tout comme il faut!*

Obviously, monitoring the Tr/CTr game was central.

The seductive glue often needed to be diluted and the analytic container was incessantly frayed by the patient: for example, making holes in the spatial–temporal fabric. At times this would mean her skipping a session, me extending it a minute or two, a late arrival, a message or a phone call from "elsewhere" to reschedule, catch up on, or cancel a session at the last minute. They were often related to expressions of negative transference manoeuvres, if not real attacks on the bond, but also tests of its holding power – as if to say: "Are you there? ... Pick up! ... I would love to but I can't ... Show me that you understand, that you're helping me and that … you care for me," and above all, "you hold me."

THE PERFUME OF MAY: TOGETHER IN A SENSORY BATH OR A DUEL TO THE DEATH?

I have chosen this session to illustrate simultaneously some of the sensory and relational tangles of T's life and for how – by chance or by having the nose for it – it brings to life an intolerable, (un)buried suffering of mine.

At the beginning of analysis, I asked T to tell me more about the "hair story", given that she had often referred to it but never talked about it.

Here follows an excerpt in which the patient wonders about her presumed being out of tune with things. She had gone to a funeral, but in an absent, closed state.

P – It's that I feel guilty seeing others cry and being out of tune with them. When I was little, I would never cry, except every now and again out of self-pity … because others blamed me … childishness. All in all, when I really think about it, in X [her childhood city] I never cried. It was in Y [her current city] that I began to tear my hair out.

A – I think "In Italian, this expression connotes a sense of desperation".

A – I say "And not only in the figurative sense".

P – And my mother would shave my head … out of desperation. I was laughed at in school and I closed up more and more. I felt like an outcast and isolated myself. I was ill at ease … I felt judged because of my hair.

(A short extract of relevance to one then quoted at length.)

P – Recently the desire to rip out my hair due to a kind of nervous boredom has come back … It's a picking at myself … not picking *at* something but *around* it … I can't stop it anymore: one hair leads to the next. What brought back this desire to pick at myself? I don't know, but these two imposing beings are present … two men desire me and are very insistent … I feel an irritation inside … and I bring it out, onto my scalp … ripping out my hair is like ripping myself out.

A – Ripping out doubts, thoughts? Is it also feeling yourself?

P – Yes, I feel pleasure in ripping out a hair ... in that moment, it's bliss, I feel pleasure mixed with pain ... the hair leaves the scalp ... I smell it, inspect the root and throw it away ... If I'm in front of the mirror, I select which hair to pluck. It is not random. I choose a hair which is healthier and stronger than the others. The sound of the rip, that ticckk! I hear it well. I always say to myself "Now that's enough", then I tell myself off ... for not having stopped. I have to do it. It all started again with white hairs. Before I never used to count them, now I am aware of every last one of them ... They always appear in the same area, at the top of the field [a slip of the tongue, she says campo – field instead of capo – head]. I feel a "tingle", a tickle, an itch. When I was a little girl, I would worry about the bald patches, but then I would tell myself that they would grow over ... But now I have to be a bit careful: it's compulsive, I have to do it.

Another short extract.

P – It's just that when I buy clothes and shoes, I'm certain that without these objects I won't be beautiful or visible, or even beautiful to myself ... I don't think, my mind wanders only to what follows next ... until I'm at the till, and then maybe ... Like the compulsiveness I feel with my hair ... luckily for now I go to the mirror and restrict myself to pulling out the white ones ... but before it was different. I don't recall feeling sad but ... I didn't care about the bald patches because my mother shaved my head anyway. Even if everyone thought I was strange, I kept to myself and I didn't care.

THE SESSION

My thoughts and inner movements are in italics in quotation marks.

That morning I get to the consulting room thinking how linden tree flowers have a sweet perfume but that I cannot even remember it ... I try hard to recall it ... it was slightly aphrodisiacal.

T is my first patient of the day. She starts off by saying that D surrounds her with flowers and perfumes to avoid losing her ... but the more he shows her his dedication, the more she sees him as an intolerable, undignified doormat which she must get rid of. She contributes to the joy of olfactory pleasure by buying precious, expensive perfumes for the house.

She recounts how she prepares succulent dinners, spending large sums of money ... she bakes sweets, especially elaborate cakes ... she could probably make a living from it, if push came to shove ... a friend of her owns a restaurant ... fantastic! She says that she decorates the table because she likes to be immersed in beauty ... She furnishes her new house attentively.

P – L likes her new bedroom, even though she often sneaks into mine. She keeps an eye on D and throws tantrums.

A – When the patient mentions L, I realize that it's been a while since we last spoke of the famous, expensive cat she bought her daughter for Christmas; it's disappeared from the family news ... her daughter's cute request comes to mind ... and with it the image of T giving in at the last moment to the request she had opposed, and visiting cat shelters and exotic cat sellers on Christmas eve ... Is it still alive? Is it dead? I wonder.

T has gone back to talking about the perfumes which D buys her and which she buys herself.

P – Things just seem to be going that way these days ... I have just discovered a very well-stocked perfume shop; it's got a nice name, strange for a perfume shop ... Sacred Heart ... do you know it?

A – "Analysts don't always have to answer questions," I muse, "luckily enough ... but even if I wanted to and I thought it were necessary, I couldn't."

"That's where I shop!" I think with surprise. In a time that was ... I had been one of the first to shop in the newly opened branch of the store ... I think of the owner, extremely competent but always ill-mannered with her visibly anorexic daughter ... the toys and perfumes of the song my aunt Flora used to hum ... Floris' perfumes in London ... memories engulf me like a cloud of perfume from the cosmetic section of a department store ... mixed up and indistinct, bewildering ... and like the different fragrances T's words tie themselves up with my memories ... I lose myself ... a whiff of pain ... am I listening?

P – ... you know, amber?

A – "Is she talking about amber, the resin in which insects sometimes get trapped, or the precious aphrodisiac ingredient in perfumes?" ... I think to myself, more in a daze all the time.

T continues.

P – ... because the fragrance notes.
A – I feel that it stuns me and has me by the throat ... the realization that my sensitivity and "competence" in the world of perfumes is gone and will never be there again ... and I no longer possess olfactory memories ... and I don't "know" like she asks me to! I try to cling to an old resolution, still unfulfilled to go back to studying smell and olfactory memories ... ah, my medical competencies ... those, too, lost.

 A knot in my throat ... it hurts .... I'm stunned.
 I come back in touch and listen.
P – ... because I've found a perfume which drives me crazy.

 A silence follows, echoing the word "crazy" as it expands in all its many meanings.
P – But who do we put perfume on for? For example, do I put it on for D? I don't think so, I don't know ... every day he attracts me sexually less and less ... and why does he give them to me as presents? For me? For himself?

 Silence. Then she goes on.
P – In the meantime, vain, I try them on ... I look at the beautiful bottles ... I arrange them in the bathroom ... I smell them.
A – "With thoughts like confetti ... narcissism ... an atmosphere of masturbatory climax ... she prolongs the "eeh" sound of smell.

 I find myself saying, without thinking too much about it:
A – ..."*Like the hair whose root you sniffed:* it was yours, ripped from you, from your body ... before you threw it away ... forever."
P – Hmm (which stands for "oh right, yes")
A – It occurs to me that after the accident I have no longer gone back to that perfume shop ... the mere thought of it bothers me ... how stupid of me! I could have trusted the shopkeeper's competence or the experience of the owner and bought a new perfume, instead of trying to fix in a kind of "smell-o-gram" of the last perfume I chose and preferred.

 Once again I lose myself.
 I am once again beside her, having perceived how much I envied her narcissistic and solipsistic olfactory triumph, because I'm struck by a brief and startling fit of pain, the pain of a hair plucked from my head.
 "Don't touch a hair of my head" is a very plastic expression. Don't use violence.
 Vulnerability in both of us?

Symmetries.

T continues.

P – ... the smell of that hair is ... the smell of life ... of your own authenticity ... it smells like it's yours.

A – ... perhaps also of uniqueness.

As if in a crescendo T goes on:

P – Yes, the perfumes which you can buy these days are very chemical, reproducible – to infinity ... but they are unique when they come into contact with a particular skin ... they combine ... that's why we can't decide at once whether or not we like them, it takes some time ... they change.

I have the sensation that she is very excited.

We both seem excited, I think. Circulating emotions. But which ones? I just know there are many and they are warm. Mixed up. (A shared bath?) A strange link between the knot in my throat (which keeps coming and going) and the lightness which replaces the usual sadness in her tone when she speaks of D's attempts (and hers) to revive (and perfume?) a love which she no longer feels. At least that what she fears but she is not sure ...

I feel that we have re-established an a-symmetry, but that it is new.

I have never felt T so deep and so close or from so nearby.

I have never felt my sense of loss so "tied up" and so "loose".

Sooner or later, I would have to talk to someone about it.

AFTER THE SESSION

It took me a long time to write notes, I lost them and then found them again after turning my consulting room upside down and only thanks to a memory flash.

One could reasonably ask the thorny question, "How can one make an honest contribution to the CTr topic if the clinical material has been excessively censored by the analyst's fear of exposure or self-disclosure, or, vice versa, if the material is too rough and exposed for fear of not showing crucial connections and resonances?"

Obligatory (and desired) discretion when writing about a particular, intense CTr experience is put to the test when one attempts to analyse single elements to offer the reader useful reflections. In any case, I will try to distinguish between two series of considerations: those which came in the heat of the moment, within the reported sessions, a minimal part of the conscious elements of the complex work of CTr (Russo, 1998); and those which, with a cool head, we can speculate on, using the debate about transference (the patient's and the analyst's)/countertransference.

First of all, the narrative sequence and the associations of the P (patient), followed by the countertransferential movements of the A. I realize that by using this order I take on the preposition *gegen* of *gegenübertragung* – in the semantic meaning of towards, around, against, in reaction to.

My emotional movements were initially of amazement, of surprise – how had the P sniffed out the wound of absent sensoriality? I had just been thinking, before meeting the P, of the aphrodisiacal and/but lost smell of linden trees, with sweet nostalgia. There was no unpleasantness or irritation in my being asked "do you know (the smell of) amber?" Mysteries of the unconscious or more simply, deciphering human communication? Then I moved on to thinking of something new happening to her, finally nesting on her own with cakes and furnishings, but also of something primal: faeces and seduction, perfume which covers and seduces, sadomasochism and the oscillation of roles. Who is showing off to whom? Who seduces whom? Who abandons whom? And the analyst, what role does she play, or better yet, what role is she brought to play?

But dead, or at least in death-throws, was also (and once again) the P's chance that a full, reciprocal love might come to light and live – in this case with a man who was devotedly in love with her.

The agony of not feeling pain for this death/impossibility/rip was, however, too much mine. Most likely, a projected counter-identification was on the scene (Grinberg, 1979).

In any case, the image of amber which traps and preserves little dead animals, a crypt, a uterus-tomb, had its own beauty and called up memories of mine, of a distant stroll along the Baltic Sea with a loved one.

Again, a long, long time ago. Too much and … too much of me. And why too much "never again" and so much "again today"?

The ring which the restored fluctuation in my attention threw out to me, like a life-saver ring, was the connection between the image of the perfume bottles nicely displayed in the bathroom which she would go to smell (obsessiveness as a defence from pain and guilt?) and the visual representation of her smelling the torn-out hair (pleasure and pain or pleasant pain. "Oh, now I feel/smell!"[5]). My comment, which started with the words "like your hair", set off a slow untangling of me (A) by her (P) and the restoration of the necessary asymmetry.

The "skin-to-skin" had been the condition, at one and the same time, of confusion, of exchange through mixing, of "porosity" in the identity barriers, of closure in a third, separating space, however virtual. But the skin-to-skin also allowed experimentation with regressive states, if not exactly experimentation with a union which had a homosexual undertone to it, in the sense of primary homosexuality (an analyst/primary sensorial seducer-mother), and so the risk of violent rip-away separations or alternatively suffocating and mortal clutching.

Awareness of the regression quality of the experience, held in mind by the A and retraced – through reverie or emotional memories – could have brought both back to the present and to the dual. The redeeming device of the setting had worked, with difficulty, at least as the third. "Sooner or later I'll have to talk with someone" was the residual stabilizer of the third-ness of colleagues and theory.

SOME CONSIDERATIONS ABOUT THE TRANSFERENCE/ COUNTERTRANSFERENCE CROSSROADS

Without a doubt, more time was needed than the handful of seconds an ironic colleague would have said to discern the normal aspects and objectives – as Winnicott would have called them – from the aspects of Tr/CTr of the A herself or even of her neurosis of CTr (Ferenczi, 1932) When we have to deal with projective identifications or projective counter-identifications (Grinberg, 1979), as in this case, the questions are very problematic and the choices (interpreting, yes or no, when and how) are not easy.

Surely it was possible to use CTr as a compass for the interpretive work, an indicator of the P's unconscious (and not only). In short, a gash – and I deliberately use a strong, physical term – had been created in the state of things during that session. CTr could have been used to elaborate the less structured levels of the P's mind, but only through the difficult work of CTr could one have got to the form of thinkability and representation of the emotions in circulation. However, the insidious question remained, "whose emotions?" The terrain was, as always in these cases, very insidious. We could think that Racker, in his attempt at systematization, would have defined it as a position of direct CTr, sustained by complementary identifications, and perhaps in the face of that particular paralysis, confusion and flooding of the receiver's reminiscences, he would have made me/us remember, taking heart, that "we are still children and neurotics even when we are adults and analysts" (Racker, 1968).

For various reasons, but above all for doubts regarding the patient's capacity to access the symbolic fully, I oriented myself so as not to fall into what could have become a subtly expulsive technique of the pain of CTr, through interpretation. I chose to stay in the pain/pleasure of the tearing of her hair which was touched, heard, smelled. In my opinion, it was of fundamental importance that I went back to my place so as not to invade the patient's space, and to restore balance in the asymmetry of such vital importance in such a situation. Only in an asymmetric position can one tolerate the CTr, with the conviction that the analyst's internal axis can spark a psychic change.

Of course, I had to reckon with the super-Ego doubt of having not "yet acquired the necessary objectivity in practice", as Freud wrote to Jung (1912, p. 476). Because of that recommended "objectivity", I thought I had caught on to an even deeper meaning. Was what happened in the session really *gegen*, hindrance?

How and how much had the patient really perceived or been influenced by my implicit signals? This might not be the central question, even if it is legitimate to ask oneself how much and in what way a sensorial minus of the analyst can create an invasion of the field. Perhaps making a virtue of necessity is the point. The ability to tolerate her peculiar, lonely pain, which expanded during the session, which up to that time had been left unexpressed. My interpretive words could easily have turned into actions or suggestions. This particular countertransferential tolerance, necessary for survival amidst the stench of death, anality and seductive glue, may have supplied hope of digestibility and signification for the cruel feelings of separation, loss and abandon and, above all, for the impelling questions of dependence and symbiotic union.

A sensory deficit, a narcissistic wound had met a semblance/mask of maniacal triumph, in defence of extreme questions.

My unconscious had been simultaneously receptor and pit, and my attention had transformed from being freely fluctuating to being prickly and static. My unconscious had been invaded by representations of the patient not immediately legible, if not for the path of experimentation-transit, even in-through the analyst's body, of the patient's knotted-up emotions.

The body, "means and the heart of treatment", had erupted with the roar of mania, of the retentive collecting or with the libidinal force of the transmitter, with the whole set of resistances of the patient–broadcaster. The signal was given by the analyst's attention, which became almost fixed on a point, in expectation of a link, and from her body in tumult.

Going through the most significant literature on countertransference, we can glean some consistent themes, from the "blind spots" which follow movements of unresolved repression, following the well-known and fortunate denomination Freud adopted from Wilhelm Steckel (1912), to Bion's (1977) invitation to investigate caesura, link, synapse, (counter-trans)ference, transitive/intransitive mood (Riolo 1998). A fundamental element is the prefix *trans*, which points back to the dynamics, to the diachronic and synchronic movement, to the exchange economy (not only all that is *infra-*), but above all to communication between unconscious territories. Communication through the various barriers, permeable or well-built, of the one and of the two, of the intrapsychic and the interpsychic. Surely there, where bodies' relevance in factual and representational reality is high (wounded body of the analyst and symptomatology on and in the patient's body), the patient's transference can become central as it transfers *into* and not *onto* the analyst, setting off the difficult work of otherness, subtly perceivable in the excess of resonance. *Heimlich* and *unheimlich* together. All this, I believe, gives the passage described nourishment.

THE BODIES: CAUTIONS, RESOURCES, PITFALLS

We always have well in mind that not only the two real bodies of the P and A meet in the analyst's room. Sometimes they are invaded by others' ghostly bodies, or not inhabited/deprived by patients' living bodies and analysts which can disappear entirely or partially, distorting or conforming themselves to an infinite range of fantasies, fears, desires. The bodies which met in that particular analysis inscribed a story and a vital trajectory characterized by a complex plot, from the genome to the symbolic. The patient who, in order to feel alive and express herself, rips her hair out, emotions and words, summoning all her senses together. The other, that of the analyst, deprived of the faculty of fully perceiving sensorially, and who is taken by the throat by ungovernable emotions, becomes mute, and at the same time cumbersome and vibrating.

We analysts hesitate to talk about our body but we know that, in some way, it is at work, silently or clamorously, to indicate the way towards finding words.

The questions of if and how and how much my patient noticed my *vulnus* remain unanswered. That she had probably registered my painful "olfactory absence" seemed plausible following the sequence: P is familiar with amber? A jumps at the visible register for amber resin which captures dead insects.

Had she picked up on my envy and nostalgia for that whole odiferous world? Probably she had sensed my absence-for-mourning, in the same way as when, at the dawn of her life she had encountered the "unburied" mourning of her mother for her own father, whose funeral she had not been able to go to because she was far away and pregnant with my patient. The children of silent, absent-for-mourning but present-for-duty mothers, we can hypothesize, develop special, investigative multisensory skills. Surely the "mother death" which Green talks about, had been for this woman – born in mourning and hanging on for dear life – an object figure of some importance.

In fact, she rubbed salt in the wound on catching its scent.

Perhaps, however, she hadn't noticed anything in the factual reality. For the sake of rigor, I can never spontaneously assume total certainty.

FROM REFLECTIONS ON A PARTICULAR FORM OF COUNTERTRANSFERENCE TO CHOICES OF TECHNIQUE

Both T's life and her analysis are substantially imbued with elements which refer to the themes of an intimate and syntonic union (a perceptive experience which tones and organizes), and of separation (detachment and violent uprooting, resulting in emptiness).

Abandonment is the dominant theme, both in its active and passive roles and inversions of them, and in the strategies which reactivate it, in the attempt to avoid it or to elaborate its traumatic dimension as an extreme defence.

Attempts at denying that she is chronically abandoning/abandoned seem to be of central importance. The paths of denial effectively wind down to the sensorial investment of the object. Moreover, the change from active to passive induces her to abandon the object before its appeal and seduction are worn down and before a meaningful relationship with the real and whole object can be established. Control over the situation is kept through self-harming rituals (ripping out her hair, now especially the white ones which show she is ageing) or through self-stimulants ("I set out the perfume bottles and sniff them"). She seems to be saying "I let money slip through my fingers to buy compulsively things which make me more attractive ... and therefore extant".

What has allowed the analyst to survive, to keep alive the hope of being able to use and render useful the analytic relationship for her who both so needed and yet was so afraid of it? To go out of unison, and then go back (in the turning-point session which I have described, for example)? To listen again (to herself)? Not to re-act?

It was probably picking up, through her body, on that imperceptible transition from a uniqueness which resides in a personal odour and in the combination of a specific skin odour with an external perfume which simultaneously makes it stand out and covers it up. The communicative function of perfuming oneself, also with an analyst who cannot sensorially perceive but who nonetheless activates, through introjected identification and nascent empathy, enough internal receptors to capture a movement in emotions. It was about picking up on the precious tenderness of the desire to stroke a cat's fur and to be stroked like a cat-child, and to perfume herself for someone as a kind of dance which is not only narcissistically seductive but also filled with reciprocal pleasure. I feel your "*discours enduillé*" going through mine.

My technical choices were determined in part by a priority for absolute interpretive caution regarding the patient's kamikaze attacks. They were, especially at the beginning, in keeping with what I had gathered in the intake interviews, amply reported because so full of precious "instructions for use" and warnings. All these things received my punctual comment, always with an element of *unsaturation* which would allow her to add meaning. Usually they were transference interpretations which opened up glimmers of light and allowed differentiation and distinction. Attention to classic parameters was maximal: those of distance and temperature, tact and timing, and above all reception and vigilant tolerance for the charm and spells, for the deadly boredom which threatened to wrap us up in repetitive accounts of the minutiae of her opaque, repetitive days. I honestly don't know if my devices were at times fragile or somewhat lacking in their containing interpretative activity, but they did allow us both to go past the "two or three times" which marked her previous therapeutic experiences. They allowed me to elaborate the lesson which I have tried to recount, at least to a small extent.

Notes

1 I had been making my way across this landscape for a while before meeting this patient, with the death of a very significant person in my world of affection and sensoriality.
2 The Italian word *svenarsi* would most faithfully be translated with "to bleed oneself", but is used idiomatically to refer to a great effort being made, as is also true in English – "to bleed someone (dry)", for example.
3 *Segnare rosso* in Italian can have more than one meaning. It can be used to refer to menarche or menstrual stains. Alternatively, in a scholastic setting, it indicates a not-too serious mistake in schoolwork. Here the verb is in the imperative: "Mark (it) red."
4 *Andare a capo* in Italian can have more than one meaning also. It can mean that a new paragraph should be started. It can indicate getting to the origin of a problem, somewhat like "get to the bottom of it". It can also mean to move into command. Here it is in the imperative: "Start a new paragraph", for example.
5 The Italian verb "sentire" can be translated with the English "feel", "hear", "smell", "taste".

Bibliography

Aisenstein, M. (2009) Les expressions du corps dans la cure. *Psychanalyse en Europe*, 63: 37–44.
Anzieu, D. (1985) *L'Io Pelle*. Rome: Borla, 2004.
Bion, W.R. (1977) *Two Papers: The Grid and Caesura*. Rio de Janeiro: Imago.
Colazzo, M. (2009) Parfums. *Psychanalyse en Europe*, 63: 55–65.

Corsa, R. (2008) L'identità violata: quando lo psicanalista perde la salute. Segreti e confessioni nella malattia dell'analista. *Rivista di Psicoanalisi*, 54: 315–335.

Fenichel, O. (1944) On the unconscious significance of perfume: John Prett. *The International Journal of Psychoanalysis*, 23, (1942), *Psychoanalytic Quarterly*, 13: 390.

Ferenczi, S. (1932) *Diario Clinico*. Milan: Raffaello Cortina, 1988.

Franchi, F., Castriota, F., Chiarelli, R. (2006) *Il Corpo Nella Stanza d'Analisi*. Rome: Borla.

Freud, S. (2008) *Lettere a Wilhem Fliess 1887–1904*. Turin: Bollati Boringhieri.

Freud, S. (1912) Consigli al medico nel trattamento psicoanalitico. *S.E.*, 6.

Freud, S. (1909) Osservazioni su un caso di nevrosi ossessiva (Caso clinico dell'uomo dei topi). *S.E.*, 6.

Freud, S. (1929) Il disagio delle civiltà. *S.E.*, 10.

Grinberg, L. (1979) Controtransfert e controidentificazione proiettiva. In Albarella C., Donadio M. (eds), *Il Controtransfert*. Naples: Liguori, 1986.

Hermann, I. (1943) *L'istinto Filiale*. Milan: Feltrinelli, 1974.

McGuire, W. (ed.) (1974) *The Freud/Jung Letters: The Correspondence between Sigmund Freud and C.G. Jung*. Princeton, NJ: Princeton University Press.

Racker, H. (1968) *Transference and Countertransference*. Croydon, UK: Medway Press, 1982.

Rosenbaum, I. (1961) The significance of sense of smell in the transference. *Psychoanalytic Quarterly*, 31: 293.

Riolo, F. (1998) Naufragio senza spettatori. *Rivista di Psicoanalisi*, 2: 98.

Russo, L. (1998) Sul controtransfert. *Rivista di Psicoanalisi*, 2: 98.

Schwartz, H.J., Silver, A-L.S. (1990) *Illness in the Analyst: Implication for Treatment Relationship*. Madison, CT: International University Press.

Segal, H., *The Work of Hanna Segal*. New York: Jason Aronson, 1981.

5

ACCESS TO THE EMBODIED UNCONSCIOUS THROUGH REVERIE AND METAPHOR

Benedetta Guerrini Degl'Innocenti

In normal development the bodily self and the psychological self together form the sense of self; the bodily self is the founding core, the container of the psychological self (Freud, 1923). Body sensations and experiences play an essential role in development and, in the same way, powerfully come on the analytic scene, whether one likes it or not, whether one acknowledges it or not. Then the inclination and capacity for psychologically oriented thinking – what is now called reflective function or mentalization – transform body experiences into affective states, thoughts that can be thought, put into words and shared.

Clinically, psychoanalysis has dealt with the mind–body issue since its outset. Freud thought of the body as *Körper* – "the body I have", the actual body, a material and visible object, a "prerequisite" to the psyche (Laplanche, 1987) – as well as *Leib* – "the body I am", a vital matter and the early core of subjectivity.

As psychoanalysis deals with the body, it operates as a language that promotes interventions and transformations within the "actual" dimension of the body. And although the symbolic language with its metaphors draws on a large variety of sources, the body is ultimately the metaphorical source of all the metaphors, the fabric out of which all the symbolic representations are cut (Benveniste, 1998; Johnson, 1987; Lakoff, 1987).

Metaphor, more than anything else, is a cognitive tool. Maria Ponsi (2010) writes:

> By emphasizing a common aspect of two objects of the world we don't only explain, we also create something new, we take a step forward in the knowledge of something unknown. [...] Using a metaphor with any object that is not yet known enough allows us to make inferences, formulate hypotheses and theories as well.
>
> (p. 2)

But metaphor is not only the basic structure of a cognitive function. Modell (2003; 2009), for example, claims that metaphor is the founding structure of the psychological unconscious process: an inborn property of the mind rooted in the body, an unconscious process that can be assimilated to dream, yet it operates in a waking state as well. As Modell (2003) says, it has the function to interpret unconsciously the affective world and to prepare for action.

Somehow, we could say that all language is a metaphor, as words are signifiers that stand for what they mean. Ordinary language is replete with metaphor, albeit often deadened in effect by over-usage or else hardly detectable because it has become so much a part of the meaning of the word (Ogden, 1997b). When metaphorical language is lacking in its lively and creative function, we are stuck in a world of surfaces with meanings that cannot be reflected upon.

Psychoanalysis is essentially a metaphorical enterprise (Arlow, 1979): many authors have stated that work in a psychoanalytic treatment can be compared to reading a metaphor. As Campbell and Enckell (2005) underlined, instead of elaborating words like a linguistic metaphor does, a psychoanalytical metaphor elaborates non-verbal representational means as perceptions, feelings, thoughts or memories. Dreams are metaphors, reveries are metaphors and, sometimes, symptoms are metaphors. Reverie is a process in which living metaphors are created that give shape to the analyst's experience of the unconscious dimensions of the patient and of the analytic situation (Ogden, 1997a). Inside the psychoanalytic process the capacity to transform reverie into more verbally symbolic forms can create expressions describing what unconscious experience is like. There are some pathologies, such as severe eating disorders and some forms of violent acts (Campbell and Enckell, 2005), in which the body seems to have lost its metaphoric power and the mind its capacity to transform, metaphorically, the experience, so much so that anorexia becomes a mute condition looking for meaning. In these cases, where the body experience has lost both its symbolic value and its structuring and organizing dimension, "the body as such" (Gill, 1994) can become the container of not-mentalized experiences, a forlorn land where suffering seems to be begging for words.

AIMS OF THIS CHAPTER

In this chapter I will describe a clinical case in which the body dominates the scene through a symptom which would usually be defined as anorexia, but I will not specifically speak about anorexia or generalize the remarks I will make about my clinical and therapeutic experience with this patient.

I will emphasize how one of the specific issues in treating this patient is her apparent inability to access the metaphorical function of the mind, understood not only as a basic structure of cognitive function, but as the founding structure of the unconscious psychological process (Modell, 2009). I will also show that this inability to think metaphorically is connected with a lack of reflective function of her mind which would allow her to feel herself as a "subject" in relation to what happens to her. Quite the opposite, her reflective function seems to work only as a way of objectifying reflectiveness. There is *the body I have*, but not *the body I am*. Some theoretical thoughts will help us understand how this deficit in the symbolic functioning and reflective thinking can be connected with markedly dysfunctional features in her early relational context. We will also see how, consequently, the patient's unconscious has been trapped in a wordless body and how this has challenged the analytic device. Much of the preliminary[1] work for a real analytic work was geared to stimulate an authentically reflective thinking.

DEVELOPMENTAL REFLECTIONS

The way in which the body can be experienced and thought about at first depends on the way the body, and more generally the individual as a person, was treated by the caregivers. Feeling beautiful or horrible is fundamentally an object-related issue (Lemma, 2010). In other words, to go "from the experience of need to the dynamic of desire" (Badoni, 2000), it is necessary to have a maternal object capable of containing, regulating and transforming body experiences into affective states.

As we know, the infant gradually acquires the mental experience of him/herself through a careful observation of the mental state of his/her object, within which the infant learns to detect the way in which the object perceives his/her feelings. If the child's caregiver is able to tune in effectively with the child (Stern, 1985), or provides a "good enough" mental mirror (Winnicott, 1967), body sensations may be transformed into subjective states which can gradually become the object of verbal expression. Empathically attuned verbal responses promote the gradual symbolic coding of affective bodily experiences, ultimately leading to the development of distinct and defined feelings. Being able to experience and acknowledge one's own affects as mental phenomena (that is, as feelings), instead of simply as bodily phenomena, therefore depends on the presence of a facilitating intersubjective context.

Recent conceptualizations of "mirroring" emphasize that, no matter how well attuned a parent is to the infant's state, his/her mirroring facial and vocal behaviour never perfectly matches the infant's behavioural expressions (Fonagy et al., 2002). Mothers, and other adult figures, "mark" their affect-mirroring displays by exaggerating some aspect of their own realistic response, to signify that these responses are reflections of the other's feelings rather than being expressions of their own feelings. The infant can recognize and use this marked quality to "decouple" or to differentiate the perceived emotion from its referent and to "anchor" or "own" the marked mirroring stimulus as expressing his or her own self-state (Aron, 2006). In other words what the mother reflects back to the infant is the experience of sameness within difference.

As Aron (2006) highlighted, the mother who exclaims "Ohhh" when she sees her child who bruises his knee marks her response by signifying that she is not reacting exactly as the child is, but that she is separate.

According to Aron (2006) and Benjamin (2004) we can talk about mirroring with its marked component as a dyadic phenomenon functioning also as a differentiating third point emerging between the infant and the attuned parent: the child's immediate response, the mother's response identifying with her child's fear, and the differentiated component of the mother's response in which she knows that the child is not dying and will get over it. The exaggeration by the mother in mirroring her baby's emotional signal looks like a kind of pretending; in other words, she is just playing with metaphors.

"Thirdness" thus emerges here from within the dyad, preparing the way for the coming of the father as a literal third object to intervene and separate mother from child. This is what Aron and Benjamin (1999), describing the origins of self-reflexivity in intersubjective space, called an *incipient third*. It is in this way that mirroring creates a third symbolic intersubjective space of representation between infant and parent allowing for and facilitating mentalization and affect-regulation. As Ogden writes, "The paradox of the little girl's transitional oedipal relationship (created by mother and daughter) is that the first triadic object relationship occurs in the context of a two-person relationship" (1987: 485).

Also the third as elaborated by the Lausanne Group is neither necessarily another person nor an object but rather a third focus within a dyad. Fivaz-Depeursinge and her colleagues (2004) have found that the triangular capacity is already in evidence from three to four months of age. At this early age, triangular relations are immediate and context-dependent. By nine months they exhibit the beginnings of an intentional stance, and with the advent of symbolic thought and the moral emotions they gain self-reflexivity. In accordance with this finding we can point out that primary triangular processes exist from very early on in life and that what is most characteristic of the oedipal stage is not triangularity per se, but rather symbolic thought, narrative structure and reflexive self-awareness (Stern, 2004).

Thus, from a developmental perspective, traumatic affective states must be interpreted with respect to the relational system in which they are formed. If we keep in mind the concept of the mother as the primary regulator who performs in relation to the child's physical states (Schore, 2001), we can think of those traumas which take place in the early phases of development as relational events. The presence of a caregiver who is able to accurately recognize the signs of affect in the infant, as they occur before words, is necessary in order to find the right words consonant with affects – before the onset of speech, initially, even though words may be used (Straker, 2006). When the caregiver is mis-attuned at the preverbal stage the child is unlikely, later, to experience an adequate consonance between words and affect and is likely to have poor affect regulation and an insecure sense of self. A faulty regulation skill, apart from interfering with the infant's natural exploration of reality, may also link the need for safety to concrete modalities, massively interfering with symbolization processes.

GIULIA

"We all have a story to tell but we don't always choose to do so. The story we cannot avoid telling is the one that our body inevitably narrates" (Lemma, 2010: 1). In these cases one may happen to feel seized by the appearance of the other, and actually this was my very first experience with Giulia.

When I meet with Giulia, she is in her early twenties. She is 5.6 feet tall and weighs 45 kg. Such scanty data clearly convey what G is made of: a bony body, hard to look at, and yet hard to avert one's eyes from. Her capacity to draw people's gaze and hold it seems as strong as her inability to express any emotion or to talk about herself. In other words, it is her body that keeps the score and "talks for her".

Insufficient integration shows up already in Giulia's difficulty in transforming facts into an autobiographical narrative, and the impossibility of developing a good symbol-making capacity is expressed in the impossibility of her language to represent affects, feelings and inner states fully and meaningfully. In other words, her story, that never becomes a narrative, is like her body, dried and depleted of life, coming out of her mouth in disconnected fragments, as if it had not been thought before, as if it had not been experienced. Her tragic body, which is covered by several layers, seems to be overcome by an effort to give shape to nothingness, whereas in her pale face two wide-open eyes seem to pierce the mystery of the other and, at the same time, look for some traces of herself in the other.

The contact with Giulia is one of those frightening experience from the outset because she almost does not look human. For a long time she would just sit there in front of me and look at me, without being able to describe herself and her emotions, stripped of fantasies and words, unable to think about herself as a reference point to describe her internal experiences. I feel that if she felt something, she would be frightened, but she seems to be able just to let me feel that fear and, in fact, I feel frightened "on her behalf". Session after session, I try to think how I can represent the fear I am feeling, and as I ask myself whether her body or her mind's ability to starve her body is frightening me more, a scene from *Alien* suddenly comes to me. In that film a group of humans get in touch with an alien monster, imbued with aggression in its purest form, which seems to be conceived to destroy all forms of human life. In the scene that comes to my mind one of the protagonists is about to eat, as he believes he has escaped the monster's attack. But suddenly, when he has just swallowed the first bite, he is racked by terrible pains and lacerated by an "alien" that comes out of his abdomen, killing him.

At once, I think that this reverie[2] – with its violent visual content – can open up some meaning and become an access to the "unconscious" elements that have not yet been symbolized, as well as being the answer to my haunting question: is it her body or her mind able to starve the body which frightens me most? Psychoanalysis offers different ways of thinking about an object like "alien" which is perfectly designed to destroy, but I need to approach an alien inhabiting Giulia as an entity I have come across for the first time, and I can only intuit its dreadful destructive potential, its unpredictability and its capacity to grow "from within". In other words, I think that letting Giulia tolerate a contact with such primitive and destructive aspects of her own mind – which is completely lacking all reflective function and symbolic/metaphorical capacity – cannot but be an attempt to transform the unthinkable "alien" into an internal object that can be thought and approached, though very cautiously at first. This "alien", that I observe through a counter-transference lens, appears to me almost as an alien form of embodied unconscious: it is alien in the sense that it does not seem to belong to the self, it seems to come "from without", and Giulia is not aware that she is invaded by it. But what makes it different from any other internal object is its capacity to hide in the body, to colonize it, to become part of it by parasiting all its vital resources. To approach it cautiously seems to me the only way to protect the "human component" that "lodges" it unknowingly, to understand its nature, to see what keeps it alive and what for.

GIULIA'S FAMILY

Giulia's primary environment seemed to be one in which physical and empathic absence, inconsistency and a failing mirroring response along with a strong intrusion of unprocessed traumatic parental aspects in the structure of the self (the alien component) intermingled.

In the narrative fragments that Giulia is able to tell me, her father seems to be lacking self-confidence about everything and, at the same time, it is as if he cannot ever be satisfied. Giulia describes him as an impulsive man, capable of going into tantrums, and yet being extremely fragile. These violent outbursts were tinted with persecutory guilt and often accompanied with suicidal threats immediately following such angry outbursts.

Giulia's father seemed to alternate between being absent and emotionally unavailable: his mind – which was colonized by fears, insecurities and frankly pathological aspects – was likely to lack a reflective function and did not seem able to provide a good mirroring experience, let alone give back to Giulia a consistent self-image through the recognition of her emotional needs. Moreover, her father always expected her to perform successfully and to achieve outstanding goals. But once she attained them, they were never good enough for him.

For many years her mother was, on her own admission, aloof and busy at work, involved in her own education and taking care of several ill relatives (in a way that Giulia defines as compulsive and exclusive of everything else). In the last years she began to pay more attention to her daughter because of the severe signs of psychological suffering that Giulia started to show. Yet this greater attention has been translated into a caring attempt that often seems infantilizing and controlling. Her mother shifts between at least three modes. In the first mode she is literally focusing completely on Giulia until she becomes intrusive, so controllingly caring and entangled that boundaries become entirely blurred. In the second mode, she responds to Giulia's smallest and weakest attempt to break loose by becoming rigid, cold and affectively inaccessible. In the third mode – triggered when the suffering of some relative dominates – Giulia feels that her mother literally disappears, as if she can be fully engaged, with no break or fatigue, but dealing just with one emergency at a time. Seemingly, both father and mother have always had great difficulty functioning as a couple and as parents; conflicts between the two of them and about what decisions to make have been relentless. Giulia has never understood what they really thought, as they could state one thing one day and the opposite on the next day.

Since she was a child, she thought that her father wanted a son and she suffered from an anxiety stemming from her gender identity conflicts.

FIRST STEPS

I start to see Giulia twice a week, sitting in front of her who scrutinizes me and looks for an answer about anything that concerns her. At times her questions are implicit, at times she asks them overtly. The peculiarity of her questioning is that what she wants to know is not my opinion about her, but "why does she think that?" or "what must she do in that situation?" I realize that thoughts for her do not seem to be representations of reality but rather real objects, facts. Sometimes she scares me, not only because of the mute firmness by which she is starving her body (and I mean that she is starving "the body she has", not "the body she is"), but also because of the discouraging poverty of her narratives, the narrowmindedness of her relational horizon and, most of all, the apparent lack of any emotional sonority or affective nuance in her language.

My greatest effort, for a long time, has aimed to counter Giulia's continuous tendency to give up on thinking, by housing in my mind most of the analytic process, offering her small bites of "plain food", made with the raw materials coming from her and characterized by low-intensity emotions. But, most of all, in the first two years of treatment she indirectly manifested the need to "take in" her primary objects within our analytic space. Which, given Giulia's severe clinical situation, literally meant to meet with her parents, mainly with her mother, but sometimes with her father too, and then use the space with Giulia as a transitional area where we could try to turn her actual parents into internal objects.

Her psychic objects started slowly to take shape in my mind. In an extreme and desperate attempt of her psyche to ruthlessly control the soma, I began to catch a glimpse of the fragments of her ideal ego mixed with grandiose, demanding and punitive super-ego aspects that are probably of paternal origin. Giulia's paternal grandfather Sandro was described as a terrible tyrant, extremely devaluing and contemptuous of Giulia's father. It seems that he treated his son like a total fool, a good for nothing idiot. Probably for this reason Giulia's father spent all his life in a desperate yet unsuccessful attempt to please him. Along with these aspects, I could see the anxiety about a needy state that she experienced as submission – a likely result of the evacuation of her mother's childish and dependent parts into Giulia. At the same time, this anxiety seemed to be powerfully fuelled by some expectations of self-sufficiency, free of all fears and needs. In fact, these expectations were conveyed to me by an ego ideal that Giulia's mother had already displayed in the very first meeting we had. In describing her daughter "before the problems began", she told me with a tangible feeling of nostalgic pride in her tone that "Giulia was self-sufficient".

Here is the first dream she brought to me after six months:

"I am at home and in the dream I see a young man — I have known him since I was born though I meet him only rarely now. In reality he is a cheerful and vital young man, he is good company, generous with everybody, but in the dream he is a squatter in my house and I feel something evil in him, something about him is frightening me. I tell him he has to leave, but he does not go. He has come with plenty of young people who are squatting both the floor above and the floor below mine. I call the police as I am standing in front of him, but then I am unable to speak on the phone: I dial the police number many times but I do not speak."

This dream seems to introduce on the analytic scenario Giulia's gender identity conflicts: her infantile body self, a good "companion", *cheerful* and *vital*, seems to get lost when puberty intrudes with the violence of the drive outbreak. What remains is the feeling of something *evil* and *frightening* inside herself: an uncanny aspect of self, unthinkable and unbearable, plenty of *squatting* parts. Furthermore I thought that some fragments of the traumatic and unresolved relationships with her parents, as "ghosts in the nursery" (Fraiberg et al., 1987), *invaded* Giulia's self as a form of trans-generational transmission. These "betalomes"[3] — as Nino Ferro would call them with one of his apt Bionian neologisms (Barale and Ferro, 1992) — are "alien" because they are not congruent with the internal experience, but at the same time they are "internal", as parts of the other-than-oneself which have been expelled and inoculated in the host organism. By using metaphorically the film that crossed my mind during my reverie, we could think that these alien elements — which penetrated and encysted early in her life — probably remained latent or were partially integrated, *in a state of incubation*, until some developmental challenge or thrust to self-assertiveness of the self awoke and triggered them. With the onset of puberty, the re-emergence of the Oedipal conflict and the sexualization of the body probably came to the fore to disorganize and rout the already weak defences that had been laboriously recruited to counter the poor cohesion of the self.

The infantile body — which seems, retrospectively, perceived as quiet and safe in an idealized way — became an untrustworthy, turbulent and uncontrollable body ruled by the drives. Giulia abandoned her body, with the "bad" part in it, and at the same time she structured an omnipotent protective armour, a *rescue capsule* that enabled the self to survive. Her "no" to food became part of the protective shield against the alien self and the distressing dangers of an invaded, unknown and incomprehensible body. This omnipotent and controlling self originally acted as an extreme protection against traumatic states of powerlessness, shame and terror; somehow, it served as a secure base, but at the same time the omnipotent and unrealistic perfection became a safety benchmark for all her activities. The way Giulia (like many patients with severe anorexic symptoms) is afraid of being intruded is quite similar to what severely abused patients experience: this fear of self-violation is connected to the presence of a powerfully intrusive object in the patient's mind. Like with abused people, this intrusion has not been symbolized in any way, but it appears immediately in its concrete dimension. It is not *as if* the other could penetrate inside; the other is inside, as we can see in another dream that Giulia had after a few months into analysis. In that dream the persecutory gazes of her family members penetrate and, with their incoherent, purposeless and violent content, attack her mind from within.

"I was with my parents and there were many other people too. I noticed that everyone was mad at me, they looked angrily at me: I could not understand what I did to be looked at like that, but it had to do with something terrible ... like I killed someone. I did not understand, but the pressure was so strong that in the end I broke out, made a scene and went mad."

The mind seems to be so permeable to the intrusive power of the gaze of the Other and apparently lacks a reflective function, that in the encounter the subject is traumatically reduced to the object. Giulia feels all the destructive power of this "alien", embodied in her body like a monstrous agglomerate in which psychic fragments of the Other, incomprehensible and unsymbolized sensory experiences, primitive and dangerous drive aspects, identity anxieties, needs felt as being uncontrollable, and much more – that I cannot yet see – are likely to be mixed together. Perhaps, by starving herself, Giulia is starving the other/alien inside her in a desperate attempt to ward it off.

But sometimes Giulia seems to be desperately looking for contact – a contact that is extremely infantile, dependent and longing for a fusion with an idealized but also very powerful and intrusive object, as it becomes clear in the following dream:

"I was flying with my mother – we were sitting in chairs like the ones at the hairdresser's. We were flying like in a video game, like on Google Earth, and

we had a special mouse, a three-dimensional one that, besides moving in the two dimensions, also had a button for depth. As we were flying above the sea, we fell down and I was seized by a terrible fear of sharks. Then, I do not know how, we managed to kick off again, but I thought we should ask A., who knew how it worked, to tell us how to use that mouse which I had never used before."

In this dream Giulia talks about her relationship with a symbiotic, fusing maternal object, where the experience of "thirdness" is unknown, and it is tinted with an omnipotence strengthened by the dimension of virtual games. With such an object one can only "fly on the surface", because to go more in depth one would need the contribution of a third, a paternal and separating element, a special device, like analysis, capable of providing depth and thickness. Without this "knowledge", the internal dimension can be felt as falling into an inside which is full of predatory and devouring objects.

DURING THE SECOND YEAR OF ANALYSIS

At some point along the treatment a few changes occurred. Giulia began to eat again, not much but with continuity. This immediately followed a period when her questions about "what to eat" had become urgent. Although I had never explicitly shared with her the alien's metaphor, I always kept it in mind and I decided to tell her that it did not seem to be possible to have a good answer to her question, as we could not be sure about which part of her was asking that question: Was it the part that fought to live or the one that seemed to attack all forms of life?

A few months later she says:

"I realize that I try to procrastinate the time I go to bed as much as possible and I feel I am doing so because the idea of going to bed is distressing. Why do you think it happens to me?"

[I notice that this time, rather than asking me why she is anxious, she asks me *why do I think* that she is anxious.]

I reply in a way she is now quite used to with me (unlike the first initial months when I felt it necessary to stimulate a representational capacity – totally lacking – through a co-construction of "hypotheses") by asking her: "Which thoughts do you feel that this state of anxiety could be related to?"

She thinks about it a few seconds and then answers: "I feel that the sensation of being all three of us, my parents and me, by ourselves, separate from one another, is anxiety-provoking."

I tell her that this remark seems to be really important. It is not the first time that she mentions her difficulty falling asleep, but it is the first time that, instead of attributing it to the fact of having to do many things after supper or resorting to pseudo-explanations given by other people about mysterious acting-out of the body (her mother tells her that anorexic women cannot sleep because they do not eat enough), she is now linking these problems to a state of anxiety, something that has to do with a thought that triggers a painful mental state, and this painful thought has to do with feeling separate.

She looks at me and seems to follow every single word I say very carefully.

She says that another thing also happens to her: lately, when she sits at the table, she feels that the hunger she felt before sitting has gone. She makes an effort and eats a little anyhow, much more than before, sure, but perhaps not as much as her father would want. Then, after supper, when everybody is watching television, she is hungry again and goes back to the kitchen to eat a bit more. This makes her feel guilty, because she thinks that she could eat at supper and eventually make her father happy.

I tell her that, also in this sequence, it seems possible to find new aspects belonging to some shift that apparently has to do only with the body, with an initial possibility to express a need, and perhaps also a desire – unaffected by the need or the desire of the other (her father's, in this case), with her being separate. I say that perhaps in what looks to her as a meaningless behaviour there is a still unaware emerging need to claim the freedom to recognize one's own needs and to choose when and how to meet them. She is always listening to my words carefully.

She says that the same thing did happen with her mother, who asked her if she would like her to cook the same kind of fish she had prepared a week before, and she immediately answered that she would love if her mother cooked it in the very same way. But then her mother prepared it in a completely different way and she dismissed her daughter's complaints by saying that she did ask her and she said it was okay. She adds that, although it seems incredible to her, she could not eat it.

It is not so incredible, I observe, if we imagine that lacking clear separateness between her and her mother, just as between her and her father, makes her feel that the ideas of the other can penetrate and sometimes even invade her, without her being able to state her point of view strongly and to confirm her difference. Under such circumstances, maybe the only defence is an extreme one, that is, closing all access to whatever comes from without. I tell her that, here too with me, she might happen to think that what I cook is not to her liking.

I think that a slow yet visible progress in our work together, on the one hand, is bringing Giulia back in contact with what is going on in her body but, on the other, she experiences it as a danger. Despite the attention I try to pay in cooking only what she is asking me (for example, by avoiding any topic that she has not *mentioned*), our interchange – as it contains my words and my thinking – conveys the presence of the other, which is always potentially annihilating and persecutory for her. But I also think that, through our interchange, her mind is achieving more effective defensive tools, and this can enable her body to slowly recover some vital functions, even though compulsively and often dramatically.

When it seemed that her body was starting to function again, a dramatic and incomprehensible event occurred. Giulia had two fainting episodes in the space of few months: she suddenly dropped on the floor and ended up with some bruises. After some doubts and an admission to hospital, doctors diagnosed the two episodes as "epileptic attacks" in the absence of any neurological evidence which could clarify their origin. Her family became very frightened and pressing in their asking me for a diagnosis – Giulia apparently much less so. Particularly her mother started to be fully engaged with Giulia in the "emergency mode", that often seems infantilizing and controlling. This allowed me to offer her the first metaphor: We are going to learn to call this aspect of her mother: "the 118", that is to say, the first aid emergency number in Italy. This metaphor expresses her mother's ability to respond massively to the need, but her inability to acknowledge some space for desire.

A bit surprised, I become aware of the fact that, actually, I am not quite worried either, or better, I feel as if I am split in two. I am *concretely* worried that there might be something organic, and at the same time I feel that, *symbolically speaking*, this is not a symptom to be cured but the expression, still unformed and turbulent, of a need in search of someone that can look after it.

At a certain point something happens, which allows us to begin to make sense of the apparently incomprehensible events of the past few months.

During a session at the beginning of the third year of analysis, Giulia talks of her difficulty in knowing what she feels but, unusually, she tries, with my help, to gather what she thinks she feels or what she knows about herself, a bit as if she were playing with building blocks. We go like that for a while, with Giulia who puts things together and reflects, while I "pass her a few pieces" which I have gathered for her. Suddenly she becomes silent and then asks me: "Doctor, do you ever have the feeling of having an empty head?"

I answer her that there may be more than one reason, and that it may be helpful for us to know how this "empty-headed feeling" makes her feel.

She says to me that it is not pleasant at all, and that it happens to her whenever she decides to think about herself.

I reply that it seems to me that thinking about herself is unpleasant because it seems to put her in touch with a sense of emptiness.

She agrees, saying that this has happened to her quite often, but that it is a new experience, maybe like thinking about herself. She is silent for a few minutes – a silence that seems very intense to me – and then she says to me:

"I feel as if I had just been born and I did not know how to organize my thoughts, as if I did not know how my mind worked." I am struck by this statement, which is the first real metaphor expressed by Giulia, and at the same time I think about the fainting episodes and two different images come to my mind: a computer that need to be reset because it has been affected by a virus, and the birth of a baby who falls on the floor because nobody is there to pick him up. At the moment I decide, as usual, to keep these two images in my mind, to use them a bit with the material that Giulia brings in the following sessions.

In a session of a few months later Giulia tells me about the strong headaches that she is frequently subject to, and of how she would like to get rid of the pain, and also of all the thoughts that occupy the whole space and prevent her from functioning.

I tell her that perhaps she would like to treat her head just like a computer: to be able to switch it off when it does not work well, and then to turn it on again after resetting it.

She looks at me, surprised, and then replies that it is indeed how she would like her mind to work: on–off.

I tell her that perhaps the black-outs that she experienced months ago were her attempt to reset her own mind: a way to expel all that stuff which occupies space, prevents her from functioning and that sometimes causes her great pain.

LAST DAYS

Currently Giulia is going through some small but precarious improvement. Three years into analysis, she has put on some weight, although she is not yet within the limits of normality, and her blood results are good. The most meaningful change in our interchange is the emergence of *'as if'*.

As she is talking about her wish to speak again with her former boyfriend, she says:

"It is as if I want to check whether I did the right thing when I broke up with him."

Why is she saying *'as if'*? I ask her to try to understand what use she makes of it.

"Because I am never sure what I am really feeling ... It is as if I cannot yet trust myself."

In this case Giulia seems to use *'as if'* to formulate a cognitive hypothesis: she is not yet sure whether she is able to give the right name to what she feels and she tries to compare it with something she knows *by science* and not *by conscience*, so to speak. *'As if'* serves to know but also, and at the same time, to maintain a safe distance: she does not feel, it is *as if* she feels.

Sometimes I can see how she is integrating split parts of herself and showing greater tolerance for her frail and needy aspects.

"Although last night was a bad night for me, instead of feeling the usual confusion in my head and having guilty feelings this morning, I told myself: 'Do you see that in doing so you just feel bad?' And I thought I had to tell you this, because I felt that my voice reminded me of yours."

I comment that her observing part seems to miss some of its implacable, disparaging and persecutory dimension, in the manner of Grandpa Sandro (the much-feared paternal grand-father, a real implacable tyrant who would never be satisfied), and instead has an element of grumpy care, in the manner of a Swiss tutor. Maybe this is happening because the threatening feeling stemming from the thought of asking for help is mitigated, and her turning to somebody for help does not necessarily mean any longer that she is petty and despicable.

"When I came to you I felt so strong, now I feel so weak. I have always been afraid to be dependent ... I feel very dependent on coming here now; I think that now I could not do without it but, like you are saying, not all the addictions are toxic."

CONCLUSIONS

With patients like Giulia who does not know what they feel and whose ability to symbolize is in some way paralyzed, unformulated affective experiences can be entrapped in a wordless body.

Working analytically with patients like Giulia, who are very concrete in their thinking and whose use of language is characterized by an inability to experience a metaphor as a metaphor, requires, sometimes for a long time, slow and patient work of recognition and sharing of the emotional states as they reveal themselves beyond words. This recognition is achieved through a slow but tenacious effort to distinguish between self and not-self and bring the body closer to affects by helping the construction of an internal core provided with agency and self-reference.

There is no doubt that the first epiphany of the unconscious should be, most importantly, an emotional experience, yet for Giulia, whose emotions are entirely embedded in her objectified and over-controlled body, unconscious experiences can only be "seen" and reflected upon when represented to her own consciousness metaphorically (Arlow, 1979; Edelson, 1983). The analytic use of reverie, as a largely inter-subjective form of re-presentation of the unconscious experience of analyst and patient (Ogden, 1997), enables the process by which unconscious experience is made into verbally symbolic metaphors that re-present unconscious aspects of ourselves to ourselves.

I believe that my reverie during the session with Giulia has opened a *transitional* channel of communication: I mean *transitional* in terms of an intermediate area of experience where imagination could be born and paradox could reign. In accordance with Winnicott (1953), I used this term referring to the possibility of opening an area of the mind where reality and unreality coexist, which is to be observed but left unquestioned; an area of the mind we both could cooperate to develop intersubjectively yet implicitly, in order to allow its origins and nature to remain private.

I do not *give* my reveries to Giulia, but I transform them into "building blocks" that could look like something, but also like something else. I think that my reverie, as a well-finished product of my mind, would have probably been experienced by her as something extremely concrete and alien and, consequently, as something so intrusive that it could have evoked instantaneous defences to ward it off. The complex and dramatic image of the alien as a tangle of powerful and uncontrollable drives hidden in the body, continuously processed and transformed in my mind through the contact with Giulia's thoughts, activated a metaphorical and symbolizing function in the analytic field. The images/metaphors that from time to time came to my mind during the sessions with Giulia worked as play material in child analysis: objects with which to shape the mind.

Notes

1 Throughout the first two years of therapy the work with Giulia was basically not-interpretive, due to her incapability of "grasping" the symbolic content in my interventions.
2 In accordance with Bion (1962), I consider the reverie of the analyst as a psychological intersubjective tool that, just like the reverie of the mother in the early stages of life, can transform unbearable and unthinkable sense data into alpha elements (functions), that is, into mental states that can be thought, understood and shared.
3 *Betaloma* is an expression that Antonino Ferro and Francesco Barale invented to describe clumps of beta elements which contrast with thought; this concept is related to those analytic situations in which projective identifications, as a prevailing way of communicating by the patient, risk paralysing the analyst's thought.

References

Arlow, J.A. (1979) Metaphor and the psychoanalytic situation. *Psychoanalytic Quarterly*, 48: 363–385.
Aron, L. (2006) Analytic impasse and the third: Clinical implication of intersubjectivity. *The International Journal of Psychoanalysis*, 87: 349–368.
Aron, L., Benjamin, J. (1999) The development of intersubjectivity and the struggle to think. Paper presented at the Spring Meeting, Division of Psychoanalysis (39), American Psychological Association. New York City, 17 April.

Badoni, M. (2000) Se la paura prende corpo. *Psiche*, 1: 35–39.

Barale, F., Ferro, A. (1992) Negative therapeutic reactions and microfractures in analytic communication. In Nissim, L., Robutti, A. (eds), *Shared Experience: the Psychoanalytic Dialogue*. London: Karnac Books, pp. 143–165.

Benjamin, J. (2004) Beyond doer and done to: An intersubjective view of thirdness. *Psychoanalytic Quarterly*, 73: 5–46.

Benveniste, D. (1998) Play and the metaphors of the body. *Psychoanalytic Study of the Child*, 53: 65–83.

Bion, W. (1962) *Learning from Experience*. London: William Heinemann.

Campbell, D., Enckell, H. (2005) Metaphor and the violent act. *The International Journal of Psychoanalysis*, 86: 801–823.

Edelson, J.T. (1983) Freud's use of metaphor. *Psychoanalytic Study of the Child*, 38: 17–59.

Fivaz-Depeursinge, E., Favez, N., Frascarolo, F. (2004) Threesome intersubjectivity in infancy. In Zahavi, D., Grünbaum, T., Parnas, J. (eds), *The Structure and Development of Self-Consciousness: Interdisciplinary Perspectives*. Amsterdam: John Benjamins, pp. 21–34.

Fonagy, P., Gergely, G., Jurist, E., Target, M. (2002) *Affect Regulation, Mentalization, and the Development of the Self*. New York: Other Press.

Fraiberg, S., Adelson, E., Shapiro, V. (1987) Ghosts in the nursery: A psychoanalytic approach to problems of impaired infant–mother relationships. In Fraiberg, L. (ed.) *Selected writings of Selma Fraiberg*. Columbus, OH: Ohio State University Press.

Freud, S. (1923) The ego and the id. *S.E.*, 19: 3–68. London: Hogarth Press (1961).

Gill, M.M. (1994) *Psychoanalysis in Transition: A Personal View*. London: Karnac Books.

Johnson, M. (1987) *The Body in the Mind*. Chicago, IL: University of Chicago Press.

Lakoff, G. (1987) *Women, Fire and Dangerous Things*. Chicago, IL: University of Chicago Press.

Laplanche, J. (1987) *New Foundations for Psychoanalysis*. Cambridge, MA; Oxford: Blackwell, 1989.

Lemma, A. (2010) *Under the Skin: A Psychoanalytic Study of Body Modification*. London: Routledge.

Modell, A.H. (2003) *Imagination and the Meaningful Brain*. Cambridge, MA: Bradford Books, MIT Press.

Modell, A.H. (2009) Metaphor: The bridge between feelings and knowledge. *Psychoanalytic Inquiry*, 29: 6–11.

Ogden, T. (1987) The transitional oedipal relationship in female development. *The International Journal of Psychoanalysis*, 68: 485–498.

Ogden, T. (1997a) Reverie and metaphor: Some thoughts on how I work as a psychoanalyst. *The International Journal of Psychoanalysis*, 78: 719–732.

Ogden, T. (1997b) *Reverie and Interpretation*. Northvale, NJ: Jason Aronson.

Ponsi, M. (2010) Le metafore nella psicoanalisi clinica. Paper presented at the annual meeting between Psychoanalytic Institutes of Bologna and Firenze. Bologna, 11 December 2010.

Schore, A.J. (2001) The effects of secure attachment relationships on right brain development, affect regulation and infant mental health. *Infant Mental Health Journal*, 22 (1): 7–66.

Stern, D.N. (1985) *The Interpersonal World of the Infant*. New York: Basic Books.

Stern, D.N. (2004) *The Present Moment in Psychotherapy and Everyday Life*. New York, NY: Norton.

Straker, G. (2006) Signing with a scar: Understanding self–harm. *Psychoanalytic Dialogues*, 16: 93–112.

Winnicott, D.W. (1953) Transitional objects and transitional phenomena: A study of the first not-me possession. *The International Journal of Psychoanalysis*, 34: 89–97.

Winnicott, D.W. (1967) Mirror role of mother and family in child development. In Winnicott, D.W. (ed.), *Playing and Reality*. London: Tavistock Publications, 1971.

6

THE BODY IN PSYCHOANALYSIS

Cristiano Rocchi

My thesis is that the basic foundations of self-reflective capacity lie on our body sensations.

(Lewis Aron[1])

INTRODUCTION

This is not a chapter to be considered as dealing with psychosomatics. In fact, I would like to focus the reader's attention on the analyst's reactions during the psychoanalytic treatment and more particularly on the role played by the "hyper-presence of the patient's bodily absence" on the analyst's body–mind.

Moreover, I would like to add that my position is definitely Monist and therefore I am in tune with Grotstein when he suggests that while the mind–body theme constitutes a single holistic unity and mind and body are always inseparable, they *"seem to lend themselves to the Cartesian artifice of disconnection so that we can conceive one or another for the sake of discrimination"* (Grotstein, 1997, p. 205, emphasis added). This also entails that I am distancing myself from certain positions especially of the French school. For instance, I don't agree with Green (1998) when he maintains a Monistic approach does not necessarily entail a homogeneous unity and somatic and psychic organizations differ in their structures. Obviously I believe that articles like that by Marty (1952), just to quote one among many, "Les difficultés narcissiques de l'observateur devant le problème psychosomatique" ("The narcissistic difficulties presented to the observer by the psychosomatic problem"), are of the utmost importance to approach these issues; however, my standpoint is quite different from such a way of thinking. Indeed, in the light of my Monism, I do not believe that a distinction such as that made by Green that the *body* refers to the libidinal body (erotic, aggressive, narcissistic), whilst the *soma* refers to the biological organization (Green, 1998), is a fruitful one. All these positions are in fact, in my opinion, intrinsically dualistic and as I mentioned, I opt for assuming a Monistic position. [2]

I certainly agree with Bronstein (2011) when she wisely writes, "We can broadly say that the different psychoanalytical approaches to the understanding of psychosomatic phenomena depend in great measure on the emphasis that different theories place on specific aspects of Freudian theory".

Except for some of its trends, psychoanalysis after Freud, and notwithstanding Freud I would say, is trapped in the epistemologic frame of the Cartesian body–mind dualism, which derives mostly from Plato's ideas, as the Greek philosopher introduced the concept of *soul*. [3] For him the soul was "the engine of the body"; the soul was the steersman of the ship (body). The Greek mentality the Western culture comes from had been strongly bodily before the Athenian philosopher. The body for the pre-platonic Greek philosophers had been immediately *expressive* rather than *representative*. Plato insisted we cannot trust the body, because the information it provides is exceedingly subjective. The philosopher from Athens believed that it was necessary to introduce an objective plane and observe the world – thus our body as well – through numbers and ideas. For Descartes, living beings, as machines, could be entirely reduced to matter – *res extensa* – but since they were gifted with words and thoughts, they also had a soul – *res cogitans*. The Cartesian soul, the Cartesian *mens*, is only "a thing that thinks" and is purified by all requirements more closely linked to corporeity. This dualism between body and mind is still the one that currently decides on this "disjoint unity", as I define it, in Western culture and consequently also in most psychoanalysis. In fact, stating that the psychoanalytic approach is intrinsically unitary as it considers the mind as an intimately dynamic entity linked to and based on the bodily processes does not seem to be enough to maintain that it is not substantially part of a dualistic framework. Vice versa, in my opinion, Freud (1926) had tried to promote this reunion, "In the light of the intimate connection between what we distinguish in physical and psychic, we need to admit that the day will come when [...] new routes will open leading from somatic biology and physiological chemistry to the phenomenology of neurosis", and also *"the abyss that separates the bodily from the psychic continues to exist due to our experience and for our practical efforts"* (p. 412, my italics). Finally, towards the end of his life, he wrote, "Psychoanalysis explains that the presumed concomitant processes of somatic nature constitute the true psychic" (1938, p. 80, my translation).

The dualistic view of the mind–body relationship has led psychoanalysis, or at least a large part of the many types of psychoanalysis, to fall into two main misconceptions closely related to each other: (1) to make use of the concept of linear causality (i.e. psychic event causes physical disorder); (2) to reaffirm indeed the body–mind split: if I believe that a psychic event affects the body – or that a physical event affects the mind – the split is implicitly stated. But conversely, in supporting the view that body and mind are separate when I have to explain an event occurring in one of these containers, I will be made to believe that one of the two realities has affected the other. Hence an important question ensues: how can psychoanalysis find similarities between somatic symptoms and imaginary equivalents? There are at least two possible answers. The first is that psychoanalysis may enable the re-establishment of the mental sense of somatic functions.

The second answer is that psychoanalysis may help to uncover the causality of the biological mechanisms inside the symbolism of unconscious phantasies. These two theses are mutually exclusive. To speak about the mental sense of somatic functions means that the methods of mentalization trace out the physiological operation from which they originate. Gaddini (1982) considers the primal phantasies of the self as phantasies inside the body (different from phantasies on the body, which implies a separation that had already taken place between mind and body), which make up a mental expression of somatic operations. In this way, the mental mechanism of the introjection would be the subsequent developmental elaboration of its early somatic root of oral material incorporation, in the same way that the mental mechanism of the projection would be an evolution of the early physiological mechanism of faecal excretion. What is implied here is the mental sense of the somatic operation, at first embodied in the soma and in the concrete physical functioning; later on it becomes autonomous and mentalized in the psychic symbolism. If we claim, instead, that psychoanalysis, within its epistemic model, may track down the causal genesis of a biological mechanism in the symbolism of unconscious phantasies, we are proposing something entirely different. In fact, we are doing no more than extending the model of hysterical conversion to the structures ruled by the SNA (Autonomic Nervous System) and to the inner organs of smooth muscles that are assumed to have a sexual and conflicting symbolism. This is widely known to have been the first explanation of psychosomatics put forward by early psychoanalysts (Deutsch, 1959; Garma, 1953; Groddeck, 1951) which has been revitalized by a few modern authors who adopt the so-called model of "pre-genital conversion" (Chiozza, 1976; Mushatt, 1975; Savitt, 1977; Todarello and Porcelli, 2006).

I do not subscribe to either of the above-mentioned theses. I perhaps locate myself closer to Ferrari's position because his thesis seems to me to be the least dualistic within the psychoanalytic thought about this issue: to mean the body as the original matrix of the mental functions and to consider the "psychic system" in this perspective as a refined differentiation of the biologic development of the human body. Just like (although with specific characteristics) the immune or the endocrine systems. I like Ferenczi's observation and I am very convinced by it. For instance in "Bioanalytic Corollaries", in the *Thalassa* Appendix (vol. III, 1924):

> Vasomotor and trophic disorders stand on the borderline between neurotic and organic diseases, which is a purely artificial distinction. Lipothymia for instance, at first sight, is just the consequence of an insufficient cerebral blood supply; the bioanalytic conception would add that the regulation of arterial blood pressure regresses to a period before the upright position, when the blood supply of the brain did not require yet such a high splanchnic activity.
>
> (Collected Papers, vol. 3 p. 296)

In fact, I think that it may be possible to give, with hindsight, a meaning to a psychic or somatic pathology and consequently track down, at a subjective level in the consulting room a meaning in a physical pathology shown by the individual and setting a context within their biography. However, I cannot subscribe to a model according to which statements such as "That man's ulcer is caused by a badly internalized mother" are made possible (this is an example of the type of comments I heard at a meeting on the subject of somatization). To sum up, I deem appropriate the assumption of a possible internalization of a malevolent mother "imago" giving rise to a disturbed inner object–relationship that consequently makes such patient prone to build unhealthy relationships, thereby contributing to his illness; however, I wouldn't go so far as to establish a cause–effect link between the maternal representation and the onset of the ulcer. One thing is to say specific corporeal happenings of the psychosomatic area may suggest some meaning or "the system of the organic functions includes psychic meanings holding the potentiality to express themselves in the corporeal substance" (Franchi, Castriota and Chiarelli, 2006, p. 40).

Another is to say the mind makes things happen to physical matter that is separated from it. To summarize my position, I envisage a framework within which it might be possible to abandon the mind–body dichotomy and in which there is readiness not to privilege reason over affects. I am close to the thought of Matte Blanco who in his essay on the bi-logic of the unconscious ("The unconscious as infinite sets. An essay in bi-logic", 1975; Italian translation 1981) maintains the great importance played by the emotion–thought relationship, believing that there may not be a thought that is not linked to an emotional experience. Rather, the latter precedes the former thought and acts as its "mother", says the Chilean psychoanalyst. On the other hand, within a neuroscientific environment, even Damasio (1994) denies the emotion–reason dichotomy when maintaining that reason is guided by the emotional evaluation of the consequences of the action; while emotion has the ability to influence the decision-making processes and mental life takes place through the use of information from the nervous structures in charge of the elaboration of the affective–emotional responses and at the same time in relation with the contents of memory, which reemerge during the experience. Le Doux (2002, p. 286) shares the same position when he defines the emotion as "the process through which the brain determines or calculates the value of a stimulus".

In agreement with Solms (1996), I consider affect (as in the German *das Affekt* as Freud himself introduced the term) to be a widespread concept, encompassing all those processes rooted in the body which, once conscience is reached, can be perceived according to the case (see scheme), either somatically or as emotions. They can only be given a meaning retrospectively (for example from the pain in the spleen to the sensation of heat, palpitation, anxiety, anger, excitement).

> The psychic and somatic manifestations are simply two ways of expressing the same thing. The inner happening, which is unknowable and called affect, is registered simultaneously on either surface of perception: it is perceived as emotion on the inside surface of conscience and as a somatic state on the outside surface.
>
> (Solms, 1996, p. 495)

What Ferenczi wrote on this account in *Serpent-hiss* (vol. IV, 1932), "Asthma-anger Anger-bronchial muscle contraction (bronchioli) with pressure from below (abdominal muscles) (bronchial colic)", is very evocative.

If it is the activation of conscious processes necessary to register the affect as a somatic or psychic event, it is at this very level that the split takes place, that is to say at the level where the conscious activity comes in. I would say we are close to Freud's last writings.

> Psychic phenomena depend largely on bodily influences, powerfully affecting in turn the somatic processes ... awareness [Bewusstheit TN [4]] cannot be the essence of the psychic, it is only one of its qualities, rather it is an inconstant quality, which sometimes is present and quite often is not. The psychic in itself, besides its nature, is unconscious and probably of a species similar to all the other processes of nature we became acquainted with.
>
> (1938, p. 283)

This activity is not independent from the culture where the subject is immersed. It is my strong belief that mind and body are subjects devoid of a really separate existence; their distinction depends on the observational vertex used. All this has also probably brought about the creation of instruments for research and treatment, which are different for each of the two fields. In any case, even if the distinction of mind–body sounds impossible to overcome, at least in our Western thought, like the dichotomy nature/culture or natural science/humanities, it (despite being so widely criticized) continues to maintain a strong epistemological status.

> If we understood that the problem does not concern the nature of reality, rather our way to perceive it, namely that "body", "psyche" and "mind" are categories of our consciousness and paradigms we try to decipher the experience with, and that the processes we are dealing with are untold in themselves, then we need to direct our attention to the states of consciousness.
>
> (De Toffoli, 2007)

Besides, De Toffoli writes in the same presentation,

> In his work, *Mind and Its Relation to the Psyche-Soma* Winnicott deals with "the age-old gap between mind and body" by quoting Jones' words: "I do not think that the mind really exists as an entity." "Yet," he remarks, "in clinical practice we do meet with the mind as an entity localized somewhere by the patient". He then continued stating that "the mind does not exist as an entity if the individual's psyche-soma has come satisfactorily through the very early stages of development. Mind is then no longer a special case of the functioning of the psyche-soma and psyche and soma are not to be distinguished unless according to one's point of observation. One can look at the developing body or at the developing psyche. I suppose the word psyche here means the imaginative elaboration of somatic parts, feelings and functions, that is, of physical life" (Winnicott 1953, p. 293). Therefore, even for Winnicott the distinction is of epistemologic nature and belongs to the point of observation, rather than the nature of reality.

Concluding this introduction I suggest the following:

1. *Being* for man is not somatic nor psychic. It is my strong belief that mind and body are subjects devoid of a really separate existence; their distinction depends on the observational vertex used. All this has probably brought out also the creation of instruments for the research and treatment, which are different for each of the two fields.
2. At a specific level of abstraction psyche and soma are mutually created entities; i.e. "gestures, sensations and experiences create psychic representations and the psychic structure, the image of the body, in its turn, affects regulation, perception,

self-perception of the body" (Harris, 1999, p. 254). The idea I am trying to express is visually represented by the well-known drawing by Escher *Drawing hands*, where, as the author himself comments:

> the right hand is busy drawing the sleeve of a shirt. At the moment the work is still in progress, further away on the right, he has drawn a left hand in such full details that it comes off the surface and gradually, as a living part of the body, draws the sleeve from which the right hand emerges.

The meaning of this, in my opinion, is that the psychic system, originating in the body (see above) remains closely linked to the body, and despite its dependence on it, the psychic system will interact with it in forceful and dynamic ways.

3. The constructions of a corporeal self, as a physical image of ourselves, occurs and can only occur inside dyadic and multiple relationships. The body is still a body in a social space; the corporeal states, including maybe the gender experience, are not comprehensible outside the interaction matrix. These statements are in keeping with my belief that the experience of having a body is not inborn. Indeed, it is the result of repeated interactions with the external (physical and social) and internal (exteroceptive, proprioceptive sensations, etc.) environment. In this respect I am getting closer to the position of Merleau-Ponty, who claims the body is not only a neutral background for experience, but also a reality, concrete and unitary in itself. It is not only a thing, but a condition, a context through which a relationship with other bodies can be carried out.

4. It is essential, in my opinion, to acknowledge the subjective experience of the clinician, that is to say, to acknowledge what happens to the analyst in the analytic relationship, whether consciously or not – this can include the analyst's emotions, thoughts and images, but also all his somatic events ("Severe headaches after a session of mutual analysis nearly three hours long", *The Clinical Diary of Sándor Ferenczi*, 1932, p. 60).

As mentioned in the foreword, my thesis is that the bodily countertransference formed by the crossing between the presence–absence of the patient's body and the analyst's body, constitutes both the field of survey and the instrument of treatment at the same time. As I introduce T, I will try to lead the reader into vicissitudes which are marked by the presence–absence of the body.

T

More than a year after the end of the analysis (which lasted almost ten years, during which the patient survived three instances of breast cancer), and exactly six months after the last contact, one day in June T called to say she needed to see me, because she was feeling ill. On the phone, she informed me that she had been diagnosed with a cancerous formation on the ovary and uterus. The physicians did not know yet whether it was a primary cancer or a metastasis: she was supposed to undergo surgery and probably chemotherapy, the prognosis was inauspicious and she was told that her life expectancy might be about six months. Soon after our third meeting (once the diagnosis had been confirmed and the treatment protocol identified), we agreed to start immediately meeting twice weekly with a view to progressing to three times weekly, as soon as it was feasible.

So we started that further odyssey, accompanied, at times by the shared belief of carrying out a kind of a slalom around cancers, with the heavy breath of death on our neck (nursing our omnipotence, we used to say to each other "*we have already denied the victory of cancer over her life three times*"). This tranche of analysis lasted almost two years; after the radical surgery, which consisted of total abdominal hysterectomy, bilateral adnexectomy and omentectomy, the patient started an eight-month course of chemotherapy, with very good results.

At the end of the last course of treatment, the CAT scan revealed a virtual absence of cancer in the affected area and no worrying signs in other parts of the body at risk (lungs, abdomen). It seemed a dream come true. A fairly peaceful year ensues, during which the patient comes to analysis, although regular attendance is interrupted from time to time by her desire to travel. T wants to see some places and she goes everywhere, while she feels physically able to pursue this. We talk about her travels; we both agree that travelling is a way to obliterate deadly thoughts. After all, she really did deserve to visit places such as Patagonia, Iran, Prague, which she had never visited before: a worthy reward for her tormented life. We agreed that she could call me, in case of urgent need, during her hours of analysis, to pay regularly even during her absences (this is a rule I apply to all therapies, but in this case I would have liked to leave it out). I wanted her to feel free to be able to contact me whenever in need and at the same time I wished to be able to offer my help and keep myself within a separate mental setting, sufficiently sheltered and protective. In addition, we also considered the possibility of using Skype, in case she could not get to my consulting room, so that we could carry on with the sessions despite the worsening of her condition. In such circumstances, the problem is the mental setting of the analyst.

Actually, at the beginning I found myself in a situation quite unlike the one I had to deal with when, during the first analysis, T had developed the two tumours. When I was told that the physicians had warned of the possibility of a six-month life span, I immediately found myself, though not on purpose, having to look after a terminally ill person until her death. When T had become aware of this, she reprimanded me: actually, she wanted me to be alongside her in her fight, despite the facts and despite virtually no chance of surviving, according to the physicians' prognosis. (Maybe her wish contained a more unconscious wish to recruit my healthy body and mind in helping to fight the cancer, as a colleague later suggested me). However, our previous psychoanalytic experience had been based on a similar and perhaps omnipotent hope which we should have pursued. She said that she was a new patient, but the link she was looking for was the one from the past, which had kept her analysis alive as well as herself, maybe. In order to regain that position of hope and omnipotence, I had to undertake a massive countertransference work, sometimes also with the help of a group of colleagues. When T, holding the CAT scan in her hands, told me the cancer of the genital system had been eradicated, it proved a great moment indeed.

After a year spent without any particular shock, T starts the session by talking about a skid she suffered while driving her car. I suddenly became aware of what was going on. Clinical tests detected a brain tumour. Surgery, chemotherapy, dashed hope, despair: T continued her sessions up to four weeks before her death. She felt like coming despite her weakness, while the drugs were destroying her, day after day. She spent her last week between home and hospital and when she did not come, we agreed that we could use the phone or Internet in order to carry on with the sessions, via Skype, at the beginning using video mode. However, later on she refused to let herself be seen, swollen and disfigured as she was, because of being on steroids and therefore we continued only by audio.

Previously I mentioned *"almost till the end"* as analyst and analysand had always got on well with each other; yes, actually it was *"almost till the end"* because, suddenly something that I could no longer handle, burst into the analysis. When T was no longer able to come and wished, indeed, to keep in touch with me, we both agreed on the use of the Internet to carry on with our virtual sessions. During her last weeks, she was deteriorating badly, and the drug treatment she underwent also took its toll on her psychic structure. Her general condition is well described by this email she sent me between two telephone sessions:

> yesterday I had a terrible day, when I came back home I felt very weak, and suddenly I started thinking that this physician that my sister had seen is nothing but a radiotherapist. That the story of the stereotaxis on the neck did not seem likely considering it is in that position ... etc. ... moreover, he deals with another kind of tumours (meanwhile my sister kept asking me on the phone ... "When will you call me back? A minute? Five or two?") Then I decided to take a benzodiazepine and I felt better but my head was empty. I remembered that before P's arrival for the injection, I had to go to the loo ... and I remained there sitting on the water closet for about an hour, unable to do anything, very weak and I felt so frightened, so deeply frightened that I thought had I fallen off the water closet, I would stay here all night and I couldn't call anyone. As soon as I was able to stand up, at once, I asked A. for someone to stay here at home with me and A. sent for a woman for the night. All that happened before the second phone call to you. At about 2 am I felt a strong pain in my breast, I wondered whether to go to the casualty department or not, later on I called Lucia who suggested taking another benzodiazepine. I agreed and the pain wore off.

I was no doubt exhausted. I was no longer able to pay attention, I kept diverting my mind, I forced myself to keep listening, but I could not activate the analytic ear. I believe that space was necessary in order to process the very heavy and deadly personal experiences impregnating our phone talks. It is well known that a paralysis of thought may occur in such situations. I think, however, of something specific concerning the "virtuality" of the relational situation: the paradox was that T's sick, dying body was so present that its concrete substance, as she was not physically present in my consulting room, increased her extreme heaviness more significantly, along with my inability to contain and support it.

Actually, there was another issue concerning my body, which could not be used in the physical absence of the other. Speziale-Bagliacca (1999, p. 58) quotes: "the patient's body always communicates, the analyst's body receives (vibrates out of sympathy) only when it is able to do it." Well, my body could not vibrate, it was like an ectoplasm mortified by the absence of the other who might use it as a recognized object in its being. I could perhaps receive and record unconsciously, but I could not process anything. I could not do it because my body (and my mind) was not allowed to come into play and interact with the body and (the mind) of the other. The mind was deprived of one of its containers, attacked also by the identifications with T's sick body. In addition, this might explain, at least, some temporary, physical problems of mine and certain, compensatory libidinal hyper-activities after the virtual sessions. I wrote in my notes:

> I realize that something is missing in our relationship, I do not know what it is, but I feel that something in me is no longer in resonance with T; the burden of work in the previous years and a couple of severe patients I had to take care of, keep me very busy and the space, the mental energies, the libidinal resources are what they are. However, it was not only that. It is as if my thoughts functions were blocked, with T.

There are authors like A. Lemma who maintain – rightly so – the importance of the visual relation when working with patients concerned about their physical aspect: "Although words may have a containing function, for some patients the visual relation counts more – at least until some internal roads are built to understand their use of the body and their experience of glances" (2005, tr. it. 2011, pp. 11–12). One could therefore postulate that even in this case, with T., the issue of the absence of the mutual glance may have determined some serious impasses. My hypothesis does not exclude that even the absence of the visual sense may have influenced the analytic relation, although in a non-decisive manner. The decisive variable was rather the absence of T.'s body and since the body was profoundly ill, her massive presence inside the mental setting of the analyst – what I call the "hyper-presence of the absent body". A hyper-presence that determines a non-self-recognition of the body–mind of the analyst.

One Sunday I received a phone call and an email from her sister in which she said that T had been taken to hospital. On Tuesday of the following week, she would die after a ten-day coma.

The sad narration of the epilogue of this event, of this human relationship, should not make us lose sight of the psychoanalytic context in which it occurred. T had been very important for me, not only because our shared destinies for about fifteen years created an extremely profound relationship, but also because I had the chance to carry out a huge work of clinical–theoretical reflection. The countertransference, although it is obvious to say it, is extremely, if not excessively pressed with patients like T. I cannot help attributing to the long psychoanalytic work with her, the strong drive I gained to pursue interest in what I am inclined to call the "analyst's subjective experience", including the countertransference *stricto sensu*.

This strong emotional drive became like a spotlight that illuminated shady areas on which I had lingered precociously long ago, but I had not been able to investigate yet, maybe because I feared to put some theoretical–technical foundations of mine in a difficult position. From the clinical point of view, I had to face up to some situations that could not be managed suitably other than with a countertransferential work that, however, had also a sort of "outpouring" on the theoretical level. So, the desire to confront certain positions of mine with colleagues, either close ones, at times also involved in this analytic event as "off-screen" assistants, or distant ones that could read what I went on writing, had been a significant drive and a source of support in working with T. It also helped me with other so-called "difficult" patients, such as some borderline, seriously depressed, or mainly psychotic personality structures.

CONCLUSIONS

The intensity of death feelings, the physical weakness and the drug treatment affected T's psychic work. Anyway, as I was able to realize from our very first meeting, though in an embryonic stage, T was a person with complex problems in the field of separation–individuation. From the very beginning, this led me to formulate a specific hypothesis. To illustrate, here is a passage from my notes from that period: "I believe that in the course of the analysis I will be able to enter her mind in order to explore it, but that will bring out, on my part a tolerance, from which she will have the perception and the certainty to be accepted in mine" … to "be able to stay inside the pocket of your jacket" to use one of T's expressions during her first years of analysis; this image sometimes turned into its mutual symmetric counterpart: "during the days I will be away I would like to take you away in my pocket." At the same time, some of her comments, as when she asked us whether it was possible to dissolve them rather than eradicate them made me immediately understand how pertinent her question was (since the term analysing comes from the Greek *analyein*, "dissolution"). Actually, it was the occurrence of a cancer in the brain, i.e. the organ of thought, which eventually stopped the analysis and T's life for good. In addition, all that happened, in my opinion – and I understand that this hypothesis may sound more than risky – was that, along with the somatic danger of the patient, the emotional–cognitive system of the analyst was harmed. I was no longer able to feel and think.

An excess of pathology (tumour derives from the Latin *tumere*, which means to swell), is equal to an absence (the absence of my own thought); a hyper-presence (of death) is equal to a hyper-absence (of the thought). Further, my non-ability to think was linked to the absence of T's body, where by absence of the body I mean both the physical absence from the session and the absence of the healthy body. The mental situation was quite different when T was away on a trip and we carried on with our sessions by Skype. In those cases, the absence of the body was surely upsetting, but not as upsetting as when that absence turned into a huge drawback, i.e. the heavy shadow of death. In some situations, one might wonder to what extent, we could continue our professional stance; our affects are at stake, either towards the patient, or towards our profession. Events such as fatal illness and death, in my view, exceed the human capacity to think. Only a strong faith in our discipline – supported by peer supervision groups with the help of special and specific interlocutors – can relieve us from that anguish of missing a protective shield, which we experience, in such situations. Besides, faith is not always enough.

The analyst's body, like everybody else's, activates naturally his own senses; if anything, the point is to take this activation up as an element of strength. Let us take, for example, my mirror reactions to "subject bodies" of the patients: physical transient problems and compensatory libidinal hyper-activations.

These reactions testify to what extent the analyst is at play (and inside the play) within all sensorial levels and how these levels are, each one and as a whole, active canals of perception, elaboration and response to the patient's "materials", whether verbalized or expressed in a nonverbal way.

An acknowledgement of the body is requisite and it can be the *locus* for unravelling the tangles brought into analysis. Similarly, the absence of the body may lead to a "thought block" and stop the elaboration that is essential to the course of therapy. I would like to come back to the session via Skype, which I carried on with T while she was dying: "T's sick and dying body was so present that its concrete absence stressed once more its extreme heaviness along with my inability to hold it. In fact, there was the issue of my body: in physical absence of the other it was not to be used." If the virtual nature of the setting was the only issue here, it leaves the question of the "non-usability" of my body, which did not arise during the previous phone sessions when T, free from tumours, absented herself in order to travel.

Most likely, the impasse was linked to the specific configuration "presence–absence of the body of the patient/non recognition of the body of the analyst" of this phase. A double evasion permeating the analytic couple and my body as an analyst: mortified for not being used by T. as an object recognized for its existence, I could not activate any more my analytic ear and think. I think the potential space (as Winnicott defines it) was missing, that allows psychic reality to manifest itself while living an experience; such experience also occurs through the perception and mutual acknowledgement of the two separate bodies involved, in my experience. Bion (1970) observed that real change takes place at a purely experiential level, something that cannot be either represented or known. Marion Milner (1955) conceived an undistinguished area, which was not internal like Mrs Klein's, yet it existed between the other and me and she called it illusion and linked it to creativity and insight. Well, within the analytic relationship with T, just getting close to something I had mentioned, became impossible! We could speak about the total collapse of that function of the analyst well described by Ogden (2004, p. 1353): "The function of being uninterruptedly the human place where the patient is becoming whole. Both a psychological and a physical dimension." Moreover, going back to Winnicott again: his "going on being" (1949, p. 293) is not supported anymore, since the holding made of the analyst body (mother) dissolved when the body of the patient (daughter) stopped being a body.

The strain on the analyst appeared strikingly as he admitted to be body himself. Of course, T.'s case was very dramatic, but even turning the focus away from the final stage, the recognition of the body of the analyst (the analyst had to recognize it before the patient did) required and led to a weighty countertransference work.

As I was saying, it was the analyst's mind set at stake, as he had been called by T. to be at her side in the battle against all odds rather than to accompany her to death. It was, again, necessary therefore, to introduce the analyst's body as analyser element (through the corporeal countertransference) at the point where absences and superabundances occur. However, how do we approach this, given that, in terms of theory, psychoanalysis does not take into account the analyst's body? This was confirmed by the same study group where my ideas came to light, a group I am obliged to because otherwise I would have never written it. Except in a situation where the countertransference implication of the analyst was evident, as he suffered from the same disorder as his patient did, never were those presenting clinical cases called into question as to their bodily experiences. Which is, to say the least, curious in a group of analysts who had met for years to reason about the body in analysis!

We should not be too astonished by this absence, nor criticize the attitude that has promoted such silence about the body; instead, we should try to find the roots of the resistances, inside certain psychoanalytical schools, which do not allow for the active presence of the analyst's nor the analysand's bodies in the analytic relationship.

In my opinion, the absence of the body raises a theoretical gap or maybe a constitutional paradox within psychoanalysis: it is a cure that necessarily involves joining two bodies, but one that imposes a law of incorporeality at the same time.

It is necessary now to (re)-introduce the analyst's body into the consulting room at conceptual level. Now, although psychoanalysis is a talking cure, my firm position is that two steps are necessary to go into a greater understanding (meant both as the term of taking in and deciphering) of our patients, more particularly, notably the difficult ones; in general, even of those who are not affected by a personality disorder and therefore with an overall better mental functioning because some somatic and psychic states are difficult to analyse and because they can however be traced in any personality. Both steps entail the adoption of a psychoanalytic viewpoint including the following:

a) To conceive the psychoanalytic session as a situation where inter-psychic, relational, interactional elements are steadily and inescapably present inside the frame that is built within analysis, which consists of the thoughts, emotions and somatic events of either component of the dyad, though each has their role and the relationship is, on the whole, asymmetrical;
b) To (re)introduce the body of the analyst – taking up the subjective–somatic components as a possible analyser element. (As Ferro proposes, we need to stay in touch with what might be the analytic status that a particular communication, such as stomach pain, has in the analytic session (2009, p. 73)), mostly where a bodily absence or an overabundance appear.

These processes, of course, involve the countertransference, particularly the body countertransference, which will have to be proved as attentively as possible, using our patient as the best colleague (following Bion, 1978, 1983) to guide us in such complicated matters. Moreover, the analyst's use of his own body as an analyser instrument of real life facts that can be defined as somato-psychic, may provide the analysand with a new dimension to go deeper into self-cognition. That is to say: "if I recognize before you, the patient, the absence or the presence of my body, I offer you the possibility to recognize the presence or absence of yours." Moreover, the recognition can only happen if the analyst's body becomes a means, i.e. an analytic instrument, as much as his mind. I assume that Riccardo Lombardi refers to this when speaking about "the role of analysis in facilitating the construction of a language to enable corporeity to speak" (2002, p. 370). As Adrienne Harris points out "So the analyst's body becomes one of the points of codification or representation that cannot be symbolized verbally, but, nonetheless very present in the intrapsychic life and cast into the interpersonal space" (1999, p. 246). This operation can provide the foundations for carrying out works that may lead to the building of the analytic function, the inalienable heritage of the analysand at the end of a successful analysis.

Notes

1 Lewis Aron, Frances Sommer Anderson (2000) *Relational Perspectives on the Body*. Hillsdale, NJ, The Analytic Press, p. 23.
2 It is obviously impossible, here, to deal thoroughly with the mind–body issue, also using, as would be useful if not correct, the huge quantity of philosophical papers on that subject. I would only like to point out that, to be precise, within a philosophical horizon, at the moment I am close to Quine's position when he states, for instance, "More has often been read in the proclaimed reduction of mind to body: something like a reduction of psychology to physiology or more particularly to neurology. I see no hope of that, much less of a reduction of ordinary mentalistic talk to neurology (...). Mental events are physical, but mentalistic language classifies them in ways incommensurable with the classifications expressible in physiological language" (W.V.O. Quine (1987) "Mind versus Body", in *Quiddities: An Intermittently Philosophical Dictionary*, Cambridge, MA, London: Harvard University Press, p. 133). It is a statement showing the materialistic, metaphysical profession of faith of the author ("mental events are physical events") along with the clear logic–epistemologic awareness of the impossibility of success of any reductionist approach on the mind versus body issue. I *fully* agree with it.
3 It is believed the word "soul" was introduced by Plato in the 4th century BC (for some, even by his master Socrates). Soul, psyche and mind are used like synonyms in common language, although this is not appropriately correct. For instance, while speaking in terms of modern language, in the case of René Descartes, I believe that he meant "structure" by and "function" by mind. However, it is true that the story of the concept of soul coincides with the one of the concepts of psyche: as a matter of fact, soul derives from the Greek *ànemos*, "breath", "wind" and psyche from *psychè*, "breath", "blow", but also "life" (from *nephesh,* a Jewish term for life, precisely). And it was the same Descartes who introduced the term "mens" (mind) to mark a discontinuity in his thinking from the ancient, more particularly Aristotelean concept of the soul as a principle of all the psychic and metaphysical faculties of the living body. In this work, however, although I am aware of the various

semantic nuances, I will use psyche and mind in an interchangeable manner. I will also do the same with body and soma (see above).

4 Here Freud is using "Bewusstheit" rather the more common Bewusstsein (das), perhaps taking it from Nietzsche's *Die fröhliche Wissenschaft* (1882) "Bewusstheit ist die letzte und späteste Entwickelung des Organischen und folglich auch das Unfertigste und Unkräftigste daran" (*Erstes Buch*, 11: *Das Bewusstsein*) ["Consciousness is the last and most recent development of biologic and therefore the most uncomplete and vigorous one". Own translation]. However, *Bewusstsein* (Engl. consciousness), would point out an ability resulting from the human evolution, namely the ability to perceive its own mental states and processes, a psychologic reality, while *Bewusstheit* (awareness) would be the state, the condition, the fact of being aware and can be used to point out those states of awareness reached with the help of a psychological technique.

References

Bion, W.R. (1970). *Attention and Interpretation*. London: Tavistock Publications [Reprinted London: Karnac Books 1984].

Bion, W.R. (1978). *Four Discussions with W.R. Bion*. Perthshire: Clunie Press [Reprinted in *Clinical Seminars and Other Works*. London: Karnac Books, 1994].

Bion, W.R. (1983). *Seminari italiani*. Rome: Borla.

Bronstein, C. (2011). On psychosomatics: The search of the meaning. *The International Journal of Psychoanalysis*, 92: 173–195.

Chiozza, L. (1976) La interpretación psicoanalítica de los fenómenos somáticos. In Chiozza, L. (ed.), *Cuerpo, afecto y lenguaje*. Buenos Aires: Alianza,.

Damasio, A.R. (1994) *Descartes' Error: Emotion, Reason, and the Human Brain* [Italian translation 1995]. Milan: Adelphi.

De Toffoli, C. (2007) *Si Deve Creare il Corpo Prima di Poterlo Vedere*. [You Need to Create the Body Before Seeing It], Presentation to the Centro di Psicoanalisi Romano, Rome (Unpublished).

Deutsch, H. (1959) Psychoanalytic therapy in the light of follow-up. *Journal of the American Psychoanalytic Association*, 7: 445–458.

Ferenczi, S. (1924[1919–1926]), vol. III, *Opere*. Milan: Cortina, 1992.

Ferenczi, S. (1932[1927–1933]), vol. IV, *Opere*. Milan: Cortina, 1992.

Ferenczi, S. (1932) *The Clinical Diary of Sándor Ferenczi*. Cambridge, MA: Harvard University Press, 1985.

Ferro, A. (2009) Psychosomatic pathology or metaphor: Problems of the boundary. In *Mind Works: Technique and creativity in psychoanalysis*. London: Routledge, chapter 3, pp. 76–106. (The New Library of Psychoanalysis.)

Franchi, F., Castriota, F., Chiarelli, R. (2006) *Il Corpo Nella Stanza D'analisi*. Rome: Borla.

Freud, S. (1926) The question of lay analysis. *S.E.*, 20: 177–258. London: Hogarth Press, 1959.

Freud, S. (1938) Some elementary lessons in psychoanalysis. *S.E.*, 23: 281–286. London: Hogarth Press, 1959.

Gaddini, E. (1982) Early defensive fantasies and the psychoanalytical process. *International Journal of Psychoanalysis*, 63: 379–388.

Garma, A. (1953) The internalized mother as harmful food in peptic ulcer patients. *International Journal of Psychoanalysis*, 34: 102–110.

Green, A. (1998) "Theory". 1: 19–63. Reply to Claude Smadja and Alain Fine. In Fine, A., Schaeffer, J. (eds), *Interrogations Psychosomatiques*. Paris: Presses Universitaires de France, pp. 99–103.

Groddeck, G. (1951) Psychosomatische Forschung als Erforschung des ES: Aus einem nicht gehaltenen Vortrag. *Psyche – Zeitschrift für Psychoanalyse*, 4: 481–487.

Grotstein, J.S. (1997) "Mens sana in corpore sano": The mind and body as an "odd couple" and as an oddly coupled unity. *Psychoanalytic Inquiry*, 17: 204–222.

Harris, A. (1999) Il corpo nella teoria e nella clinica relazionale. *Ricerca Psicoanalitica*, 10 (3): 245–272.

Le Doux, J. (2002) *Synaptic Self: How Our Brains Become Who We Are*. New York: Viking.

Lemma, A. (2005) *Under the Skin: A Psychoanalytic Study of Body Modification*. London: Routledge (tr. it. 2011, Sotto la pelle. Milan: Cortina.)

Lombardi, R. (2002) Primitive mental states and the body: A personal view of Armando Ferrari's concrete original object. *The International Journal of Psychoanalysis*, 83: 363–381.

Marty, P. (1952) Les difficultés narcissiques de l'observateur devant le problème psychosomatique [The narcissistic difficulties presented to the observer by the psychosomatic problem]. *Revue Française de Psychanalyse*, 16: 339–362.

Matte Blanco, I. (1975) *The Unconscious as Infinite Sets* (It. tr. 1981). Turin: Einaudi.

Milner, M. (1955) The role of illusion in symbol formation. *New Directions in Psycho-Analysis*. London: Tavistock Publications.

Mushatt, C. (1975) Mind–body environment: Toward understanding the impact of loss on psyche and soma. *The Psychoanalytic Quarterly*, 44 (1): 81–106.

Nietzsche, F. W. (1882) *Die Fröhliche Wissenschaft*. Cologne: Anaconda Verlag, 2009.

Ogden, T. (2004b) On holding and containing, being and dreaming. *The International Journal of Psychoanalysis*, 85: 1349–1364.

Quine, W.V.O. (1987) Mind versus body, *Quidditties. An Intermittently Philosophical Dictionary*. Cambridge, MA, London: Harvard University Press.

Savitt, R.A. (1977) Conflict and somatization: Psychoanalytic treatment of the psychophysiologic response in the digestive tract. *The Psychoanalytic Quarterly*, 46 (4), 605–622.

Solms, M. (1996) What is the affect? In Ekins, R. (ed.), *Unconscious Mental Life*. London: Karnac, pp. 45–82.

Speziale-Bagliacca, R., (1999) Ferenczi: il corpo, il contenimento e il controtransfert. In Borgogno, F. (ed.), *La partecipazione Affettiva dell' analista: Il contributo di Sándor Ferenczi al pensiero psicoanalitico contemporaneo*. Milan: Franco Angeli, pp. 107–120.

Todarello, O., Porcelli, P. (2006) Trattamenti in medicina psicosomatica. In *Psicoterapie, Farmacoterapie e Neuroscienze*. Milan: Franco Angeli.

Winnicott, D.W. (1949) Mind and its relation to the psyche soma. In *Through Paediatrics to Psycho-analysis*. London: Hogarth, pp. 243–254, 1982.

Winnicott, D.W. (1954) Mind and its relation to the psyche-soma. *The British Journal of Medical Psychology*, XXVII, 201.

7

THE BODY IN THE ANALYTIC CONSULTING ROOM

Italian-British conversations

Barbara Piovano

> The point of diving into a lake is not immediately to swim to the shore, but to be in the lake; to luxuriate in the sensation of water. You do not work the lake out – it is an experience beyond thought.
>
> (John Keats)

INTRODUCTION

If it is true that traditional medicine has dedicated itself exclusively to a reductive understanding of the body and has neglected the patient's assumptions and emotions, it is equally true that "psychoanalysis has ignored the bodily phenomena, as though they were not as important to our understanding of psychic life as verbal communication and feelings" (Matthis 2005, p. 14).

Today the body enters the consulting room as a meaningful presence, and not only in the analysis of children and adolescents. It no longer makes sense to ask ourselves whether the body in analysis should be considered an encumbrance or a resource if we consider that every physiological and pathological event always expresses itself *simultaneously* on the two levels of the mental and the organic. Nor do we still believe that the body does not possess thought – in the wake of Gaddini (1987), "the mind is everywhere in the body" (p. 315), and of Bion (1979) who in *The Dawn of Oblivion* imagines a mind that descends from the space of "air" until it meets a body that "feels" and "thinks" (Bion, pp. 5–6).

Freud, in the last phase of his life, bequeathed to us some rather enigmatic statements on the relationship between the unconscious, the psyche, and the body, permitting us to imagine an open dialogue between body and mind and to think of an unknown area where body and mind expand until they meet and merge into a kind of unity.

We are led by some rather cryptic and incomplete statements to reflect not only on the relationship between the unconscious, the psyche, and the body, but also on transformations in the concept of the unconscious stimulated by the polysemic and polyphonic developments in the field of psychoanalysis I refer to in the following enigmatic statements: "it [psychoanalysis] explains the supposedly somatic concomitant phenomena as being what is truly psychical, and thus in the first instance disregards the quality of consciousness" (Freud 1938b, p. 157); "the psychical, whatever its nature may be, is in itself unconscious" (1938a, p. 283); and "psyche is extended; knows nothing about it" (1938c, p. 300).

This chapter is the product of my deeper thinking on the mind–body question and my way of understanding the clinical thinking of a British-Italian study group composed of psychoanalysts from Britain and Italy. The group has met twice a year since 2003, and it shares the project of writing a book on its object of study: the body in the analytic consulting room. This group has focused particularly on: (1) the attention paid to clinical manifestations of the body and the clinical approach toward them; (2) the patient's previous history of somatic pathologies and symptoms; and (3) the bodily phenomena presented in the course of the analysis and during a single session, as well as the analyst's *receptivity* and responses to these.

In the first part of this essay, I propose to give a panoramic view of many aspects of the mind–body question that were touched on in the group and of experiences of corporeity in the analytic field (the living body in the analytic experience), grouping them into sections. After reviewing some of the group's readings, which explore the mind–body relationship and the subject–object relationship – the two axes of the process of symbolization – I formulate some working hypotheses and elaborate some aspects of technique that are considered relevant to the topic of the corporeal dimension in analytic work. Brief clinical vignettes taken from analyses of patients of mine illustrate the emergence of both the patient's body and the analyst's body in analysis, and the way in which theory and clinical work are integrated.

In the second part of this chapter, dedicated to the body in child analysis and to the contribution of child analysis to adult psychoanalysis, I will elaborate what I consider to be my own personal contributions. I consider the last part of the chapter equally personal; here I highlight some conceptual and cultural similarities and differences between the Italian psychoanalytic culture and the British one, both in general and with particular reference to the approach to the mind–body problem in the analytic consulting room.

WHICH BODY DOES THE ANALYST DEAL WITH?

In a rather schematic and incomplete way, for the sake of brevity, I will list the ways in which the body is most often described in encounters in the consulting room:

1. The vital and expressive body. It communicates at the preverbal or extraverbal level and integrates communication at the verbal level through choice of clothing, type of gaze, body movements, postures, gestures, acting out, silences, sensoriality, and sensuality.
2. The hysterical body, i.e., the signifying symbolic body. In hysteria, the body speaks via somatic symptoms; these symptoms symbolize psychic conflict and are symbolic inasmuch as they refer to an imaginary, fantastic body (McDougall 1974, pp. 440–441).
3. The sick body. More and more often, the analyst finds himself offering "analytic" treatment to patients who are physically ill – even to terminal cancer patients who fail to recognize reality in order to protect the self from disintegration (Vigneri 2010; Rocchi 2013). To the physical pain or illness that the patient brings to consultation or to analysis, or that develops during treatment, it is appropriate to assign the same level of dignity as that given to psychic pain, both from an ethical point of view and from a scientific one. In fact, physical and psychic aspects are two facets of the same entity, according to the current prevailing monistic view of mind and body, which considers these to be two sides of the same coin – two ways of expressing the complex

and multidimensional nature of the human being (Solano 2013; Matthis 2000; De Toffoli 2009, 2014).
4. The body usurped by the intellect. Sometimes an analyst must relate to a patient whose mind is split from his body, or, as Ogden (2001) would say, a patient who has a pathological mental disposition detached from bodily experiences. Such a patient's thinking is characterized by anxious preoccupation with absolute self-sufficiency and omnipotent control, both of bodily sensations and of relations with external and internal objects. When hypertrophy of the mind is accompanied by a bodily symptom, the latter must be understood as an attempt to withdraw the psyche by the intellect in order to lead it back to the original association with the soma, and to neutralize not only the seduction of the psyche on the part of the intellect, but also the usurping of the psyche by the intellect (Winnicott 1949).
5. The body that signals a relational disturbance that can be expressed only in the bodily register of language. The body makes itself felt in order to signal relational vicissitudes with significant persons, when the somatizing patient has not developed a psychic space in which meaningful correlations can be activated between sensations, emotions, and thoughts, and where conflicts can be contained.

HISTORICAL REVIEW: THE MIND–BODY RELATIONSHIP

The bodily and interactive roots of symbolization

I will briefly review some of the authors whom we read in the study group and who examined in depth the mind–body and subject–object relationships and addressed the two supporting axes, the bodily and the interactive, of the processes of symbolization.

From the body to the mind

Even though in modern thought there is a shared unitary vision of mind and body, the psychoanalyst has long thought of the mind as something that slowly emerges from the biological life of the body. Psychoanalysis has always pointed the way from thing to symbol, following the trajectory toward representation that was theorized by

Freud: drive – psychic representative of the drive (*vorstellungsreprasentanz*) – thing presentation – hallucinatory satisfaction of the desire – difference between perception and hallucination – recognition of the external object – learning the language – word representation (Racalbuto 1994, p. 19).

Winnicott (1949) notes that "one can study the mind of an individual as it specializes out from the psyche part of the psyche-soma" (p. 244) and defines the self first of all as a bodily self. He defines the psyche as the "*imaginative elaboration of somatic parts, feelings, and functions, that is, of physical aliveness*" (p. 244, italics in original).

Bion, quoted by Carignani (2006), *in the initial phases of his work*, defines the proto-mental system as something in which the physical and the psychological/mental find each other in an undifferentiated state. "The proto-mental system I visualize is one in which physical and psychological or mental are undifferentiated" (1961, p. 102). "If, as far as psychological disorder is concerned, the system is postulated as proto-mental, it is equally, from the point of view of physical disease, proto-physical" (p. 108).

Subsequently, Bion maintains that *mental functions and the mind emerge from sensorial and emotional data, and not vice versa* – i.e., thinking can be generated only by the transformation of sensorial and emotional data*:* "we can therefore accord a chronological priority to beta-elements over alpha-elements" (1962, p. 35). "Beta elements are a way to speak of things that are not thought" (1974, p. 66).

Ferrari (1992), in his model of the Concrete Originary Object, maintains that the mind wakes up from the body cocoon, that the body already contains in itself the potential to become thought, and that mental functions are activated autonomously by the body. The body is the basic matrix from which mental activities arise – a *living* and changing body that emits sensations and emotions by which it is constantly modified – and it is also the object of the mind, since it is that from which the mind springs (it is not the result of a process of introjection). In this way, Ferrari's model distinguishes itself from the Kleinian perspective, which considers the breast and the external mother's body (which become an internal object as well) the psychic object on which the mind focuses.

Gaddini (1987) writes that "the mind's development is a gradual accomplishment advancing from body to mind, a sort of emergence from the corporeal which coincides with the gradual mental acquisition of a sense of physical self" (p. 316). He adds that "psychoanalysis can advance only in the opposite direction, from the mind to the body ... up to the initial stages of mental differentiation from bodily functioning" (up to the point at which a biological process acquires a mental quality).

The subject–object relationship

Since the child's psyche-soma is located from the moment of conception in the intersubjective context of the mother–child relationship, it is not correct to speak of an entrenchment of the psyche in the body, or of the mind as something that slowly emerges from the biological life of the body, without taking account of the fact that these processes are developed within the mother–child dyad. In the same way, we might question the idea of a chronological succession in which the mind arrives afterward, given that body and mind are simultaneously and synergistically developed in the context of the primary relationship.

The importance of the *role of the primary object* and the quality of relational experiences in promoting *psyche-soma integration,* the *regulation of affects,* and *processes of symbolization* is underlined and shared by analysts who use different languages and refer to different theoretical models. One thinks of Winnicott's (1960) intuition regarding the impossibility of thinking of the neonate as a unit separable from the mother; of Bion's concept of reverie; of Bowlby's (1969, 1973, 1980) experiences of attachment; of Stern's (1985) affective attunement; of Tronick's (1998) processes of mutual dyadic affective regulation; and of the respective therapeutic application of these conceptualizations that anchor the development of affective symbolization and of thinking to the quality of the caregiver–child relationship.

LISTENING TO THE BODY: SOME WORKING HYPOTHESES

Without any pretext of formulating a theory of technique, I will focus on some key assumptions that have emerged from our study group's discussions, concepts that I consider important for their inclusion of the bodily dimension in analytic work.

A type of listening that permits a full and integrated expression of all the various idioms and languages that the person has at his disposal allows the analyst to reach the patient at all levels of his personality (his psychophysical organization) and foster mind–body integration, bearing in mind that translating body language into an iconic and verbal language may lead to dissonance and misunderstanding in communication. In actuality, many different forms of thinking exist – as well as various codes of thought – that express multiple self states, often traumatically dissociated: subsymbolic codes of implicit and procedural thinking (the thinking of the body); iconic codes of thinking (visual thinking, using images); and linear codes for verbal thinking/symbolic representations (Arnetoli 2007, p. 2).

The analyst's body can become the "instrument and the heart of the cure" (Ferraro quoted by Jaffè 2013) in the sense that, by *entering into contact with his own body* and with his own psyche, the analyst can transform sensorial experiences and proto-emotions into psychic experiences and capture thoughts at a nascent stage. In fact, often, the patient's body seeks a path toward representation through the analyst's body. In this regard, Bollas (1987) writes that the patient's instinctual drives try to find the way to mental representation through the analyst's soma, in that the patient is entrusting himself to the safe bond that exists between the analyst's psyche and soma.[1]

The analyst's interventions take into account the patient's prevailing *level of mental functioning (symbolic or presymbolic)*, and which of these the patient brings to a particular session or part of a session, as well as his *relational modes*: the sensory use of the object with an object-sensation, the relationship of adhesive continuity with the object, and projective identification with a containing object.

The observation and registration of the patient's *nonverbal communications* are integrated with listening to the patient's verbal communication. The analyst pays attention to the way in which the patient arrives and takes leave, how he lies on the couch, his gestures and facial expressions, his way of moving and tone of voice, pauses in the discourse, and his mood swings. These details, in the context of the patient's dreams and associations, allow unconscious fantasies – among other mental processes – to be brought to light.

In vis-à-vis analysis, there is greater pressure on the analyst to "look at the patient as a body in its person" (Khan 1971), and to decodify the patient's bodily expressions as messages, just as the patient can resonate with and read the analyst's body. In the vis-à-vis analysis of an adolescent patient of mine, the greater part of the communication for a lengthy phase of the analysis occurred *at the extraverbal and preverbal levels,* through clothing choices, the gaze, bodily movements, postures, gestures, acting out, long silences, and *the language of dreams without associations.* It was necessary to stay at a subsymbolic level of communication until the patient was capable of grasping the connection with symbolic aspects proposed by the analyst without that connection being heard as an incomprehensible translation in a foreign language (Piovano 2010).

Countertransference is an essential instrument for decodifying bodily events in the session or over the course of an analysis, and for suggesting an appropriate reply to the patient. The analyst's bodily countertransferential reactions allow him to approach emotions and affects that are still unspeakable and unthinkable, and the countertransferential elaboration of bodily states can have transformative value (Bollas 1987).

On this topic, Lombardi (2002) maintains that sharing the experience of an emerging corporality in the analytic relationship makes it possible to approach the experience of "the uncanny" body in a patient who has a dissociation between body and mind, or a negation of corporality, or a feeling of contempt for his own corporality. Sensorial and emotional movements at play in the analytic relationship take shape as "a conversation for four voices, those from our heads taking turns with those from our bellies" (p. 375).

From the body to the dream and from the dream to the body

The relationship between the body, the capacity to dream, and dreams themselves would merit a separate chapter. I will limit myself here to mentioning some categories of dreams that have a connection with the body that I have frequently noted in my clinical work.

Some dreams indicate that a *space for the dream* has been constructed – a space where experiences, images of the self, or conflicts that previously manifested as sensations, uneasiness, or bodily afflictions can be represented.

Toward the end of an analysis, after an early spontaneous miscarriage, and after having seen the image of a non-living embryo inside an inadequately formed gestational sac, a patient of mine communicates fantasies and experiences that, in her dreams, take the form of a lizard. I think that the representation of the lizard was the result of her capacity to symbolize, achieved after years of containment and empathic listening, during which I had tried to provide a sense of sensorial, emotional, and bodily states that were not yet symbolized, and to give a name to unformulated needs and anxieties. The lizard brought to my mind early phases of the analysis in which it seemed to me that the patient was becoming more real, alive, and human, precisely through her 360-degree exposure to my gaze, my listening, and my voice. The analysis had reached the point at which "deep" autistic material could be symbolized; through the symbol of the lizard, a basic issue could be expressed: the patient's own autistic-like response to her mother's absence (Piovano 2008).

Other dreams, through a barely articulated language rich in images, can point to an asymptomatic bodily alteration of which the patient is not yet aware. A patient of mine, after her first sexual experience at the age of thirty, felt as an "impalement," recounts the following dream, transmitting a sense of disquiet, bewilderment, and strangeness, without any associations: "The two folds of my genitals [she points with her finger] descended down, down .... I touched them and they were insensitive, jagged like a rooster's crest, and there was a big hole. I told myself: 'Since there's a hole, I'll get a piercing there.'"

Two years later, while she is having a sexual relationship with her boyfriend, she discovers by chance that she has a benign, virus-related tumor (papilloma virus, commonly named "rooster's crest"), and she hypothesizes that the infection might have been contracted during the period when she told me about the aforementioned dream. I asked myself whether greater attention to a possible somatic source of the dream, instead of to its meaning, could have oriented me toward a possible somatic illness that came to be represented and pointed out in the dream.

TOUCHING CURE, TALKING CURE

I have chosen these two formulations to highlight two dimensions of analysis that pertain to a series of theoretical and technical constructs that, inasmuch as they allow us to reach the patient at various levels of his psychophysical organization, may be particularly indicated for patients who turn to an analyst for help with a psychosomatic pathology and who present bodily problems during the analytic treatment.

Many authors have underlined the importance of a relationship that speaks to the patient's needs for *contact* – through words that are enveloping, touching, moving – and his needs for a rapport and for transformation in the direction of symbolization (Racalbuto 1994; Quinodoz 2002). In the analytic relationship, states of sensorial, visual, and acoustic-musical reverie are essential in leading the patient toward representation. *Acoustic* reverie refers to psychoanalytic listening, separated from visual content and concentrated on sound, put into play in order to reach a "prelinguistic understanding" with the patient through "resonant listening" (Di Benedetto 2000). Meltzer (1975) speaks of "deep musical grammar," referring to a common psychic origin of both musical thinking and emotional life. Music, together with the human voice, can be the vehicle of symbolic forms of emotions.

The use of psychoanalytic treatment for categories of difficult patients has changed the psychoanalytic conception of interpretations and has emphasized the transformative potential of unsaturated interpretations and narrative transformations. *Unsaturated interpretations* are interventions used to semantically define ambiguous and polysemous comments that aim at encouraging associations and connections. *Co-narrative transformations* are transformations that take place through sharing with the patient the meaning apparently manifest in the patient's communication (Corrao 1991; Di Chiara 1992), without explicit interpretations being formulated.

Another distinction may be made between transference interpretations as comments that must be specific to the emotional and fantasied meaning of the session in progress and interventions that are not interpretive (Stern et al. 1998; Tuckett 2008; Foresti 2013).

Much has been said about the therapeutic action of *non-interpretive interventions*. They are transformative to the degree that they allow the patient to repeat pathological mental patterns in a new context, open to new experiences of the self. In cases where there is a symbolic and representational deficit, these interventions permit the experience of communicative modalities at the preverbal level within the relationship (Ogden 1989; Neri et al. 1990) – modalities that coexist with or precede the processes of psychic elaboration that assume separateness and the capacity to symbolize.

I refer to moments of intimacy based on experiences of attunement/sharing of both the patient's and the analyst's sensorial and emotional states, to the analyst's negative capability (Bion 1970), to moments of meeting (Stern et al. 1998) – encountering opportunities that involve a reorganization of the patient's implicit relational knowledge (and the analyst's), to fusional moments (distinct from confusional ones), which are located at a nonverbal, procedural, intersubjective level, allowing the patient to experience a psychosomatic and sensorial unity with the analyst. This affective experience, which in some cases the patient has never had, makes the perception of separateness and otherness progressively more tolerable (less catastrophic), and favors recognition of the specificity of objects and emotions (Tagliacozzo 1985).

In some clinical situations, entering into contact and resonating with the patient's bodily and sensorial-affective states through a bodily and emotional presence can be an important transformative and curative factor, as can be seen in the following clinical vignette.

Mario, a 25-year-old patient of mine who had hair loss, experienced a regrowth of hair after some months of analysis. I attributed the remission of this symptom and his improvement chiefly to my offering a regular setting (which was continually threatened by the intrusion of a mother who flooded him with words, as I observed in the first joint consultations with mother and son) and a couch with a hand-embroidered doily on the pillow. The latter was characterized as a cradle/stroller, in a metaphor that I chose and that was shared by Mario. Together we played with the possibility that this cradle might have encouraged the rebirth of his hair.

Fantasies aside, Mario used the couch to relax and to await an abatement of the tachycardia and intense sweating with which he always arrived at his session. Sometimes, in contrast, he squirmed about on the couch and cracked his knuckles, as though he found no peace – transmitting a state of agitation that he only rarely connected to his state of mind or to an unpleasant event.

I think that an important curative factor might have been the silence: a silence that afforded him an undisturbed isolation – that is, a way for him to be alone while in company. I interrupted this silence with movements of my body or with some request for him to communicate his mood to me only when it transmitted a sense of emptiness or of death to me in the countertransference. Mario perceived my bodily movements and the modulations of my breathing as signs of my libidinal–emotional presence, and he contacted me with his own movements, or with comments on the weather or on what he had done since the previous session, when he felt that too much distance was being created between us.

At the beginning and end of the session, and when he lay down on or got up off the couch, and even when he turned his head on the pillow, he was placing his problem "under my eyes" – allowing me to touch with my eyes his alopecic spots and to share and verbalize his concern about his suffering.

In another excerpt during a later stage of the therapy, I wrote: "The analytic couch, which initially offered physical containment of his extreme sensorial bodily excitement, in time became the battleground where Mario was struggling to build his boundaries and symbolically own his own body, contrasting the regressive tendency to fuse with the mother's body, and enter into a relationship with me by talking about his extreme shyness and fear of strangers. The body gives way to speech."

THE BODY IN CHILD ANALYSIS

If one considers that the analyst's mind, the analytic function, and the analytic instruments are the same whether one works with children, adolescents, or adults; that thought and language have sensorial and motoric roots; and that interpretive activity is addressed to intrapsychic and interpersonal configurations in the analytic field in which it unfolds, then theoretically, an analyst who has certain personality characteristics could cure patients of different ages and with different pathologies.

I refer ideally to an analyst whose emotional experience and whose thinking have their roots in his own sensorial–bodily experience – that is, an analyst whose body continually communicates about itself, gives form and substance to the psyche, and contributes to the birth of thought – an analyst who lets himself be affected by the patient's bodily experiences, and who can tolerate a breakdown of his own thinking in order to trace within the patient, through the analogy of preconscious psychic functioning, unrepresentable mnestic inscriptions.

I maintain, however, that the child analyst, thanks to experience acquired in clinical practice, may have a greater capacity to move with agility along both the vertical axis (mind–body) and the horizontal one (the relationship), as well as the capacity to maintain an *interbodily dialogue* (Colazzo 2010) that gives "flesh" to emotional life and thought, and to foster transformations from the presymbolic to the symbolic.

Moreover, the child analyst develops a natural ability to put himself into contact with his own child and bodily self (and to reach the child self in the adult), to move in areas along the border between mind and body, and to dwell in a state of dialectical, transformative tension between unformed–formed, somatic–psychic, indifferentiation–differentiation, internal and external, familiar and strange – before giving associations or interpretations.

The relationship established with the child analyst bears the stamp, the mnestic trace, of the child's bodily relationship with the primary object, where bodily experience and object relations are almost blurred (Thanopulos 2013). The child analyst becomes drawn into actions that require his presence physically, emotionally, and mentally. He is not permitted *not* to be there in body and mind, soul and body. The child analyst must maintain the analytic function while interacting with the child at a bodily level as well, since the child uses his body to communicate and to play.

The child analyst is also called upon to recognize the sensorial and motoric shapes that make up the vocabulary through which the child tries to express his states of being in the relationship. If this doesn't happen, the child risks re-experiencing in the transference the rejection of authentic aspects of the self, aspects that were not seen in the early relationship and that are encapsulated in dark zones of the mind and in *secret parts of the self*. In his relationship with the analyst, the child repeats and *acts* (like an adult) – in the most evident and dramatic way, with great richness of detail – the unconscious fantasies that originate from primitive bodily sensations and perceptions.

The function of the analyst's reverie consists of different aspects of *bodily*, affective, and mental reverie, and fosters the transformation of archaic functions of the mind (primary anxieties, sensoriality, and proto-emotions) into psychic experiences – feelings, affects, and thoughts. It is thanks to the work of *positivization* (Godfrind 1993) – that is, the analyst's attempt to express in words his perception of the child's sensations, emotions, and affects – that the latter constructs his *sensorial self* and his bodily identity.

The affective and emotional space and climate created between child and analyst promote the affective experience of the relationship in its transferential aspects (nascent transference, the developmental and organizing dimension of the transference – Moccia

2007) and in those of a relationship with a new object with evolutionary potential. This relationship is constructed and evolves in parallel with the development of the process of symbolization. Countertransference permits one to grasp traces of missing elements and traumatic impingements in the primary environment and of early defense mechanisms, set in motion for the sake of psychic survival in the course of experiencing the event, and to go back to the characteristics of the primary environment and the primary object (for example, the object that does not possess qualities of sufficient separability, the intrusive object, etc.).

In particular, the analyst's bodily countertransference (Mathew 1998; Piovano 1998; Pozzi 2003) permits him to gain access to the child's bodily experiences and to transform them into images and "*imagée*" interpretations – equivalent to the "creating anticipations" that as a rule function spontaneously between mother and child – which foster the construction of images in the child (Golse 1992).

An important function of the child analyst is to discourage the child from the use of protective defensive maneuvers (Mitrani 1996) – for example, the use of autistic forms and objects – and to promote gradual disillusion with respect to the me/not-me distinction through the introduction of transitional areas and the elaboration of catastrophic anxieties connected with the recognition of alterity and of object loss. This is a necessary passage to help the child render the unthinkable as thinkable and to symbolically re-find the lost object.

BRITISH–ITALIAN CONVERSATIONS ON THE MIND–BODY PROBLEM IN THE ANALYTIC CONSULTING ROOM: SOME CONCEPTUAL AND TECHNICAL CONVERGENCES AND DIVERGENCES BETWEEN THE TWO PSYCHOANALYTIC SCHOOLS

The word *conversations* is used in the title of this chapter to emphasize not so much the conversational aspect of our group's get-togethers as the "coming toward each other" (from the Latin *con-vergere*) that characterized our meetings. To begin with, this coming together involved working with language: great effort was made by the Italians to express themselves in English, and the English participants showed great patience in translating "Psychoanal-ese" into English.

In the title, I speak of the *analytic consulting room* in order to incorporate those elements of the setting (including the analyst's internal setting) that renew very old experiences of contact/non-contact with the object, and that take shape along the border between mind and body. To these areas one can attribute the function of reconstructing the sensory floor of the ego that is equivalent to Bleger's (1967) meta-ego, necessary for the foundation of a core identity. In fact, the setting-body-environment (the analytic consulting room, the rhythmic nature of regular hours) as the polymodal source of sensorial stimuli (tactile sensations, and auditory, olfactory, kinesthetic, and visual ones) offers a first level of sensorial integration – "a background of sensorial containment, that is barely perceptible, of all the subsequent states of subjectivity" (Ogden 1989, p. 54, quoted by Civitarese 2008; translation by G. Atkinson). The aspects of *invariability and of a nonprocess* of the setting meet normal needs for adhesion and fusion, guaranteeing the basic cohesion that is necessary to the structuralization of the self.

What follows must not be considered a report, but rather an attempt to communicate my subjective experience in the study group and my reflections on this experience. It seemed to me at the outset that the highest priority of the group was to mitigate the encounter with the "other than self," introducing *transitional areas:* the spontaneous reference to English authors who were familiar to both Italians and English, and the introduction of readings in English translation by Italian authors who have elaborated on the early areas of functioning of mind and body in psychoanalysis – for example, Gaddini's *basic mental organization* and Ferrari's *concrete originary object*.

Right from the start, I found myself facing a paradox. That is, the English maintain that the Italians have greater familiarity with the body and with the bodily language, and thus are more capable of interacting with the patient at the sensual and sensorial level, and of moving in the relational and prerepresentative area. However, the Italians – "who know English psychoanalysis much more than the English know Italian [psychoanalysis]" (Campbell 2009, translation by G. Atkinson) – have learned a great deal about psychosomatic levels and about unmentalized states of mind from English-speaking authors (for example, Bion, Winnicott, Marion Milner, Bollas, Tustin, Mitrani, etc.).

Aware of the fact that I am undertaking an ambitious task, I will try to describe and conceptualize something of my experience in the study group, underlining some conceptual and technical similarities and differences between Italian psychoanalysts and English-speaking psychoanalysts that I came to appreciate. Let me state in advance that the following comments, besides being excessively schematic for the sake of brevity, are intended to convey my subjective experience in the group, as mentioned earlier, and are not necessarily generalizable to the British and Italian psychoanalytic cultures overall.

British colleagues adhere closely to the clinical material and their observations and interpretations arise from it, though they are obviously filtered by their respective theories (explicit or implicit) of reference. In their chapters, attention to clinical evidence predominates over theoretical discourse. The clinical material and the analyst's discussion of it are presented in a detailed, exhaustive, and saturated manner, at times leaving little space for the reader's imagination or reflection.

British colleagues are more concerned with decodifying constellations of unconscious fantasies and capturing the unconscious fantasy manifested in the analytic relationship. They use interpretation of the transference with greater self-assurance; they are more capable of catching aggression and do not hesitate to interpret it in order to produce *insight* in the patient, or when it could cause an impasse in the analytic relationship. They interpret weekend separations almost systematically, and in this they are supported by their choice to privilege intensive, four- or five-times-per-week sessions.

The Italians, moving in a relational area that extends to the concept of the analytic *field*, give greater space to their reverie (i.e., the analyst's thoughts, feelings, fantasies, conjectures, daydreams, and bodily sensations that are more profane, common, and banal, which usually seem completely disconnected from what the patient says and does in a particular moment – Ogden 1997). They sometimes communicate the analyst's associations and countertransference experiences to the patient.

Italian psychoanalysts recognize the transformative value of *non-interpretive interventions*, especially in patients who have not developed a psychic container and who would hear the interpretation – especially interpretations that emphasize alterity and difference – as an alienating intrusion.

The Italians theorize the experience of a "good fusionality" (Neri et al. 1990), that is, of the vivifying and structuring aspects of fusional moments (different from confusional moments), which allow the patient to experience a psychosomatic unity with the analyst, accompanied by a sensation of being two in one – an intersubjective preverbal experience that some patients have never had. On the other hand, for some of my British colleagues the word *fusion* is synonymous with undifferentiation and emphasizes pathologically regressive aspects of the analytic relationship, while experiences of shared sensorial and emotional states between patient and analyst presuppose a differentiation of one from the other.

Italian psychoanalysts show a greater degree of flexibility in crossing boundaries between theories and in integrating traditional concepts (drives, the unconscious, transference, countertransference, projective identification) with more recent ones (enactments, intersubjectivity, self-disclosure, co-construction) in order to understand clinical material from various perspectives, and to meet the patient at various levels of his psychic organization – that is, from the most archaic, autistic, and psychotic levels to the more neurotic ones. British colleagues tend to object to this wide-ranging, comprehensive (Bolognini 2008), and "polyphonic" ("with many voices sometimes in harmony with each other") (Roussillon – personal communication, November 2009) aspect of Italian psychoanalysis. They rigorously maintain that, even when one works with seriously disturbed patients, an eclectic approach – one that tries to utilize diverse frames of reference in order to understand diverse clinical phenomena – may result in neglecting contradictions or exporting concepts beyond the context (Campbell 2009).

Reflecting on my assumptions in the light of the study group, it seemed to me that, independently of the number of sessions, and staying within the realm of the model of psychoanalytic cure (different from the training model), one may be able to recognize common ground in the shared use of the concepts of transference, countertransference, interpretation, role reversal, personification, and interpretive action. Both the Italians and the English work on the relationship (its transferential and relational aspects) and on emotional exchanges. It seems to me, however, that the Italians may lend more attention to countertransference and thus to the analyst's subjectivity, thereby opening up an intersubjective perspective (Gill 1984).

The elaboration of the chosen topic – the body in analysis – has produced a common way of thinking, despite differences in working styles and theoretical and cultural backgrounds. The psychic and the somatic are not phenomena belonging to different realities, but aspects of the same reality that is born and developed in the relationship. The complex question of the body–mind relationship and the origin of the psychic is dealt with in clinical practice from a relational perspective that places the relationship and emotions generated in the relational context at the center of the treatment. The analytic relationship becomes the place where *a dialectic movement between body and mind and between self and object* can be realized and articulated, and the psychoanalytic experience, for both analyst and analysand, becomes the occasion for an emotional attribution of meaning to somatic events – or, vice versa, for a somatic *incarnation* of psychic experiences.

In the presentation and discussion of clinical cases in the study group, I have sought to consider and share many starting points for reflection on the opportunity or necessity of working in the self– other and mind–body boundary area (along the line of a continuous fusional whirlpool) in order to visit (to examine) the earliest psyche – the origin of a psychic apparatus that was born of the body. I have tried to find the early meaning of experience – that is, of those experiences lived as an initial working through of somatosensory states (Mangini 2009). These are experiences that repeatedly *present* themselves without any possibility of a connection to *representations* or verbal expressions, in that, *originally*, an organized thought, or logical or verbal structures, are not yet available (Racalbuto 2009).

I will now attempt to delineate some differences between British and Italian psychoanalysts that derive from differing intellectual traditions and the diverse cultures of the psychoanalytic organization to which they belong. First, the English have a "neo-positive" and "post-positive" approach that tends to focus on what happens in the consulting room. That is, they privilege an attentive, rigorous, and active reading of the patient's discourse and of transferential and countertransferential movements.

The Italians, applying Heisenberg's principle of indetermination to the complexity of the psychic apparatus (Foresti 2013) and of intersubjective relationships, trust in the development of dynamic intersubjectivity and of the analytic process within the analytic setting. Here I am referring to the analyst's external and internal settings, which already in themselves activate transformative phenomena. In addition, they favor the "dreaming together of the analytic couple" proposed by analysts who refer to the technical aspects of the analyst's reverie (sensorial, acoustic, and visual – Ogden 2004; Grotstein 2007), and to talking as dreaming (Ogden 2007) and transformation in dreaming (Ferro 2009).

In conclusion, I would like to emphasize the creative importance of this meeting of colleagues from the Italian and British psychoanalytic societies, which lies in the working out of a technique that promotes the development of the mind through modalities of listening and intervention that assume contact with and exploration of the sensorial and imaginative material that travels along the border areas between body and mind and between self and not-self.

★*Translation by Gina Atkinson, M.A.*

Note

1 But is this bond between the psyche and soma of the analyst really that safe (Dermen, personal communication, February 2009)? The late Rosenfeld – interested in "what is going on in the relationship" – asked himself, in commenting on a patient whom I brought to him in supervision, a patient at the beginning of a second analysis with me – why, in the final phase of the first analysis (undertaken with a well-known analyst!) the patient somatized with a persistent low back pain. He hypothesized that the patient's body became the receptacle of the analyst's separation anxieties, unelaborated and evacuated into the patient through a massive acting out: the anticipation of the end of the analysis at an earlier date than that suggested by the patient (personal communication, September 1985).

References

Arnetoli, C. (2007) Centro di Psicoanalisi Romano. Una prospettiva relazionale sul corpo. Meeting "Prospettive psicoanalitiche sul corpo," 24 February 2007 (Unpublished).

Bion, W.R. (1961) *Experience in Groups and Other Papers*. London: Tavistock. [Italian Translation: *Esperienze nei gruppi*. Rome: Armando, 1971.]

Bion, W.R. (1962) *Learning from Experience*. London: William Heinemann. [Italian Translation: *Apprendere dall'esperienza*, Rome: Armando, 1972.]

Bion, W.R. (1970) *Attention and Interpretation*. London: Karnac Books 1984. [Italian Translation: *Attenzione e interpretazione*. Rome: Armando, 1973.]

Bion, W.R. (1974) *Brazilian Lectures*. London: Karnac 1990 [Italian Translation: "Seminari Brasiliani." In *Il cambiamento catastrofico. La griglia/caesura/SeminariBrasiliani/Intervista*. Turin: Loescher, 1981.]

Bion, W.R. (1979) *The Dawn of Oblivion*. London: Clunie Press/Ronald Harris Trust.

Bleger, J. (1967) Psicoanalisis del encuadre psicoanalitico. *Revista de Psicoanalisis* (Apa), vol. 24 (2): 241–258.

Bollas, C. (1987) *The Shadow of the Object: Psychoanalysis of the Unthought Known*. London: Free Association Books, 1994.

Bolognini, S. (2008) *Secret Passages: The Theory and Technique of Interpsychic Relations*, trans. G. Atkinson. London: Routledge, 2011.

Bowlby, J. (1969) *Attachment and Loss, Vol. 1*. New York: Basic Books, 1983.

Bowlby, J. (1973) *Attachment and Loss, Vol. 2: Separation, Anxiety, and Anger*. New York: Basic Books, 1976.

Bowlby, J. (1980). *Attachment and Loss, Vol. 3: Loss, Sadness, and Depression*. New York: Basic Books, 1982.

Campbell, D. (2009) Introduction. Paper presented at the Fifth British-Italian Dialogue, February 7–8, Bologna (Unpublished).

Carignani, P. (2006) Il corpo nella psicoanalisi. In Carignani, P., Romano, F. (eds), *Prendere Corpo. Il Dialogo Tra Corpo e Mente*. In *Psicoanalisi: Teoria E Clinica*. Milan: Franco Angeli.

Civitarese, G. (2008) *The Intimate Room: Theory and Technique of the Analytic Field*, trans. P. Slotkin. London: Routledge, 2010

Colazzo, M.P. (2010) Perfume. Paper presented in the British-Italian Study Group (Unpublished).

Corrao, F. (1991) Trasformazioni narrative. In *Orme*. Milan: Cortina, 1998.

Dermen, S. (2009) Fifth British-Italian Dialogue, February 7–8, Bologna (Unpublished).

De Toffoli, C. (2009) The body as a signifier of body mind transformation. Paper presented at the Fifth British-Italian Dialogue, February 7–8, Bologna (Unpublished).

De Toffoli, C. (2014) *Transiti Corpo-Mente: L'esperienza della Psicoanalisi*. Milan: Franco Angeli.

Di Benedetto, A. (2000) *Before Words: Psychoanalytic Listening to the Unsaid Through the Medium of Art*. London: Free Association Books.

Di Chiara, G. (1992) *L'incontro, Il Racconto, Il Commiato. Tre Fattori Fondamentali Dell'esperienza Psicoanalitica. Saggi Sulla Relazione Analitica*. Milan: Cortina, pp. 43–62.

Ferrari, A. (1992) *L'Eclissi del Corpo*. Roma: Borla. [English Translation: *From the Eclipse of the Body to the Down of Thought*. London: Free Association Books, 2004.]

Ferro, A. (2009) Transformations in dreaming and characters in the psychoanalytic field. *The International Journal of Psychoanalysis*, 90: 2009–2030.

Foresti, G. (2013) "More-than" or "more about"? Breve e incompleta storia delle ipotesi sull'interpretazione psicoanalitica. *Rivista di Psicoanalisi*, 59 (33): 645–663.

Freud, S. (1938a) Some elementary lessons in psycho-analysis. *S.E.*, 23: 279–286.

Freud, S. (1938b) An outline of psycho-analysis. *S.E.*, 23: 139–208.

Freud, S. (1938c) Findings, ideas, problems. *S.E.*, 23: 299–300.

Gaddini, E. (1987) Notes on the mind–body question. *The International Journal of Psychoanalysis*, 68: 315–329.

Gill, M.M. (1984) Psychoanalysis and psychotherapy. *The International Journal of Psychoanalysis*, 11: 161–180.

Godfrind, J. (1993) *Les deux courants du transfert*. Paris: Presses Universitaires de France.

Golse, B. (1992) L'enfant autiste, sa pensée, son corps et ses images. *Psychiatrie de l'enfant*, 2: 481–518.

Grotstein, J. (2007) *A Beam of Intense Darkness: Wilfred Bion's Legacy to Psychoanalysis*. London: Karnac Books.

Jaffè, R. (2013) Transmission of somatic and sensory states in the psychoanalytic relationship. Paper presented in the British-Italian Study Group (Unpublished).

Khan, M.M.R. (1971) "To hear with eyes": clinical notes on body as subject and object. *The Privacy of the Self*. London: Hogarth Press, 1974.

Lombardi, R. (2002) Primitive mental states and body: A personal view of Armando B. Ferrari's Concrete Original Object. *The International Journal of Psychoanalysis*, 82: 363–381.

Mangini, E. (2009) Ricordare e rimuovere l'originario psichico. In Mangini, E., La Scala, M. (eds), *Le Fonti dello Psichico*. Rome: Borla.

Mathew, M.A.F. (1998) The body as instrument. *Journal of the British Association of Psychotherapy* 35: 17–36.

Matthis, I. (2000) Sketch for a metapsycholgy of affect. *The International Journal of Psychoanalysis*, 81: 215–222.

Matthis, I. (2005) Emotional life: A perspective close to the body. *Scandinavian Psychoanalytic Review*, 28: 11–21.

McDougall, J. (1974) The psychesoma and the psychoanalytic process. *The International Journal of Psychoanalysis*, 1: 437–459.
Meltzer, D. (1975) *Explorations in Autism*. Perthshire, UK: Clunie Press.
Mitrani, J. (1996). *A Framework for the Imaginary*. London: Karnac, 2008.
Moccia, G. (2007) Articolazioni, varietà clinica, evoluzioni. In Niccolò, A.M. (ed.), *Attualità Nel Transfert*. Rome: Franco Angeli.
Neri, C., Pallier, L., Petacchi, G., Soavi, G.C., Tagliacozzo, R. (1990). Fusionalità. Scritti di Psicoanalisi Clinica. Rome: Borla.
Ogden, T.H. (1989) *The Primitive Edge of Experience*. Northvale, NJ: Jason Aronson.
Ogden, T.H. (1997) Reverie and interpretation. *Psychoanalytic Quarterly*, 66: 567–595.
Ogden, T.H. (2001) Reminding the body. In *Conversations at the Frontier of Dreaming*. New York: Jason Aronson.
Ogden, T.H. (2004) This art of psychoanalysis. *The International Journal of Psychoanalysis*, 85: 857–877.
Ogden, T.H. (2007) On talking as dreaming. *The International Journal of Psychoanalysis*, 88: 575–590.
Piovano, B. (1998) *Parallel Psychotherapy with Children and Parents*. New York: Jason Aronson.
Piovano, B. (2008) The function of the analyst's boundaries in the psychoanalytic relationship. *International Forum of Psychoanalysis*, 17: 91–103.
Piovano, B. (2010) Acting, dreaming, thinking in adolescence: An analysis from the beginning to the end. *International Forum of Psychoanalysis*, 19: 27–33.
Pozzi, M.E. (2003) The use of observation in the psychoanalytic treatment of a 12-year-old boy with Asperger's syndrome. *The International Journal of Psychoanalysis*, 84 (5): 1333–1349.
Quinodoz, D. (2002) *Words that Touch: A Psychoanalyst Learns to Speak*. London, New York: Karnac, 2003.
Racalbuto, A. (1994) *Tra il Fare e il Dire*. Milan: Cortina.
Racalbuto, A. (2009) Pensare l'originario della sensorialità e dell'affetto nella costruzione del pensiero. In Mangini E., La Scala, M. (eds), *Le Fonti dello Psichico*. Rome: Borla.
Rocchi, C. (2013) The body in psychoanalysis. Paper presented in the British-Italian Study Group (Unpublished).
Solano, L. (2013) *Tra Mente e Corpo. Come si Costruisce La Salute*. Milan: Cortina.

Stern, D.N. (1985) *The Interpersonal World of the Infant: A View from Psychoanalysis and Developmental Psychology.* New York: Basic Books.

Stern, D.N., Sander, L.W., Nahum, J.P., Harrison, A.M., Lyons-Ruth, K., Morgan, A.C., Bruschweiler-Stern, N., Tronick, E.Z. (1998) Non-interpretive mechanisms in psychoanalytic therapy: The "something more" than interpretation. *The International Journal of Psychoanalysis*, 79: 903–921.

Tagliacozzo, R. (1985) Angosce fusionali: mondo concreto e mondo pensabile. *Rivista di Psicoanalisi*, 31: 290–298.

Thanopulos, S. (2013) The "body with its drives" and its clinical implications. Paper presented in the British-Italian Study Group (Unpublished).

Tronick, E.Z. (1998) Dyadically expanded states of consciousness and the process of therapeutic change. *Infant Mental Health Journal*, 19 (3): 290–299.

Tuckett, D. (2008) *Psychoanalysis Comparable and Incomparable: The Evolution of a Method to Describe and Compare Psychoanalytic Approaches.* Edited by R. Basile, D. Birksted Breen, T. Bohm, P. Denis, A. Ferro, H. Hinz, A. Jemstedt, P. Mariotti, J. Schubert. London: Routledge.

Vigneri, M. (2010) La morte e l'origine dei percorsi simbolici. Riconoscimento e disconoscimento della morte nelle culture e nella clinica. In *Intendere la Vita e la Morte*, Milan: Franco Angeli.

Winnicott, D. W. (1949) Mind and its relation to the psyche-soma. In *Through Paediatrics to Psycho-Analysis.* London: Hogarth, 1975. [Italian Translation: La mente e il suo rapporto con lo psyche-soma. In *Dalla pediatria alla psicoanalisi.* Florence: Martinelli, 1975.]

Winnicott, D. W. (1960) The theory of the parent–infant relationship. *The International Journal of Psychoanalysis*, 41: 585.

8

WHEN THE BODY SPEAKS

Bodily expressions of unrepresented affects

Luigi Caparrotta

INTRODUCTION

The aim of the paper is to illustrate some of the difficulties the analyst may encounter in detecting, unravelling and attending distorted and hidden expressions of affects by presenting two clinical cases. There is clearly a wide difference in the nature and presentations of the two clinical cases and uses of their body. However, there are also some commonalities. In both cases the developmental infantile trajectory seems to have remained blocked at the imitation phase. The challenge brought about by their respective adolescence exposed unconscious conflicts related to different uses of their bodies, which is the common pathway for the expressions of affects. While in the first clinical vignette the analyst is presented with a serious episode of self-harm to make sense of, in the second case the analyst is presented with the sudden onset of physical ailments to disentangle. In both cases the analyst becomes conscious of the full force of the patients' struggle in the expression of their aggressive affects only after the attack on the body in one and the presence of afflictions in the other. These clinical situations highlight the importance for the analyst to be aware that the patient's body becomes a vehicle of repressed and split off affects.

DEVELOPMENTAL CONSIDERATIONS

It is well established that the infant becomes aware of his own self, the external world and hence reality through the discovery of his own body. This awareness is gradually acquired via the recognition, regulation and integration of multimodal sensory and motor experiences from the most primitive type, such as the sense of smell and hearing, to touch and taste, which along with sight, will eventually become increasingly more refined. As Fenichel (1945 p. 37) pointed out, the first reality is what can be "swallowed", while Spitz (1955) aptly described "the mouth cavity" as "the cradle of perception". The poet John Betjeman (1936) elegantly describes childhood "as measured out by sounds and smells and sights before the dark hour of reason grows".

From the developmental point of view, the awareness of one's own body including its boundary constitutes one of the many pathways to self-representations as first stated in Freud's dictum: "The ego is first and foremost a body ego ... [And] ... it may be regarded as a mental projection of the surface of the body" (Freud, 1923). This statement was much later revisited by Sandler and Sandler (1998 p. 126) who more comprehensively translated it as meaning: "self-representation is first and foremost a representation of the body self". In addition, the body ego, including its discovery via the mother, is considered to be the forerunner of the ego organisation. This process however is unique for each individual and certainly not passive in that "the body ego is not just a passive observer, but a fervent actor in doing its job" (Lehtonen et al., 2006).

Gaddini (1969) formed the view that the imitation stage was a fundamental developmental step, which along with introjection,[1] constitutes part of the structure towards the process of identification in the service of adaptation and the reality principle. In 1981 he pointed out the following:

> For the infantile mind, what the entire organism is in contact with from the sensorial point of view, and through tactile experiences in the first instance, does not stand for environment, but for the boundary of the self. The primitive perception is imitative from the physical point of view and consists in the modification of the body in response to a stimulus .... "To imitate in order to be" ... is essential for the infant so that he can "be" what he is lacking of [...] The formative process of the self is based on the aggregation of fragmented sensorial experiences (tactile, olfactory, etc) [...] linked to the mother–environment.
> (p. 10)

He also said that the development of the mind should be considered as:

> A gradual process from the body to the mind i.e. a sort of emergence of the body which coincides with the gradual mental acquisition of the bodily self [...] this would not be achieved without the arduous emerging process from a non-objective body, that is to say that of the functioning mother–infant unit.
> (p. 5)

It must be stressed, however, that in the normal mother–infant interaction the process of imitation is mutual, in that the mother equally responds or initiates imitation by "mirroring" facial expression and gestures of the infant while at the same time – consciously or unconsciously – introducing culturally appropriate, contingent and newly modified imitative behaviour. Even so, "strict imitation alone won't do" – warns Stern (1985, p.139) – unless it is cemented by mutual exchange of affect between mother and infant. Hence the imitation phase, during the gradual process of identification, has to be combined with an appropriate degree of "affect attunement", whose function is that of defining the quality of the relationship. By dovetailing with one another, imitation and affect attunement pave the way to the formation of feeling state or affective self-state, thus setting up the basis for secure attachment as well as future interpersonal and social sharing (Gergely, 2007, p. 72). Gaddini (1981) goes on to say that, when imitation is not integrated with introjection, then imitation tends to persist and may lead to psychosomatic manifestations as a result of deficits of mental representation and capacity for introjections; hence the affective self-state is compromised. This point has been elaborated further by the Paris School of Psychosomatics and in particular by Aisenstein (2006) and Aisenstein and Smadja (2010). They suggest that failure in psychic structuring, even before the acquisition of language, the somatic solution, better defined as "acting in the body", is frequent.

THE ANALYTIC SITUATION

In considering the analytic situation more in detail, we can equally regard the patient–analyst interaction as a mutually constant conscious and unconscious interchange of bodily and affective signals between analyst and patient across all sensory-motor modalities and emotional experiences. While noticing, verbalising, linking and eventually interpreting some of these experiences – within the transference and countertransference parameters – could be regarded as the mainstay of any analytic work, sometimes some of the signals originating from our patients (and I dare say also from the analyst) are underestimated if not totally overlooked. This failure in my view tends to occur particularly during the work with patients who, while giving the impression of following the rules of free association and thus appearing to be accessible, also appear to defensively compartmentalise compulsive self-harming thoughts and fantasies or overwhelming affects, which cannot be verbalised. By this I mean that while these patients appear to be ostensibly cooperative and engaged in the analytic process, i.e. "in tune" with the analyst, they may also silently develop a parallel "out of tune" highly destructive process or an exciting erotised affective component unconsciously undermining, if not undoing, the former. This dual compliant and defiant process is clearly deceptive. It may lead us not only down false alleyways, but may also give us a false sense of security. For example, compulsive and relentless self-harming urges are sometimes communicated by means of throwaway "crying wolf" remarks during an otherwise engaging narrative, making it difficult for the analyst to attribute the right importance at the right time. Consequently, our ability to discern spurious signals from real underlying distress can be seriously hindered. When these ambiguous modes of communicating distress ominously and silently reach unbearable and uncontainable "feeling states" of extreme proportion in these patients, actual impulsive damaging acts against their own body may rapidly ensue. These self-destructive acts can take us completely by surprise and present us with a major setback in the analysis. On these occasions it is always helpful to unravel the meaning of these acts with colleagues.

Some of these severely disturbed patients may also be suffering with unyielding conflicts regarding their sense of identity including their sexual identity; hence they may use, abuse (or may even suppress) in their body unconscious affects and impulses in an attempt to externalise (or get rid of) their identity confusion. Borderline personality disordered patients in particular may also unconsciously use the analyst (or indeed "any other") as a vehicle onto whom they project "unwanted or alien parts of themselves" (Rosenfeld, 1987;

Bateman and Fonagy, 2004, p. 89). In such cases, when the analyst is absent or unavailable, these patients feel totally and utterly alone with themselves and have no option but to resort to attacking in their own body those very alien or unwanted parts, which they now feel reside within themselves. In order to get rid of the ensuing overwhelming affects and sources of conflicts linked to these alien parts, self-harming becomes then the only conscious solution immediately available to them, thus compelling them to give into it. In these cases, a structural environment based on empathy and mirroring may facilitate contrasting and objective experiences of the self (Auerbach and Blatt, 1996).

Some of the above issues will be examined in more detail in the first clinical illustration. This clinical vignette highlights in particular the struggle in a patient suffering from significant identity conflicts, which became so unbearable as to lead to a hideous and unexpected act of self-harm. Soon after the beginning of the analysis an un-integrated feminine identification became painfully exposed. This occurred amidst contradictory and misleading expressions of affective states, which during the sessions were often intermingled with an apparently coherent narrative along with a reasonable mode of relating. The second clinical illustration refers instead to a group of patients whose ability to express their overwhelming emotional and affective life is hampered by a pervasive sense of shame and which seems to find its way to the surface only through bodily channels. More specifically I shall illustrate the sudden development of a number of physical ailments in a patient covering up a range of unrepresented highly exciting affects.

BODY ISSUES ENCUMBERING THE MIND

In my first clinical example I would like to highlight how the supremacy of aggressive impulses and highly charged sexualised fantasies obscured the function of the mind in a particular patient. In a desperate attempt to ward off mounting aggressive and sexualised fantasies, which became particularly relentless in between sessions and during holiday-related absences of the analyst, a rapid onset of compulsive self-destructive thoughts eventually gave way to a sudden actual self-harm during the initial phase of the analysis. A basic disharmony of body–mind relationship (Ferrari, 2004; Lombardi,

2009) underpinning a deep seated sexual identity conflict gradually came to light.

Justin, an unemployed gentleman in his thirties, presented for analytic help a few months after a close relative died from a long illness. He reported being very upset and exhausted by a series of illnesses and life-threatening complications in his wife, who was apparently enjoying reasonably good health by the time he sought help. It felt as though the recent bereavement, the removal of the work structure and being less needed by his ailing wife considerably diminished the vital roles he heavily relied on and exposed the foundations of a rather brittle sense of identity. Being needed at work was essential to the maintenance of his self-esteem, while the enduring sufferings of his loved ones provided him with a vehicle for a form of "altruistic surrender" (Sandler and Freud, 1983). Consequently, when he was made redundant from his job, his self-esteem plummeted; while the end of the afflictions in his family temporarily put a stop to an unconscious masochistic gratification stemming from the compulsion of making himself constantly available and "running the track", as he once put it. My understanding was that while these events took place, a number of unresolved sufferings and unattended needs in himself inevitably came to the surface.

Besides the above reasons, he admitted that what drove him to seek help at this juncture was that he felt tormented by an out-of-character crush for a young man. Indeed, he was virtually ready to ditch his beloved wife and two young children in order to pursue this unrequited infatuation. In one of my initial comments I pointed out that along with his losses he was perhaps also struggling with a more worrying underlying fear of destroying everything he had managed to build for himself so far. He sternly reported that he took his relative's death in his stride, like with many other unpleasant or uncomfortable events in his life, and "simply got on", hardly paying attention to their impact on his emotional life. Crying or indeed showing any real emotion was in his view a sign of being fickle and weak. He could not tolerate any helplessness in anyone, let alone in himself and, although he felt naturally predisposed towards helping others, he also realised he would often "do it" in a rather perfunctory fashion. In the course of the analysis, however, it became clear that he underestimated his deep emotional attachment to his loved ones, against which he defended by presenting a rather hard veneer.

After settling into his sessions, Justin's infatuation – understood as representing his longing for an ideal youth and body he never had – gradually receded. The waning of this apparently ego dystonic obsession left him increasingly aimless and highly disturbed. He began to express death wishes and was plagued by compulsive aggressive and sexual thoughts/dreams. While trying to take control of mounting "racing mad thoughts", constantly threatening his precarious sense of reality, he was also desperately attempting to retrieve that perfectionistic and "orderly person" he used to be. At the time I observed that, although he gave the impression that his distress seemed of recent onset, his previous compulsive need for order indicated that he must have been warding off disordered and fragmented states of mind for much longer.

I became very concerned about the seriousness of his clinical condition; hence decided to establish a clear analytic and extra-analytic frame, including medication and the assistance of a psychiatrist to rely on particularly during my absences. In the meantime I did my best in order to help him to think about ways of "structuring" his time between sessions and weekends as his wife was often away for work while his children were busy with their schooling and sporting activities. These "parameters" (Eissler, 1953) along with other comments and interpretations enabled Justin to discover a much cherished, though often thwarted in the past, artistic side of himself.

The self-harming thoughts however remained unremitting. While reinforcing the more functioning and creative side of his personality, I found myself taking them less seriously. Justin seemed to respond positively to my approach and began to use painting in order to communicate his underlying distress. The compulsive self-mutilating fantasies were still in the background; however, I took the view that so long as he talked about them and I could take up the unconscious aggressive component towards me and his loved ones, he would be less at risk of acting them out.

He spoke of his wish to "hack off" parts of his body he intensely disliked such as his toes. I tried to help him become aware of his longing for an ideal pre-pubertal sexual body, which he originally projected into the teenage boy (Freud, 1910), while having to come to terms with the disappointment of his own ordinary adult body. His own image before puberty may have contained the unconscious fantasy of having a body different from the one he had in reality (Laufer and Laufer, 1984, p. xiii). He acknowledged the devastating and crippling consequences of such self-harm actions, thus reassuring himself and me that he was not going to act on his compulsions. One day, however, he reported that he wanted to cut off the tip of his nipples. This compulsive thought rapidly became delusional and he quickly felt compelled to act upon it before being able to make sense of it with or without my help. This desperate and bizarre mutilating act, which took place out of the blue in two stages between sessions amidst a mixture of anxiety and dissociation, was carried out ostensibly in order to offset another compulsive thought related to his wish to rekindle contact with another woman. She was a past fling of short duration with whom he experienced "the complete sexual satisfaction" he never achieved with his wife. His reasoning at the time was that this mutilation was the only way with which he could offset an irresistible compulsion of contacting this ex-lover for sexual gratification. If he pursued this contact and was found out by his wife, this action would jeopardise the relationship with his wife and children to whom by this time he was totally devoted and was terrified of losing.

Behind his rationalisation of this extreme act, however, it became evident that Justin was also developing disturbing conflicts arising from an increasingly strong attachment to me and was terrified that I would get rid of him. This attachment was maintained through reporting homosexual erotic fantasies between sessions, which were both pleasurable and highly frightening in equal measure. Hence, on a more unconscious level, this attack to sensitive parts of his body represented a concrete solution in order to offset not only the compulsive sexual fantasies about his ex-lover, but also as a punishment against his overwhelming highly erotised homosexual attachment to me.

The attack on his nipples was also a desperate attempt to do away with his forbidden sexual desire he projected into them. By getting rid of his nipples, he could feel neat and rid of an un-integrated feminine identification. His out of control erotomania highly threatened the cohesion of his body self; hence the solution to remove any feminine narcissistic investment by discarding his nipples as they were foreign bodies (Kohut, 1972).

He reported dissociation and virtual detachment during this act, as a defensive manoeuvre against his unconscious sado-masochistic way of relating and maintaining his object relationships. However, excessive self-focus can lead to dissociation and the self-mutilation may help to restore a sense of agency and self-awareness (Auerbach and Blatt, 1996). This act made me wonder whether he used his body "to feel" what he could not otherwise represent in his mind. In our psychoanalytical discourse we often speak of body manifestations, body feelings, body image and so on. But how much can words and language (and perhaps even thought) hold, let alone express? Is it possible to paradoxically "discharge" into our bodies what we are unable to "feel" with our mind (Limentani, 1977; Kilborne, 2010)?

I took up his unconscious aggressive wish to punish me lest I would abandon him and leave him at the mercy of his unfulfilled erotic and destructive fantasies. I also made it very clear that I was not prepared to helplessly witness and tolerate further attacks to his body. If he did not feel safe during the analytic treatment I would have no option but to resort to psychiatric assistance with a view to admitting him to hospital. I also warned him that a repeat of such action would seriously jeopardise any future analytic work with me and thus, paradoxically, through these self-destructive actions his very fear of abandonment would then be confirmed. Frantic phone calls and messages ensued, which arose from an anxious need to make sure that he had not destroyed me with his actions.

Subsequently to the cutting, it became clear that Justin had not been feeling at home with his body (Erikson, 1956) for a long time in that he had been hiding a long-standing loathing for his body. For example, I learnt that Justin had developed a highly disturbing relationship with his body from an early age. Often left to fend for himself in a little African village surrounded by natives, he recalled experiencing a mixture of excitement and anxiety at the idea of being left in the "unknown". Fearing humiliation and teasing from the native children because of his skin colour, Justin often acted as though he was a forlorn little waif, often playing with dolls and eventually becoming a keen animal lover. Meanwhile the children in the village started mocking not only his colour but also his mincing demeanour, a trait which was still visibly present.

As puberty set in, and Justin's male body gradually developed, he secretly harboured an ever growing hatred towards his penis, which in his opinion was "mis-shaped" and compared unfavourably with his brother's. At one point he even tried to strap his penis in an attempt to alter its shape and control its growth. In retrospect I wondered whether severing his nipples could be understood as a displacement of the attack on his penis.

Brought up in a "hugely puritanical household with no room for swear words", he developed a strong sense of magical thinking, and often felt "watched and judged" by higher forces. He believed that if he had bad and sexual thoughts he was "doomed", i.e. he was bad and deserved to be punished for simply having such bad thoughts. Consequently, libidinal and aggressive desires were considered totally unacceptable. It could be argued that vulnerabilities and desires remained located in parts of his body where he could frantically try to control them lest they otherwise would doom his mind.

Not surprisingly, these highly distorted negotiations of his pubertal development and conflictual repudiation of his sexual body led to an unfulfilled adult sexual life increasingly coloured by humiliation, shame and disgust. Justin's sexual development became very confusing. It contained sado-masochistic elements and was interspersed by heterosexual and homosexual encounters. Eventually it became mainly restricted to masturbation in his adult life until he met his wife. However, even with her he experienced his sexuality and body as variable and inconsistent.

While the erotic homosexual transference became dangerously inflated, there was a clear idealisation of what he perceived as being my power. Justin often experienced me as a mixture of being a "good man" as well as an attentive maternal figure both of whom he unconsciously wished to control and possess. He often thanked me for being his "saviour", while in his distress he was unconsciously denying any hostility towards me for betraying him and becoming a neglectful analyst as a result of leaving him in between sessions and holiday times.

He arrived earlier than usual to one session following my holiday break. He had trouble getting through the front door. He said he was feeling very well but quickly added that he had been thinking about me anyhow. [With his early arrival it seemed to me that he could not accept feeling left out nor countenance the feeling of wanting to intrude into someone else's session.]

I said that perhaps he was afraid that I would stop thinking about him if he was well.

He became very upset at the thought of feeling well. That would mean that he had to separate from me. He then went on to say that he had a sudden fantasy that if I was to became ill he would look after me. [I thought that this was a clear reference to the homosexual/narcissistic transference towards me.]

I said that perhaps his wish to make me as helpless as the relative he used to look after would make him feel that he could have me all for himself.

The following day he said he felt guilty for wishing me ill and added that he probably meant that he wished to give me a taste of what it was like for him to be in the position of being the carer. He then mentioned a dream in which he was travelling by tube, but because it was too crowded he was perilously hanging on to it from the outside. While travelling he noticed loose electric cables coming down from above. They brushed past him and he was afraid of being electrocuted. He associated this to a poor action film he saw with his children the previous night and the fact that he came by tube to his sessions. [While he was recounting his associations, I was reminded of the time he had experienced suicidal thoughts including the wish to throw himself under a train].

I said that in the previous session he made a reference to feeling particularly well and soon after became tearful at the thought that one day he would have to leave me. Perhaps – I added – the anxiety of being left out and unprotected yesterday and during my break, while I was too busy attending other people in the consulting room (crowded train), was too much to bear and made him feel exposed again to dangerous and (self) destructive thoughts (electric cables) as a way of punishing me.

DISCUSSION

Justin was clearly a man full of contradictions. He was generous to the point of being gullible. He was just as naive as candidly honest. His capacity for empathy and difficulty about maintaining boundaries would often lead to exaggerated altruism. Besides his conscious love and devotion to his wife and children, his compulsive care giving became his way of assuaging long-standing self-loathing, self-punishment, shame and guilt. During the first part of the analysis he appeared to listen to my comments with clear intention and soon learnt to use them in such a way that he gave the impression he was developing insight. Little did I know he was "pretending", i.e. he was hiding behind what I would now describe as a well disguised imitative attitude, perhaps for fear of disappointing me with his secret regression and lack of progress.

My understanding was that he was unconsciously searching for a soothing and responsive maternal object as well as a potent paternal figure who would rescue him from a pre-oedipal un-integrated imitative phase, which was later exposed by the onset of adolescence. In the course of the treatment I underestimated how my absences unwittingly fostered in him a regressive condition, which stemmed from an intense anxiety about separation. Indeed, his capacity to differentiate between self and other was severely impaired. This made me consider his mother's capacity for mirroring and reflecting back in order to provide affective meaning to his mental states, leading to an impaired capacity in Justin to recognise and attend to his own affective states. In addition, the confusion brought about by the development of his sexual body in the context of lack of representation of affects in his mind highlighted even further the severe split between the ownership of his sexual body and his affective life. Whilst he ostensibly grew into a man he was passively giving into the regressive pull of wishing to remain a little boy forever.

With regard to his male body, his sexual development presented him with unbearable body changes he was not prepared for. Thus, during his puberty he defensively tried to control these changes by developing vivid dysmorphic fantasies related to his body shape and to his penis in particular. In other words, he was fighting to regain control of his pre-pubertal, omnipotent and conflict-free body in order to offset the conflict-laden physical pubertal changes of a more masculine and potent body, whose aggressive component he was terrified of and yet dangerously captivated by. As Laufer (1991) would cogently put it, he felt compelled to find means of controlling his penis in a desperate attempt to stop these bodily changes from taking place.

In the course of the analysis I learnt that Justin had been grappling for a long time with compulsive thoughts and magical thinking of which he felt deeply ashamed, and hence hid them. By attacking his body he was concretely ridding himself of what he considered were disgusting sexual and aggressive thoughts in his mind projected into his body.

Eventually the analytic experience, despite the severe act of self-harm and other very painful episodes, managed to help him to reconnect his body to his mind and gradually enabled him to unravel the meaning of his bodily struggle in the light of his unconscious infantile wishes and desires.

THE ROLE OF BODILY AILMENTS AS UNCONSCIOUS COMMUNICATION

In this second clinical example I wish to highlight the onset of an interesting dynamic between transference and countertransference, which hinged on unconscious communication of strong affects and which could only find their expression through the body.

Hayley was a bright 34-year-old when she entered psychoanalytic treatment. During the first consultation I detected an unusually distinct incongruence in the way she presented herself. Her demure countenance sharply contrasted an apparent air of self-assurance. An inquisitive and cheeky gaze seemed to be out of tune with a rather mask-like facial expression while her way of smiling contained something forced and fixed in its rigid nature. In other words, I was struck by her initial unconscious body language and gestures, which were distinctly out of keeping with her ostensible self-confident presentation. This apparent confidence I later understood as stemming from a superimposed tomboyish demeanour, which she unconsciously developed in order to offset a fear of identifying herself with an anxious and engulfing hypochondriacal mother.

She gave the impression she enjoyed coming to the sessions, but I soon noted in Hayley a peculiar ability to keep me at arm's length. Thus, I became overwhelmed by her persistent distance, which did not allow me to capture her inner affective life.

Following a number of comments on my part about her sense of shame, her fear of intrusion and her wish to control me lest I would threaten her need to maintain a sort of [pseudo] self-sufficiency, she eventually revealed that she had been secretly smoking dope in the evenings. This "secret" solution was borne out by her need to keep herself "cut off and above the rest of the world". We came to describe this retreat as the "bubble", the origin of which went right back to her latency years during which she developed a fantasy of being a producer in charge of a theatre where she could control and hector various actors. Following this disclosure, the "bubble" solution was gradually relinquished.

Most importantly, however, Hayley developed out of the blue, throughout most of her analytic journey, a number of significant physical ailments, which hampered the continuity of her sessions. The first physical manifestations were intermittent hives, which I interpreted as representing an unconscious allergic manifestation to the analytic work. Subsequently, she became extremely preoccupied with her sight. After discovering that she had been suffering from a "lazy eye", she berated her parents who should have detected it and corrected it in her earlier years. Another day, after finally admitting that she was beginning to enjoy her sex life, she reported she developed a genital condition requiring emergency surgery. Following the sudden break-up of a long-standing relationship she developed amenorrhoea for many months. Later on she suffered from a serious urinary tract infection followed by severe sinusitis leading to acute swelling of her face. She also developed numerous colds and dental problems. The most peculiar aspect of these medical conditions of varying severity was that she reported them in a matter of fact way, giving me the impression that they did not matter much to her. But most interestingly, they tended to clear almost as suddenly as they appeared.

In the following section I shall present session material in more detail during a week after the third year of analysis where I try to illustrate my grappling with Hayley's suppressed emotional life while keeping track of and connecting it to her bodily experiences.

Tuesday session

Following my previous week's holiday and after she cancelled her Monday session for medical reasons, Hayley slowly and carefully lay down on the couch while her stomach rumbled.

> *P.* ... My body speaks for me. Yesterday they stuck me in a hospital gown, naked, undignified waiting to be examined by a junior doctor. He was rough. He terrified me by talking about a cyst and needing a second opinion from the consultant. Thankfully it was a false alarm as there was no cyst.
> [Long pause]
> *A.* Did they identify the source of the infection?
> *P.* They suggested it could be a gallbladder infection ... I remember my mother ending up in hospital with a similar infection in my early adolescence .... The whole hospital experience made me feel depersonalised and aware of how vulnerable, exposed and dependent I was .... I'm also preoccupied with A's lack of

response and my dependence on him. I cannot convey to you how full of rage I felt towards him, taking his sweet time ... It is all-multifaceted, a bit like African music or poetry. All of this I like, I love the complexity, which I can allow and appreciate, but it also drives me mad. I want things simple and sorted ... I now have the image of minimalist art.

A. You mentioned being made to feel vulnerable by the doctor and dependent by A. Perhaps my going away made you feel wary of me, vulnerable and painfully aware of your dependence on me.

P. You are right, but yours it is a predictable dependence, unlike other unpredictable dependence [I thought that her comment indicated her need to be in control]. Other people can make more loose arrangements. I sometimes like that, but sometimes I struggle with real looseness of things ... It is the not knowing that drives me mad. The same uncertainty applies to my new date. We got to know each other quite well. Perhaps he is frightened of getting close to me physically. I did not go into it. I'll enjoy longing for it. Other times I feel like saying: Let's get on with it. Now, after all the analysis, I have learnt to wait and let things be. I know it, but I am not finding it easy ... [Pause] ... For some reasons the artist Damien Hirst comes to mind, he preserved real body parts in formaldehyde. They are kept alive and yet dead, but also stopped from rotting. I would not take things out there, I rather wait to preserve them in my own way, but by preserving them I kill them. For example, the train was running late, the previous one was cancelled. I wanted to take it easy and looked out of the window. It was spring time, beautiful, there was a scent in the air; I was reminded of past time when I was a child, in the school with the sun on my skin, my adolescence. All this was taken over by the agitation of being late [to the session]. I saw past a wonderful warehouse and experienced the happiness of being part of the world. I wanted to bottle that happiness. I fantasised about the money coming through so that I could buy a bit of a warehouse. The contentment disappeared and greediness came in: by wanting to have I lose the contentment of belonging ... time of passing clouds during last week-end ... wonderful music and jam sessions of Afro-Caribbean nature ... I want to preserve something. I want the pleasure and a more reality based wish to have something concrete.

A. It sounds as though you feel teased by the conflicting thought of wishing to have your cake and eat it too.
P. [She smiled] ... The bubble was like Damien Hirst, keeping things alive, playing with them, but also killing them. I must say I have come a long way since I started. [Here she was clearly referring to her pretence of keeping things alive].

During Wednesday session she dreamt about a film in which a male nurse looked after a ballerina in a coma. She wondered: "How can he take over this woman? He talks to her and becomes her mind. He breathes life into her …. I needed someone to breathe life into me, as if I felt like a mindless ballerina. My neediness comes in waves … I am in a bit of a muddle.

I said: "I wonder whether it is your loneliness that makes you feel in a muddle and confused. Perhaps you wish I was always available including week-ends helping you to identify sensations and emotions or even breathing life into you."

She spoke with shame of her dependency on people. She wondered whether she came over as too intense and was disappointed that she could no longer be the apple in people's eyes as she felt as a child. I made a comment about her fear of uncovering intense emotions, including her sexual desires, which led her to suppress them and preserve them, in this way not dissimilar from Damien Hirst's dead/alive works of art. She wondered why she felt so uncomfortable about revealing her emotions and I said that perhaps she needed to protect herself from the fear of being rejected if she became too intense for me.

On Thursday she spoke at length about her sense of powerlessness while witnessing distressing events at work.

In the following week she appeared highly controlled. She spoke about feeling uncomfortable in her previous sessions, but now she felt fine. She wondered whether she was playing hide and seek with herself. I asked her what she meant by hide and seek and linked it to her wish to play hide and seek with me in her attempt to disclose her emotional life. She asked herself how much she was alive or dead to herself or others. She also mentioned she had heavy periods which were possibly responsible for the dip in her mood. I reminded her that her periods had been dead for a long time. She admitted feeling vulnerable over the w/e and wondered why she needed to damp down her feelings. She recalled her father banning the word hate from her household. I said that having an intense mixture of positive and negative emotions was forbidden and shameful in equal measure.

DISCUSSION

The original fantasy-bubble of being in charge of actors during Hayley's latency years represented in my view a transitional, regressive fantasy where Hayley could omnipotently control her objects. It enabled her to retreat into a safer place and away from her fear of identifying with her ailment prone mother, who experienced Hayley as having the perfect body she never had. Hayley's ailments therefore represented paradoxically an unconscious primary imitation with a sick mother.

I also believe that it protected her from the fear of growing into a sexual woman. The ensuing underlying emotional and bodily changes at puberty, not dissimilar from Justin's presentation as previously described, exerted an uncomfortable pressure she tried to resist. By unconsciously suppressing her emotions she was also trying to hold on to a phallic identification – being a tomboy – thus attempting to disown her sexually feminine body.

As the "bubble" gradually dissolved during the analytic process, unmanageable strong feelings of attachment and dependency became exposed, which she warded off by maintaining a significant distance from me in the transference. Her unconscious need to be in control, particularly present in the early stages of her analysis, was brought to bear through her capacity to mesmerise me and induce a sort of hypnotic–somnolent state of mind, thus making it difficult at times for me to follow her or indeed feel able to come up with useful interpretations (Brown, 1977). In addition, her monotonous staccato voice, whilst lying on the couch in a rather controlled and motionless way, further reflected her controlling and aggressive wish to remain distant. "Hate was banned from my household", hence it was no surprise that Hayley had to underplay her rage towards A by transforming it into music and poetry. By the same token her unconscious aggressive impulses stirred up by powerful feelings of attachment and dependence on me, transformed her emotional state into being "half dead – half alive". Thus, her suppressed emotional life could only find its expression through bodily channels. By exposing her feelings of vulnerability – which for her meant femininity – through her symptoms she was unconsciously testing my acceptance of her (feminine) ill body. I often wondered whether she unconsciously used her "ills" in order to make sure that I remained anchored to as well as responsible for her "physical self".

The discrepancy between Hayley's countenance and underlying affect in her initial presentation may have been the result of a poor integration of her phallic identification with the perfect feminine self in an attempt to comply with her mother's needs for perfection. She equally pretended to be the "perfect self-sufficient patient" by purportedly containing her highly charged emotional life until serious medical conditions eventually came to the fore. In my view the appearance of these symptoms paradoxically fostered even more an unconsciously regressive pull to the maternal object evinced in the transference with me. Perhaps Hayley, in order to feel "half-alive", had no option but to go through bodily sensations such as itching (hives), pain and swelling (sinusitis, abscess), unstable vision (lazy eye) and burning (urinary tract infections): all manifestations of different underlying emotions. She had thus attempted to express a range of unrepresented affects of an exciting nature by unconsciously using a variety of shame-inducing body sensations created by her ailments. In a word, Hayley, like Justin, felt at the mercy of a body "speaking" on her behalf.

Eventually, as her medical conditions receded, Hayley began to communicate more forcefully her emotional repertoire, which included a long-standing pent up rage towards her mother. After this process she began to accept her mother at a more adult level, which eventually enabled her to negotiate the separation from her and be less frightened of her ordinary feminine self.

FURTHER THOUGHTS AND CONCLUSIONS

In this chapter I have illustrated a developmental perspective in my understanding of two patients' inability to express their affective life. When their verbal communications could not convey the full extent of their underlying affects, they were compelled to use their body – consciously in one and unconsciously in the other – in order to discharge or express some of their powerful unprocessed emotional states.

I began with the issue of imitation as a fundamental developmental stage necessary for the process of identification during the mother baby interaction in the context of affective mutual resonance. When this process is hampered, the child's ability for self and affect representation is compromised, resulting in a poor self-image and sense of identity.

In the analytic situation the analyst has to be constantly on the alert for the pitfalls of the imitative nature of the narrative while parallel bodily signals may indicate the silent presence of unexpressed and strangulated affects.

I have chosen two clinical examples whose poor self-identity demonstrated a pre-oedipal developmental failure, which became reactivated during their adolescence. Both patients unconsciously resorted to their body in order to access and express their affective life including their forbidden aggressive impulses. In particular, the clinical illustrations bring into sharp relief the predicament of patients who use (and abuse) their body as a way of communicating what may not be represented as yet in their mind. In these circumstances the patient's body becomes "an other" – an object experienced as foreign, hence not owned by the subject – and prone to be unconsciously used to express split off and/or repressed emotional experiences.

However, there are important differences to take into account between these two clinical cases both in terms of severity and their defensive use of dissociation between their mind and their body. While Justin's struggle is more at the level of the "body he has", which becomes an object imbued with a magic pre-pubertal fantasy, Hayley demonstrated a better capacity for symbolisation and elaboration, which allowed her to gradually acknowledge "the body she is". In addition, the use of the body in the first patient could be conceived as of a perverse nature (Glasser, 1986), in that instead of identification he makes use of "imitation" in order to unconsciously model himself on the object (core complex). Whereas in the second patient the use of the body could be understood as of hysterical nature, in that Hayley communicated through an unconscious imitation of a sick maternal object.

I also wish to stress that the analyst needs to be particularly mindful of more ominous parallel self-destructive processes, which may be overlooked particularly when the analyst is lured down false alleyways or may end up being obfuscated by the patient's compartmentalised and disguised narrative. In other words, while the analyst and patient may appear to be fully "in tune" with one another, it may be that this process detracts the analyst from attending to other "out of tune" manifestations of distress or of hidden affects, which can only be expressed through bodily channels.

Finally, while the analyst's task is to name, facilitate, expose and interpret a variety of emotional states with a view to acting as a bridge between bodily manifestations and thought inhibition, we should not underestimate how much the analyst's absences can also bring into the fore powerful regressive reactions in particularly vulnerable patients, whose relationship to their body is constantly at odds and disconnected from their suppressed emotional life.

ACKNOWLEDGMENTS

I wish to acknowledge the invaluable help of my British-Italian colleagues, who enabled me over the years of bi-annual discussions to develop, conceptualise and put into practice various ways of understanding body communications.

Note

1 Indeed, according to Loewald (1960) "part of what is introjected is the image of the child as seen felt, smelled, heard and touched by the mother".

References

Aisenstein, M. (2006) The indissociable unity of psyche and soma: A view from the Paris Psychosomatic School. *International Journal of Psychoanalysis*, 87: 667–680.

Aisenstein, M., Smadja, C. (2010) Conceptual framework from the Paris Psychosomatic School: A clinical psychoanalytic approach to oncology. *International Journal of Psychoanalysis*, 91: 621–640.

Auerbach, J.S., Blatt, S.J. (1996) Self-representation in severe psychopathology: The role of reflexive self-awareness. *Psychoanalytic Psychology*, 123: 297–341.

Bateman, A., Fonagy, P. (2004) *Psychotherapy for Borderline Personality Disorder*. Oxford: Oxford University Press.

Betjeman, J. (1936) Cornwall in childhood. In *John Betjeman Collected Poems*. London: John Murray. 1958.

Brown, D. (1977) Drowsiness in the countertransference. *International Review of Psychoanalysis*, 4: 481–492.

Eissler, K.R. (1953) The effect of the structure of the ego on psychoanalytic technique. *Journal of the American Psychoanalytic Association*, 1: 104–143.

Erikson, E. (1956) The problem of Ego identity. *Journal of the American Psychoanalytic Association*, 4: 56–121.

Fenichel, O. (1945) *The Psychoanalytic Theory of Neurosis*. New York: W.W. Norton.

Ferrari, A. B. (2004) *From the Eclipse of the Body to the Dawn of Thought*. London: Free Association Books.

Freud, S. (1910) Leonardo da Vinci and a memory of his childhood, *Standard Edition*, 11: 63.

Freud, S. (1923) The ego and the id, *Standard Edition*, 19: 26–27.

Gaddini, E. (1969) On imitation. *International Journal of Psychoanalysis*, 50: 475–484.

Gaddini, E. (1981) Note sul problema mente-corpo. *Rivista di Psicoanalisi*, 27: 3–29.

Gergely, G. (2007) The social construction of the subjective self: The role of affective mirroring, markedness and ostensive communication in self-development. In Mayes, L., Fonagy, P., Target, M. (eds), *Developmental Science and Psychoanalysis: Integration and Innovation*. London: Karnac.

Glasser, M. (1986). Identification and its vicissitudes as observed in the perversions. *International Journal of Psychoanalysis*, 67: 9–16.

Kilborne, B. Personal communication. 18 April 2010.

Kohut, H. (1972) Thought on narcissism and narcissistic rage. *Psychoanalytic Study of the Child*, 27: 360–400.

Laufer, M., Laufer, M.E. (1984) *Adolescence and Developmental Breakdown*. New Haven, CT: Yale University Press.

Laufer, M.E. (1991) Body image, sexuality and the psychotic core. *International Journal of Psychoanalysis*, 72: 63–71.

Lehtonen, J., Partanen, J., Purhonen, M., Valkonen-Korhonen, M., Kononen, M., Saarikoski, S., Launiala, K. (2006) Nascent body ego: Metapsychological and neurophysiological aspects. *International Journal of Psychoanalysis*, 87: 1335–1353.

Limentani, A. (1977) Affects and the psychoanalytic situation. *International Journal of Psychoanalysis*, 58: 171–197.

Loewald, H. (1960) On the therapeutic action of psychoanalysis. *International Journal of Psychoanalysis*, 41: 16–33.

Lombardi, R. (2009) Body, affect, thought: Reflections on the work of Matte Blanco and Ferrari. *Psychoanalytic Quarterly*, 78: 123–160.

Rosenfeld, H. (1987) Impasse and Interpretation: Therapeutic and antitherapeutic factors in the psychoanalytic treatment of psychotic, borderline, and neurotic patients. In *New Library of Psychoanalysis*. London: Tavistock.

Sandler, J., Freud, A. (1983) Discussions in the Hampstead Index on "The ego and the mechanisms of defence": XI. A form of altruism. *Bulletin Anna Freud Centre*, 6: 329–349.

Sandler, J., Sandler, A.M. (1998) *Internal Objects Revisited*. London: Karnac.

Spitz, R.A. (1955) The primal cavity: A contribution to the genesis of perception and its role for psychoanalytic theory. *The Psychoanalytic Study of the Child*, 10: 215–240.

Stern, D. (1985) *The Interpersonal World of the Infant*. London: Karnac.

9

A SKIN OF ONE'S OWN

On boundaries, the skin, and feminine sexuality

Patricia Grieve

> The ego is first and foremost a bodily ego; it is not merely a surface entity, but is itself the projection of a surface [i.e. the ego is ultimately derived from bodily sensations, chiefly from those springing from the surface of the body. It may thus be regarded as a mental projection of the surface of the body].
> (Freud, 1923, p. 26, [Footnote, 1927, loc. cit.])

This chapter aims at exploring, through a clinical case, the relation between body boundaries, psychic boundaries, and the experience of the skin in connection to both. The development of feminine sexuality and its vicissitudes are also considered in the context of early conflicts.

Winnicott developed Freud's description of the body ego in an interesting way. He thought that the process of the psyche coming to dwell in the body was not a given, but the outcome of a fine and complex developmental process involving the mother's holding and handling of the baby's body. He described this outcome as "personalization", his neologism for the opposite of "depersonalization", that is, "the development of the feeling that one's person is in one's body" (1945, p. 151); or, "the achievement of a close relationship between the psyche and the body" (1963a, p. 223), a link that is broken in mental and psycho-somatic illness.

The skin is the bodily matrix for the achievement of a body image with clear boundaries; in health, as Winnicott expressed it, it constitutes the limits of the self. The skin, as "the limiting membrane of the body and therefore of the personality" (1969, p.115) provides us with useful metaphors, but, more powerfully, as psychoanalysis has shown, these metaphors are anchored in primitive bodily experiences that are the unconscious roots of our psychic life. Primitive somatic and sensorial experiences are inscribed as somatic memories, which may later be represented in the psychic apparatus. S. Isaacs' pioneering work (1940–1952) was perhaps the first attempt to conceptualize and explore the beginnings of psychic life and the primitive forms of representation, on the frontiers of body and psyche.

Gaddini (1987) observed how, at birth, the loss of the boundary created by the amniotic membrane, becomes a stimulus to primitive mental functioning, in the shape of memory, inscribed in the body, in order to repeat the experience of finding clear and containing limits. The mother's hands and body, as a holding environment, provide these boundaries, in the absence of which the individual becomes caught up in a repetitive search for sensorial experienceswhich may substitute for this lack.

The softness and temperature of the mother's body, her skin, voice, and body rhythms, provide an enveloping and holding environment; the internalization of these maternal functions, and the imaginative elaboration of these, and other sensorial experiences, are bound together by the construction of what Anzieu (1985) would conceptualize as "skin ego", the earliest organization of the body ego based on the representation of the surface of the body as boundary and as container. This is the basis for the achievement of "oneness", and of several organizing differences: me-not-me, inside–outside, body–psyche. The skin ego, therefore, has protective and containing functions not only with regard to outside intrusions, but also in relation to internal upheavals; initially, both are equally disruptive: the continuity of being provided by maternal care configurates a sense of integration, and enables the gradual differentiation of internal and external stimuli. These stimuli may then be experienced without becoming a threat to the continuity of existence, which may rupture the sense of oneness held by a skin that is gradually becoming differentiated from the mother's; that is, becoming a psychic skin.

Post-Freudian psychoanalysis widened the frontiers of our discipline through the exploration of the origins of psychic life and the development of the ego, providing us with a theoretical framework that enabled new generations of analysts to observe, understand and explore the primitive functioning which may coexist with an apparent "neurotic" psychopathology, and revealing the archaic anxieties linked to a fragile sense of self and body limits.

The issue of boundaries, both external and internal, is of paramount importance in contemporary psychoanalysis, as Green (1972/1990) has stated, writing about borderline pathologies, where we can clearly observe a confusion between drive, object and ego. Starting with D.W.Winnicott's work, different psychoanalytic authors (for example, Heimann, 1958; Laplanche, 1987) went beyond Freud's and Klein's endogenous view of psychic development, and described the effects of the intrusion of the Other's psyche on the nascent ego of the infant. In the words of Green: "Intrusion anxiety, of which Winnicott gave the first and most successful demonstration ... [involves] ... a dysfunctioning of the frontiers of the ego which proves to be incapable of protecting the subject against the object's intrusion" (2005, p. 152).

The analytic situation, in patients with a fragile sense of psychic boundaries, and for whom the skin occupies an important place in their unconscious phantasy life, has a twofold relevance: the setting (including the formal setting as well as the internal setting of the analyst) provides for stable boundaries and represents a holding environment which silently weaves the skin ego together and restores holes and ruptures in its continuity; the transference to the analyst as object and its interpretation may allow for separation, with the dangers of a premature differentiation if this is not accompanied by the important work on the former aspect.

Analytical work with such patients requires on the part of the analyst an attitude of attention to the countertransference, given the nature of the archaic anxieties and phantasies that are activated, which involve loss of boundaries between subject and object, making the patient extremely sensitive to the psychic movements of the analyst. The analyst is also receptive to the loss of psychic boundaries, which may generate confusion in the countertransference. Given the nature of the object relation and the anxieties involved, interpretations may have, for long periods of time, the paradoxical status of being uttered from a position of a subjective object, that is, of an object not fully recognized as external to the subject, but which is also the carrier of ego functioning. The transference to the analyst as object may be perceived as a threat of intrusion.

The treatment has to tread, therefore, along a narrow path between fusion and intrusion (Green, 2005).

ON SKIN IN DREAMS, AND DREAMS AS SKIN

In a paper that appeared after the publication of "Le moi-peau", Anzieu discussed what he termed "formal signifiers" (1987). These are proto-symbolic attempts at representation of early configurations involving body, self and object, which, being imbued with archaic anxieties, cannot be transformed into symbolic representations. They are related to what Isaacs (1940–1952) described as the most primitive unconscious phantasies, close to body experience, which take place at the very beginnings of the emergence of a body ego. Anzieu links them to Aulagnier's pictograms (1975). They cannot be repressed, and are liable to invade the subject under the form of a hallucinatory experience, an anxiety dream or a nightmare. In these archaic traumatic situations subject and object are still not clearly differentiated; they are mostly connected with experiences of intrusion that threaten to rupture or overwhelm the subject, preventing the establishment of the skin–ego.

A young female patient brought, during the first years of analysis, a series of dreams which, because of their quasi-hallucinatory quality, seemed related to Anzieu's description. Most of these dreams involved the skin, in different states and functions, and they revealed, as X-rays of her psychic life, archaic anxieties which she attempted to keep at bay with increasingly failing resources. I shall follow the route marked by these dreams, and their gradual transformation towards more complex and narrative expressions, allowing for the subjective appropriation of her bodily and emotional experiences, and for the acquisition of more stable boundaries, that is, of a psychic skin.

The dreams had another particular quality: devoid of a narrative or a temporal dimension, they were more like pictures or static attempts at representing an archaic image. They carried, as Roussillon described in a recent paper, "the sensory-motor trace of the impact of the encounter with a still poorly differentiated, poorly identified object, confusing part of the subject and part of the object" (2015, p. 593). These were archaic proto-symbolic representations which could give shape to a struggle for psychic survival.

Shortly after starting analysis, my patient, whom I shall call Cristina, described a dream which had an impact on me: "A woman with her skin flayed so that her rib-cage was exposed, but alive, was telling me (the patient): 'It's all right'. I could not see her head, but I knew it was a woman. It was as if she had sacrificed herself and as if she had been devoured, in a cannibalistic way, by a man, of course: I can't think of a woman doing that."

I was struck by the expression of psychotic-type anxieties in someone whose inhibitions and phobias I had initially thought of as basically neurotic. However, we had been able to see, very soon into the treatment, that she was afraid that the analysis would leave her in a defenceless and vulnerable state. The analysis might confirm her fears of madness, or, even worse, make her mad. I understood this "fear of breakdown" (Winnicott, 1963b) as a reference to early traumatic impingements on her nascent ego, fostering the premature and defensive development of mental functioning, detached from bodily experience, in order to compensate for failures in her holding environment. Emotional growth was therefore impaired.

The dream had made her very anxious and she described it with difficulty and embarrassment. Earlier in the session my patient had said that she had refused to go out with a boy who had phoned her during the weekend (it was a Monday session). The patient found it difficult to talk about the dream, but felt the person depicted was not herself; however, she could also feel close to the suffering it expressed. I opted for an interpretation that touched on her fears related to beginning analysis, and said that perhaps she was afraid that the treatment would leave her as in "raw flesh" ("carne viva"), a Spanish expression alluding to an open wound, and also to a skinless state. Cristina confirmed that this was so.

Cristina had mentioned a slight eczema on her scalp, which had appeared during times of stress since the onset of puberty. She was also prone to blushing and to urticaria whenever she could not express her anger. During the sessions she would also pick bits of skin from her scalp and eyelids, look at them briefly in an absent-minded way, and discard them; after many years this practice gradually diminished, even though this was never put into words during the sessions.

The patient had consulted because of her difficulty in forming relationships with boys, which she found very shameful. The dream seemed to provide some answers to those difficulties, as it revealed archaic anxieties involving the integrity of the body and of the ego. At that early stage of the analysis Cristina also seemed to be revealing to me her fears about the analytic encounter as a dangerous intrusion which threatened her fragile sense of a separate identity. But I had also felt that the dream expressed my patient's fear that the analysis might be harmful to me, that the violent oral attack on the breast could represent an anxiety about the analytic encounter and the dangers of being "fed" by my words if at the same time I could be perceived as a worried or damaged analyst. A few days later I had the opportunity to convey this to her and she agreed readily, which surprised me. The headless woman of the dream could therefore represent either one of us, or both: the skin that could separate and delimit is torn.

Anzieu (1985) described a fantasy represented by a shared mother–child skin, which is painfully torn in the act of separation: Cristina's dream seemed to depict such an internal situation. Beginning an analysis had a paradoxical meaning: it might rupture the confusional dyad; but the torn skin might also leave her utterly defenceless.

However, the woman is also "alive", and this is an important detail: in spite of the pain, the destruction is not total, so there can be hope, for herself and for her object. The dreams were a significant and important help in the analytic process, without which my patient could have suffered a severe psycho-somatic disturbance, or a psychotic breakdown. Instead, she was able to begin to represent her great sensitivity through the depiction of a suffering skin.

The phrase "It's all right" seemed a characteristic way my patient had of keeping the object at bay: the mother's intrusive anxiety was more feared than potential physical damage. Cristina told of a hospitalization at the time of her puberty, when she had an anaphylactic reaction to an injection. She had preferred to suffer in silence, rather than "worry" her mother, until she was found nearly unconscious. I understood that she was also afraid to make me anxious and worried; she would then, in turn, be made more anxious by my anxiety, as she was eventually able to say.

The patient had an image of a very vulnerable mother, who was very often led to tears in discussions with the patient's father. Cristina was constantly trying to please, to placate, and to pre-empt any disharmonious situations of which she was in constant fear. We talked about the projection of her own violence on an image of her father, with which she then became identified. This masculine identification seemed to contain the primitive rage which was the residue of passively suffered intrusions early in her life. Gradually, I came to see that the dream provided a picture of the precarious state of her skin–ego, with holes and fissures, unable to separate inside and outside, and to contain.

Several months later, Cristina had a dream in which "I was in the underground, with my (female) boss, and I could see, on the platform opposite, a boy, school classmate of mine, who had also studied at N. (the foreign city where she did a post-graduate course). I had, in the past, flayed this boy's skin. He looked all right in the dream, but I was afraid of his revenge, so I tried to hide behind my boss."

She said this could represent her anger and fear towards men. It seemed like a violent primal scene with mutual flaying, in which man and woman – or mother and baby in the more archaic version – could bite and tear each other's skins. We talked about the boy as a masculine version of herself, carrying the violence with which she then felt her feminine self could be attacked. The presence of a third participant, the boss, may guarantee a containment of the violence: it is a part-object, the skin–mother or the analytic function (comprising both the analyst, the interpretive work, and the setting), providing boundaries, protection and containment.

Cristina's extreme shyness in relation to men, one of her referring symptoms, could be understood using the vivid imagery of the dream as her feeling metaphorically "skinless" and therefore needing to protect herself both by distance, and also by hiding behind other women: mother and female friends. Currently, her analyst fulfilled this function, but in a different, symbolic, way, and also because there was a hope that she might be able to internalize this skin function, transformed into a psychic, and therefore less vulnerable, skin.

Another of Cristina's symptoms, as it began to unfold in the analytic narrative, was her propensity to feel invaded by any story that she came across in her life which contained elements that might affect her, so that she put herself in the other person's place and was unable to rescue herself from being sucked into their feelings. It was as if the extremely labile frontiers of her ego were unable to protect her and her identity. Needing the protection of the mother's, or the analyst's, skin also left her, paradoxically, unprotected, with no skin of her own, no clear boundaries between herself and others.

Puberty provided an opportunity to re-signify archaic intrusion anxieties through a primal scene imbued with terrifying and uncontained violence which turned it into a terrifying clash. Cristina had suffered intense and unbearable anxieties during her adolescent years when her parents had quarrelled continuously. At night she would lie in her bed listening to the sounds coming from the parental bedroom, and not fall asleep until there was silence. Everywhere she went, she became terrified of violent people she saw everywhere, as if the violent primal scene could not be contained within the walls of the parental home, and her phobic avoidance mechanisms were failing her. The walls were no longer a protection, and she would imagine listening to noises coming from the flat next door and constantly thought of a happy future when she would live on her own, totally isolated from the threatening violence generated by any kind of closeness. It was as if the illusion of a protecting skin–wall were falling apart under the impact and the intensity of her drives which, coming from inside, made her feel invaded and vulnerable to the extreme of fearing madness. Her attempts to control and split body from mind, which had helped during her latency years, proved inadequate when confronted with the menacing changes in her body and its urges. She feared encountering violent situations everywhere, and imagined her parents getting involved in them: the confusion between external and internal realities seemed associated with the invasion of her mind, and of her body.

A series of dreams which my patient brought during some time seemed to communicate a sense of boundaries, however precarious: she is driving a car, but can't control it. She can't reach the pedals, so she can't brake, or she is not big enough to see through the windshield. I interpreted in terms of her fear of losing control of her body and being overwhelmed by excitement, linked to her pubertal anxieties, when she felt she had to hide her body behind layers of clothing which would cover her newly developed feminine shapes. The patient became more aware of her own body, and we talked of her rejection of its being unequivocally female, no longer that of a child, and the fear of what she called "the instinctual", associated with the male, as something coming from inside her and felt as a pressing and dangerous drive that she could not contain. Cristina felt too small for her body, and unable to control it, but the car, as well as representing a hard protective "skin", seemed an attempt to attain activity as a means of overcoming early traumatic situations. She associated these solutions with a masculine identification.

ORIFICES AND FEMALE SEXUALITY

Instinctual experiences held, first by the mother, then by the ego, may allow for the investment of bodily orifices as pleasurable instruments of intake or expulsion, not punctures or holes in the skin ego through which inside cannot be contained and separated from outside, dangerous objects may intrude, or valuable ones leak out. From very early on a dialectics is established between the development of the skin as an enveloping tissue, holding together the physical, and then the psychic self, and the body orifices, linked to the erotogenic zones. For these dialectics to lead to a successful integration, the body orifices need to be invested as pleasurable. Winnicott (1962) speaks of a tension between ego and instinctual development; instinctual upheavals threaten the integrity of the nascent ego when it is not protected by maternal provision, the skin function of the mother. For the girl, the relationship to body openings is particularly important and may be fraught with anxieties related to penetration and intercourse as frightening intrusions that threaten the integrity of the body and of the self. Sexual excitement can be experienced as a loss of boundaries, provoking anxiety.

Adolescence introduces a renewed investment of the body boundaries, as the representation of the sexual body altered by pubertal changes requires a severance of the infantile libidinal tie to the mother. The work of recognition and acceptance of the new sexual body transformed at puberty requires the adolescent to reinvest in their skin, with all its multiple functions, including identity and sexual exploration.

In her fourth year of analysis Cristina started dancing lessons with a group of friends, and gradually allowed herself to be touched by men, not without many internal difficulties. There she met a boy with whom, after some months, she started a relationship. A long and painful path still needed to be trod in order for Cristina to be touched, kissed, and begin intimate contacts. Then the subject of penetration caused great anxiety and phobic avoidance. She described herself as suffering from "vaginismus", a condition she had read about on the internet; I decided to hold my doubts about her self-diagnosis and wait.

A SKIN OF ONE'S OWN

A dream brought during this period provided a useful glimpse into Cristina's psychic predicaments: "A daughter of her mother's [sic] had her body entirely wrapped in Sellotape; it seemed like a punishment.

Her mother had done it. She looked and thought: 'I'm glad it's not me, because if my mother is going crazy...'" (She used the Spanish expression "se le cruzan los cables" – "crossed wires" – meaning losing temporarily one's mind).

The patient associated that the girl in the dream was not her actual sister, so it must be herself, or part of herself. She added that during the weekend (this was a Monday session) she had been talking with her boyfriend about her extreme sensitivity and she had cried. (It was during weekends that the much feared attempts at penetration took place.) And she had also talked about her parents, remembering that there was a time when her mother used to cry frequently, prompted by anything her father – or sometimes her own mother – might say. Cristina used to think: "When I grow up, I don't want to be like that with my partner." She added that with her boyfriend she had cried not only for herself, when she felt the victim, but also because she saw how it affected R (the boyfriend) and she feels very bad, because she had wanted to hurt and punish him. So she cried out of guilt, and it went on and on and she could not stop herself. (This made me think of how, in the absence of the analysis, she feels uncontained and draining herself with unstoppable crying.)

So she was crying like mother, I said, and in the dream it is mother who has gagged and bound her, in Sellotape, leaving her immobile. Why would she do this, I asked. Cristina said that perhaps she had to be gagged to prevent her from being angry and aggressive. I had been struck by the word "celo" (Spanish version of Sellotape), which is singular for jealousy, "celos". It was nearing the end of the session and I made a brief interpretation in the sense that perhaps her mother in the dream also represented a part of herself that she wanted to wrap in a hard impenetrable skin, with no openings, so that nothing comes out, such as her tears, or her rage, and nothing goes in, like feeling jealous or being penetrated (Cristina was constantly comparing herself to other girls that R might find more receptive and less "impenetrable", and she thought jealousy was behind her parents' disputes; she also used to think I had other patients who were able to change at a faster pace than she did).

The Sellotape envelope represented a still precarious attempt to construct a skin of her own, a boundary between herself and maternal intrusion. However, it isolated her from other contacts and closed bodily openings necessary for tenderness and intercourse. Cristina was now struggling to differentiate herself and was fighting against an alienating identification with a maternal imago experienced as intrusive and controlling. In her relationship with R she was painfully aware of enacting a version of the relationship between herself and this mother, with her as the controlling mother. In intercourse, however, it was the penis she feared as a potentially destructive intruder; this was an expression of her projection into the man of the residue of primitive, uncontained rage aroused by the experience of helplessness when faced with intolerable intrusion.

The following day, still associating to her dream, Cristina said she feared that R might become afraid of her moods and rages. This reminded her of her mother's attitude towards her grandmother, who could be very moody. I thought she might also be referring to a situation she herself had experienced in early childhood, and wondered if she had to develop intellectual skills to predict her mother's "moods". She described how she had felt terrified of her mother cutting her fingernails and cuticle skins. She may have experienced it as curbing her primitive aggression, and it also evoked an image of a mother with sharp scissors–nails who could scratch and puncture her skin, leaving her in a state similar to that depicted in the dream of the torn female torso. Her own biting and scratching impulses coloured this image, fusing together subject and object.

I had been feeling surprised and rather ambivalent about the consistency of the new developments in Cristina's life, fearing them to be the outcome of the wilful counter-phobic growing up, which had led her to develop at the expense of her sexual body. Given the still precarious nature of her mental boundaries, I was also worried that I might have been acting out countertransferentially in a way that my patient may have experienced as pushing her towards a genitality before she had been able to elaborate and resolve the major confusions she still felt in relation to her own feminine body and desires.

The self-diagnosis of "vaginismus" seemed to be my patient's way of establishing a protective membrane between herself and masculine penetration, and also against being penetrated by my interpretations experienced in the sense described above. Perhaps this symbolic membrane served to create a space and time in which she could begin to feel her sexual body as her own, so that penetration might not be experienced as an assault on her fragile sense of bodily and psychic boundaries.

I had decided to hold my doubts about Cristina's supposed vaginismus, not pressing for a resolution, and only interpreted that her mind and her body seemed to entertain different wishes and we had to wait for them to come together. Waiting, I felt, was essential, as Winnicott (1941) had described, until the baby could reach out and make a spontaneous gesture. This idea, which he later developed in very important ways, involved a non-intrusive attitude on the part of the analyst–mother. My patient's mother, however, had been notoriously unable to wait: for instance, she had pressed to meet R when the relationship was only beginning, disregarding what she herself knew about Cristina's difficulty in establishing a relationship with a man. Although she could never express any criticisms of her mother, she described her as someone "hyperactive", involved in all kinds of activities and a very demanding profession whereas she saw herself as having a very different pace, passive and slow, and had chosen a profession on the basis of it not being demanding or implying responsibilities, and closer to the father's. But all this made her fear she might be a disappointment to her parents, both brilliant professionals in their own fields.

Some time after having the dream narrated above, Cristina came to a Monday session saying that she and her boyfriend had finally had full intercourse, and she felt very well after that. She was reassured that she was a normal woman and that there was nothing wrong with her genitals, as she had feared. She also felt freer of the jealousy that had led her to make constant comparisons with other women.

But this victory proved not to be exempt from conflict: she felt afraid of her vagina as an opening through which infectious and dirty substances could enter her body. The conditions for attempting intercourse were stringent and she would get angry with her boyfriend for any insignificant reason, so that intercourse would not happen. I interpreted her need to control the penetration, to feel that she could open or close her body at will, symbolically, by saying "no". I acknowledged her wish to decide for herself, in her own time.

During this period Cristina brought a dream in which "there was a large hole in the middle of my hand, it was possible to see the other side but for a very fine membrane that thinly covered my palm". It seemed to condense different part–objects: both her and R's hands, and the vagina, with the thin and fragile hymen still intact. She associated to a papilloma infection her flatmate had contracted in her genitals; she herself had papilloma on her foot when she was a child. This linked to her fear of infection, which made her wish that R would wash his hands before touching her genitals. It was difficult to picture her genitals as an internal space, because this conjured archaic anxieties about what it may contain. The hymen was represented as both a protective and a fragile membrane, but still could not be relinquished, just as the patient seemed to wish to transform her phobic defences – the Sellotape skin – yet was afraid to live without them.

Anzieu writes about a feminine formal signifier:

> The skin–ego function of maintaining sexual excitation is evident in a formal signifier ... A feminine one would be: the hymen is perforated. According to Annie Anzieu, the shared mother–daughter skin is originally invested with narcissistic libido and then with sexual object libido. In order for the girl to reach the Oedipus complex, perforation and the tear of the shared skin are needed; this allows the girl to have her own envelope, able to contain her nascent desires directed towards the father. Those perforations introduce the preconception of a disflowering, with the hymen being invested by the desire to be penetrated by the father.
>
> (Anzieu, 1987, p. 33)

Body openings have particular significance in a woman's relationship to her own body, and may also render difficult the construction of a body image with clear boundaries, which are also the boundaries of her self, as separate from her mother's. Penetration was experienced by my patient as a dangerous invasion of her still fragile and precarious sense of an internal space; it also implied a passive submission by not being able to control her vaginal opening. Chiland (1980) has written "To be penetrated, which is both desired and feared, implies the loss of anal mastery". In my patient's case, we had seen the importance of anal mastery – she had an early memory of wanting to use the WC like the grown ups, refusing the pot – in her premature ego development and attainment of a fragile sense of independence. Anal mastery thus constructed was fragile because it rested on a split between body and mind and not on the mental acquisition of negation, which allows for autonomous mental functioning. Negation is a milestone in the construction of a mental skin, and of the difference between outside and inside.

A MIND OF ONE'S OWN

Some time later, after a last-minute cancellation of a Thursday session, the last one of the week, Cristina went through a period when she would become angry with her boyfriend for the smallest reason, and she would punish him with her silences. The weekend following the cancellation she had been at her parents' house and had had to leave when she became extremely anxious at imagining she could hear the next-door neighbour and her son having a violent fight: this was made worse because her parents had torn down a wall to enlarge the kitchen, a change she had opposed for years. For a very long time she had found it intolerable to be in that room because she was afraid of the neighbours quarrelling, something that, in fact, had never happened. She became so anxious that she had to leave her parent's house: she hadn't felt like that since hearing her parents quarrelling as an adolescent. It seemed that my cancellation had torn down a partition in her yet fragile internal house, I interpreted to her, leaving Cristina with uncontained rage which she found frightening.

The anxiety lasted several weeks, during which she dreamed of a big monster woman who could become violent and dangerous if those close by, including herself, did not remain still and silent: she identified with this monster woman, and it seemed as if my unexpected failure intensified her need to control her objects. I thought this image also reflected an infantile situation of helplessness in the face of an unpredictable mother, re-experienced in the transference after my unexpected cancellation.

A Monday session, some time later, seemed to herald a turning point in this change. She had had a discussion with her mother, who had been on a trip with the patient's father, and had entrusted her with visiting her grandmother, which Cristina had not done, as her grandmother refused to see her at the time which suited her. This was new; previously, Cristina had submitted to her mother's demands, and guilt seemed to pass from her mother on to her with no mediation. She refused to feel guilty, like her mother does, she said. She had also been explaining to R the history of her great fear of violence in traffic disputes, so that he would understand why she got so anxious when he drives fast. (It had been an important change in recent weeks that she was able to explain her feelings to R, instead of becoming silent.) This went back to an incident in which her father had had a violent fight which had been ignited by her mother, who encouraged her father to confront the other driver. This was a fuller account of the traumatic situation than the one she had previously given. She went on to tell of her mother provoking violent situations in public, but also with her father, something that made her angry, because her mother should not have allowed her children to witness such episodes.

This was the first time my patient had been able to criticize her mother and express anger towards her: she was beginning to see herself now as different and separate. She said she could also feel that she and R were both different from her mother and father, and not fated to repeat their relationship. There seemed to be a greater trust in the resilience and integrity of her objects and their capacity to survive her violence.

In the following weeks, Cristina began to develop an idea which gradually invaded her: she was bound to have very problematic children, therefore she should not have them. She was fascinated by a reality show about adolescents who physically abuse their parents, and she had been forcing herself to watch it, she said, because it was a hard reality that we could not ignore. I thought she was probably deriving a great deal of excitement from her position as spectator, but this could rapidly switch into her becoming, in her fantasy, one or both of the participants of the scene. She saw herself as one of the mothers, with very conflictive children, so she had decided not to have them. In her mind, the mother and the adolescent child became confused. Time was abolished, so if Cristina saw herself as an adult, with a sexual partner, she became a mother, that is, she became her own mother. If she was critical of mothers, she herself became a monstrous mother.

During this time Cristina became extremely sensitive to any violent situations she heard or read about, or imagined seeing in the street, and thought R could become violent himself. These thoughts appeared when she had began to feel critical of her mother and experience anger at seeing herself in her place, being quarrelsome with her partner. They had a delusional quality, and it seemed that the difference between external and internal realities had been abolished. The skin–partition that was being constructed in the analysis still seemed fragile and in danger of collapsing.

She had begun to see her father as originally a quiet person, driven to violence by her mother's uncontrolled provocations. This involved separating from the fusional–confusional dyad. But it meant that she was a bad daughter. We became more able to differentiate a conflicting and split image of a mother: as suffering victim, and as the violent intruder. This facilitated the process of disidentification and the lessening of the fusional–confusional link.

It seemed that the psychotic delusional thinking appeared as a threat at this juncture, and could be, therefore, a defence against differentiation. It was experienced as a repetition of her adolescence breakdown, when the difference between her sexual and violent feelings, her listening to her parents' night-time explosions, and street situations, was confused and invaded her whole mental life. Her rage and disappointment at this repetition, experienced in the transference as a failure of the analyst, allowed the patient to feel what she had experienced in her childhood and adolescence as a betrayal of the parental couple. This in turn allowed for a deeper understanding of that period of her life, as well as the possibility to begin to acquire a clearer sense of her own boundaries and of ownership of her body.

SOME CONCLUSIONS

The significance of the skin in psychic development has been studied and observed by many authors before, coming from very different psychoanalytical traditions, with, however, a great deal of coincidences. I shall quote Winnicott, who defines in a very succinct way the core of the issue: "Emphasis on the skin contains an element of ego distress" (1988, p. 42).

Anzieu (1985) emphasized the skin ego's importance in ego development, and in the distinction between internal and external realities. This differentiation forms the basis for the ownership of one's body and mental functioning, as different, and as separate from the object's. This process involved, in the case narrated, a painful move away from a confusional situation towards the construction of a separate identity, a body and a mind of the patient's own. The vicissitudes of feminine sexuality added complexity to this process.

The analysis introduced the possibility of reconstructing early trauma, consisting of repeated impingements on my patient's fragile integration, and its sequelae of primitive rage, and lack of cohesive boundaries between self and object, inside and outside, and male and female. We understood a violent primal scene fantasized by the patient in terms of a resignification of the original early trauma, as an attempt at representing it.

The analytic situation enabled the patient to use her considerable capacity to represent and symbolize her pain and predicaments through the creation of dreams. The metaphor of the skin, connecting with deep unconscious and psycho-somatic processes, contained the transformational potential which allowed for psychic change, namely, the development of a psychic skin.

References

Anzieu, D. (1985) *Le Moi-Peau*. Paris: Dunod.

Anzieu, D. (1987) *Les Envelopes Psychiques*. Paris: Bordas.

Aulagnier, P. (1975) *La Violence de l'Interpretation*. Paris: Presses Universitaires de France.

Chiland, C. (1980) Clinical practice, theory and their relationship in regard to female sexuality. *The International Journal of Psychoanalysis*, 61: 350–365.

Freud, S. (1923) *The Ego and the Id. The Standard Edition of the Complete Psychological Works of Sigmund Freud*, Volume XIX. London: The Hogarth Press.

Gaddini, E. (1987) Notes on the mind–body question. *The International Journal of Psychoanalysis*, 68: 315–329.

Green, A. (1972) *On Private Madness*. Colchester: Mark Patterson & Assoc.

Green, A. (2005) *Key Ideas for a Contemporary Psycho-Analysis*. Hove: Routledge.

Heimann, P. (1958) Notes on early development. In *About Children and Children No-Longer*. London: Tavistock, pp. 138–150.

Isaacs, S. (1940–1952) The nature and function of phantasy. In Riviere, J. (ed.), *Developments in Psycho-Analysis*. London: Hogarth, pp. 67–121.

Laplanche, J. (1987) *Nouveaux Fondements pour la Psychoanalyse. La Seduction Originaire*. Paris: Presses Universitaires de France.

Roussillon, R. (2015) An introduction to the work on primary symbolization. *The International Journal of Psychoanalysis*, 96: 583–594.

Winnicott, D.W. (1941) The observation of infants in a set situation. In *Through Paediatrics to Psycho-Analysis*. London: The Hogarth Press.

Winnicott, D.W. (1945) Primitive emotional development. *The Maturational Processes and the Facilitating Environment*. London: The Hogarth Press.

Winnicott, D.W. (1962) Ego integration in child development. *The Maturational Processes and the Facilitating Environment.* London: The Hogarth Press.

Winnicott, D.W. (1963a) Casework and mental illness. In *The Maturational Processes and the Facilitating Environment.* London: The Hogarth Press.

Winnicott, D.W. (1963b Fear of breakdown. *Psycho-Analytic Explorations.* London: Karnac.

Winnicott, D.W. (1969) Additional note on psycho-somatic illness. *Psycho-Analytic Explorations.* London: Karnac.

Winnicott, D.W. (1988) *Human Nature.* London: Free Associations.

10

"SEIZED WITH A SAVAGE WOE"

Attacks on the vitality of the body in a suicidal young man

Joan Schächter

INTRODUCTION

In this presentation I use material from the analysis of a suicidal young man to explore aspects of his relationship with his body as they emerged and dominated the analytic encounter.[1] I will consider some perspectives on the development of the body–mind relationship in order to explore how Freud's tenet: "the ego is first and foremost a bodily ego" (1923, p. 26) informs my conceptualisations of the clinical encounter and my technique.

The quote in my title: "seized with a savage woe" comes from a translation of Heine's poem "The Lorelei" (1827) in which a small boatman is transfixed by the sight of a beautiful woman high on a cliff combing her golden hair and singing her siren song, his boat founders on the rocks below and he drowns.

The patient, whom I will call Conrad, experienced his body as the "battleground" through and in which he attempted to control his overwhelming feelings and his incoherent thoughts. His body, particularly in adolescence, became the enemy that he tried to subdue through a rigorous regime of diet and exercise. When these efforts failed to create some sense of inner equilibrium Conrad became intensely depressed and suicidal. In the course of the analysis I came to understand that Conrad was psychically trapped in living out a fantasy of union with an idealised mother which involved a suicidal fantasy of killing off the bad aspects of himself. Conrad also repeatedly cut his hair very short, expressing a compulsive need to "hack it back" as he put it. This cutting had several functions: a defiant self-assertion against his mother and his analyst in the transference, cutting himself off in fantasy from the object on whom he felt dependent and with whom he felt forced into a passive relationship; an attempt to feel more masculine and aggressive in relation to peers and ultimately an attack on the vitality of his body and that of his parents with whom he was concretely identified.

Moses and Eglé Laufer (1984, 1997) have written about the psychological impact of the bodily changes initiated at puberty on the adolescent struggling with unresolved infantile conflicts. Various forms of self-destructiveness occurring particularly in adolescents and young adults also evidence the threat of passivity with its associated dread of surrender to the maternal object, against which the adolescent struggles with violence (Eglé Laufer 1996). The enormous conflict between progressive developmental forces and regressive pulls is inevitably fought out in the arena of the transference, which, rather than having the quality of a playground as Freud described (1912), assumes the character of a violent and seductive life and death struggle.

BACKGROUND TO THE ANALYSIS

Conrad was 22 when I first met him. He had made his first suicide attempt after completing his finals when he was 21, after which he was unable to sustain a regular job. His parents had divorced whilst he was at University after many years of unhappiness. Conrad suffered from acute self-consciousness since early adolescence; feeling that people could see into him and see how helpless he felt. His sense of shame, humiliation and passivity formed the backdrop of his acute depression, overwhelming anxiety and suicidal impulses. He attempted to manage his disruptive affects through an extreme regime of diet and exercise. The compulsive and violent character of Conrad's symptoms was very striking, indicating the underlying narcissistic fragility and his absolute reliance on omnipotent modes of defence.

Conrad expressed intense feelings of rage against both parents, whom he felt were living inside his head, preventing him from living his own life. He complained that they were occupied with their own emotional problems and had been unable to care for him sufficiently. These complaints conveyed the presence of parental internal objects experienced as both abandoning and intrusive. Mother was chronically depressed and father was physically violent. His younger brother's arrival when Conrad was 18 months old played its part in the creation of his intense sense of deprivation and exclusion. I heard briefly of their childhood fights and Conrad's preference for pleasing his mother whilst his brother rebelled. Both Conrad and his brother suffered from childhood asthma, and he recalled some good memories of mother's physical care when he was ill.

After the initial consultations we agreed to start twice weekly psychotherapy. Whilst I thought he needed intensive work I was concerned as to whether he would be able to support this. In the first months Conrad spoke a great deal about his obsession with food, now seeing it as "emotional hunger" which he needed to regulate through controlling what he ate and trying to "shrink" his body. In the past he had obsessively searched for the "missing ingredient" in his diet that would explain and cure his depression. He also spoke of his intense feelings of dislike and disgust with his own body, which centred mainly on fears of contamination from outside and inside. He had no sexual experience and had felt extremely inhibited with girls at University; which was an added source of shame that intensified his phobic attitude to peers.

Conrad made two further suicide attempts during the first four months of psychotherapy. He spoke of feeling desperate at these times, persecuted by his thoughts and driven by a conscious need to "silence" his mind; to obliterate what he felt were mad incoherent thoughts. Following the second of these attempts he requested admission to a psychiatric hospital. He remained an in-patient during the first break and then became a day patient for three months. He was relieved to be in a safe place but quite soon began to express dissatisfaction with the limitations; an expression of his conflict between a regressive desire to be totally cared for and a wish to be dismissively independent of parental figures. During this time, I was informed of a research scheme at the Anna Freud Centre studying breakdown in young adults which offered subsidised analytic treatment. Following discussion with him, I referred him to the scheme and it was agreed that I would continue to treat him with an increased frequency of five sessions a week.

THE ANALYTIC SETTING

The analytic situation with its structure and reliability enabled Conrad to experience a much needed sense of safety, whilst my presence and listening felt intensely exciting and threatening, evoking archaic affects and anxieties of seduction, exploitation and intrusion. His mode of talking was articulate whilst also having the function of "action language", filling all the space whilst keeping me at a safe distance and in fantasy under his control (Campbell and Enckell 2005). He was explicit about his wish to be "one step ahead" in order to make my actions predictable.

He spoke of his word being "banked up" inside me, indicating his urgent need to have a secure container for frightening parts of himself which he otherwise felt compelled to violently attack in his body.

Conrad was extremely watchful and acutely aware of and sensitive to any changes in the analytic environment, inside and outside the room. His intense dependence transmitted through his words and his body became a source of humiliation and resentment. He struggled with his wish to conform to what he believed were my expectations, to be my perfect patient as he had tried to be the special child for his mother and the inevitable conflict this produced with his wish to be an autonomous adult man. Furthermore, his striving for narcissistic perfection conflicted with his infantile and adolescent sexual impulses and desires manifested through his body, which then became the hated impediment to merger with the idealised mother. Conrad quickly came to experience me as a desperately needed but threatening, humiliating object. This intensely conflictual situation inevitably increased the suicide threat.

His relationship with and experience of his body and its contents and the ways in which his body was used to contain affects that he could not represent psychically, were central to my understanding of the analytic encounter. His excessive self-consciousness, an experience that occurs on the border between the mental and the physical, on the boundary between self and other, reflected a lack of cohesion in his sense of self and in the integrity of his body boundary (Anzieu 1989). Aspects of his relationship with his body were evident in the stiff, tense posture he adopted. Conrad developed his ritual ways of entering and leaving the consulting room. He frequently arrived early and went to the toilet, repeating the visit to the toilet after the session. For some time it was not possible to explore the meanings of this behaviour as he would experience my interpretations as a humiliation, as if I was only wishing to force him to comply and submit to my wishes. I thought his use of the toilet and the waiting room expressed both his possessively needy wish to live inside me, and his need to evacuate messy and dangerous parts of his mind and body. These transitional areas (the waiting room and toilet) also offered him the opportunity to try out forms of self-assertion. He would sometimes taunt me. What would I do if he went upstairs or refused to leave at the end of a session, could I stop him? However, he quickly became acutely anxious about my response, expecting a rejecting retaliation or my collapse into an overwhelmed state. His use of the toilet became an occasion for him to enact sexual fantasies of a phallic narcissistic kind in relation to his analyst as the admiring excited mother. His handling of his penis before and after the sessions had the function of a needed reassurance against castration anxiety. In these ways he could bring me or force me into close contact with his body and its contents.

THE LORELEI

In the transference I became the Lorelei mother, an essentially narcissistic, tantalising object occupied with her own needs and responding only on her terms. In Heine's poem the boatman loses all awareness of himself and his own situation in his desperate wish to (re)-join the Lorelei. A major theme in the first years of Conrad's analysis was his fear of being too much for me that he linked to his feelings towards his mother; the intense closeness between them that was suddenly disrupted when he experienced her as shutting the door in his face, an experience that was repeated in his daily sessions. Conrad frequently spoke of his love towards me that he feared I would not accept. Moments of emotional engagement would be followed by his anxious need to distance himself, often through intellectual talk. He avidly read psychoanalytic books, in an attempt both to impress me and to control the threatened humiliation and abandonment. Conrad oscillated between declaring his love for women and his hatred and rage towards them for "having all the power". In the third month of analysis he came to a session feeling depressed because he felt I had been too sharp in my comments concerning his anxiety about finding work and leaving the safety of the day hospital. He had felt small and then thought of suicide as a way of showing me that he had "the ultimate sanction". This sequence was often repeated, inevitably creating an anxious, guilty counter response in me. I came to notice, as did he, that I would become more verbally active when he reported feeling suicidal. At these times he could experience me as more fully attuned and responsive, repeating the pattern of childhood illness eliciting his mother's positive attention.

During a Friday session in the second year of analysis, he wondered if he would ever be able to get in touch with his sexual feelings towards his mother, whether he could allow into his mind sexual thoughts or desires towards me. He spoke of feeling more relaxed about his hair growing. He felt freer to explore all his thoughts when feeling he had space in the sessions because I did not start the session. He no longer felt so compelled to conform to his mother's expectations and ideas. He then talked of exercising and needing to have an absolutely regular predictable timetable. I pointed out how this reflected his need to counteract the freedom of thought he had just been speaking about. He agreed, adding that a year before he would have been very angry to hear this from me and would have withdrawn. He recognised that he had felt sad about leaving the day hospital and about the loss of particular relationships with women he felt had cared about him. He agreed that his over-exercising was an attempt to control if not to obliterate these feelings of sadness and loss. He returned to his intense love for his mother and how she then shut the door and did not want him anymore. He was aware of the impending ending of the session, waiting for me to make the obvious link. The movement between allowing space and some freedom of thought for both participants and abolishing or restricting this in order to create a place with the idealised mother/analyst that was at the same time a deadly space in which nothing new could develop, was evident in this session.

At moments when he became aware of his attraction to me, partially displaced onto older women he met outside, he felt intensely ashamed and fearful of wanting to attack me. He subsequently felt acutely depressed and obsessed with his diet. Following a change in time of one of his sessions, Conrad began arriving late, which I interpreted as expressing his protest. He spoke of feeling like a small child with a powerful adult. He spoke of his interest in girls and older women, fearing I would misunderstand him and react in an "outraged feminist way". He then observed how he holds on to the pillow on the couch as he does now at home when he lies down to rest. He felt embarrassed to tell me he wanted me to physically hold him whilst also feeling relieved to feel this and express his wish to me. He went on to talk of his feeling that his mother had rejected his body and how in turn that made him reject his body, starving it, exercising ferociously and wanting to kill himself.

In a Monday session a week later, Conrad spoke of his need to come to his session, hoping he would not be too much for me. He acknowledged how in the previous Friday session he had wanted to force me to think about him over the weekend through talking about feeling very depressed and suicidal. Through our analytic work he was able to see that this reflected a retreat from frightening wishes he might not be able to control. He recognised that he believed it was safer for him to feel depressed, remaining a child close to his mother/analyst at the cost of sacrificing his adult sexual identity. His depression also expressed his unconscious aggression against his potential for development, less extreme than his suicide attempts but nevertheless constituting violence against his body and sexual identity. Such violence is an attempted solution to experiences of feeling overwhelmed by the object, the only feasible solution to an indissoluble dilemma: the freeing of the self from the other through the destruction of the other within the self (Perelberg 1998, p. 4). As Campbell (1998, p. 77) and others have suggested, the suicide attempt represents a solution to the wish for merger on the one hand and terror of annihilation on the other.

A TURNING POINT IN THE ANALYSIS

An important moment in the analytic work arose in the fourth year. We had been working on his wish to be independent and his fear of being abandoned, isolated and seen as arrogant, and his violent revengeful fantasies to destroy his parents, himself and his analyst. He had left a telephone message one evening wanting to speak to me without giving the reason. He conveyed a resentful anger that I was not there to answer him when he had taken the risk to telephone. I returned home late and decided not to telephone him, aware that this was in part a counter response to feeling controlled, which was evoked by his resentful tone in which I sensed some satisfaction that I was not there, as well as a decision based on the current analytic work. This was not fully thought out and I felt considerable anxiety anticipating the next session. He arrived a minute or two late and went to the toilet. I was shocked by my fantasy, on hearing a clicking noise, that he had a knife. This inevitably evoked a sensation of fear about what might happen in the session, which of us might be subject to uncontrollable violence. He came into the session four minutes late, saying he was out of breath because he had to run to get here. He was angry that I had not phoned him back, it made him feel this was "just talk". I decided to wait, aware of not wanting to be defensive but also wary of taking up his wish to intrude into my life. He went on to speak about how depressed and self-conscious he was feeling but added that he was able to think a bit about himself and he was aware that he felt differently from two or three years ago. He returned to his anger about my not phoning back; he thought I was using the ansaphone as a protection against him.

I said I could understand his anger and disappointment that I had not responded as he wished, and his feelings of acute anxiety when he felt left alone with his feelings. He said he had felt better this morning, but he had written two letters of resignation to his Professor and PhD supervisor. I felt a familiar feeling of anxiety and frustration; whilst he was telling me that he could think more about himself in my absence, he was also speaking of his impulse to destroy the developments he had achieved as the result of hard analytic work. When I spoke of his violent revengeful wishes towards me and himself, he said he felt he was a tragic case with so much unfulfilled potential. I could then point out the evident masochistic pleasure and sadistic excitement in his fantasy of being a kind of tragic hero. At the end of the session, in response to my talking of his fear that I could or would not keep him in mind with his feelings of rage and fear, he spoke of wanting to be physically held, to hold my hand and be reassured in my presence. He felt very anxious in any moment of silence as if I had gone away. He said he had run away from these feelings before, into exercise and work, but he did not want to do this now, or take anti-depressants. He wanted to finish his PhD and he knew he could.

The movement in this session from a state of rage-filled fear to a painful acknowledgement of feelings of dependence and separateness was in some ways a turning point in the analysis. This included a transformation in my countertransference, freeing myself from a position of feeling tyrannised by the threat of suicide. My fantasy that he had brought a knife to the session reflected my conscious anxiety about his response to my not phoning him back, and an expression of my preconscious sense that it was important for me to impose this boundary of saying "no" to his wish for me to remain an ideal object responsive to all his needs. The event of his evening phone call, which came in the particular context of these sessions allowed me to more explicitly take up the paternal "third" position. His capacity to psychically move in the session as I have described, indicates a certain fluidity that was very different from the rigidity Conrad had needed to maintain in order to experience some minimal sense of safety in relation to his objects.

In the subsequent months Conrad arrived a few minutes late to his sessions and spoke of his pleasure in making me wait for him even though this made him feel anxious about provoking retaliation. He said he was aware that he tended "to fill a gap with hostility". He looked at my face when he came in, looking for hostility and trying to provoke it. Conrad was by now able to use his aggressive impulses in a more structured way in effecting a separation from his analyst experienced as an overwhelming object, rather than attacking his body. There is evidence of an internal space opening up that does not immediately threaten him with being filled with archaic confusing affects. He could begin to own and experience his intensely conflicting feelings of wanting to cope and wanting to give up, to be "enveloped" by someone so as not to be responsible for himself. It was possible to articulate in the session a malformed baby part of himself which he hated and wanted to kill, especially when he felt unable to get me to concretely look after this baby part.

Glasser's concept of the core complex (1992) provides a helpful orientation for the analyst struggling with the vicissitudes of the sado-masochistic transference. The defensive sexualisation of aggression resorted to in order to protect the nascent self against an intrusive overwhelming object created levels of confusion for Conrad. His sexual excitement in the transference evoked an urgent need to attack me to ward off the threat of a deadly entrapment. My countertransference fantasy that he had brought a knife to the session was an expression of this predicament.

SOME THEORETICAL CONSIDERATIONS ON THE DEVELOPMENT OF THE BODY–MIND RELATIONSHIP

In my view the physical body with its drives and sensorial experiences has to be taken into account, and I will now consider aspects of early development that underpin the evolution of the body–mind relationship which offer a useful perspective on Conrad's developmental difficulties. Laplanche (1999, pp. 170–173) characterises seduction as the foundational process of the human being. He uses the term "primal seduction" to describe the situation in which the mother proffers to her child non-verbal, verbal and behavioural signifiers which are full of unconscious sexual significance: the "enigmatic signifier". This primal seduction consists in part of the mother's meeting her infant's needs, but there is an inherent "profound asymmetry": the infant's passivity and openness to the actions, gestures and words of the other. Laplanche directs our attention to the primacy of the mother's desire and its effects on the infant, amplifying Freud's formulation in the "Three Essays" (1905, p. 223) that the mother "initiates" the infant's sexual life and capacity to love. This enigmatic message cannot be understood and symbolised by the infant, in particular the question of the father and the differences of sex and the sexual. It is only later, through the organising fantasy of the primal scene that these elements can be represented in the child's mind. J. McDougall (1989) has also written of the impact of the mother's unconscious messages to her infant in the aetiology of psychosomatic states. In these formulations the economic element which Freud described (1905)[2] remains central in conceptualising the infant's bodily experience within the sensorial exchanges of the maternal relationship, in which touch, smell and gaze are initially predominant. A. Green (2001) wrote of the necessity for a "trusting passivation" (p. 31), meaning the infant's acceptance of its dependence on the object for maternal care, for the construction of healthy narcissism. He points out that "accepting the object means accepting its variability, the risks that go with it, that is, the fact that it can penetrate the ego and then leave it, thereby reviving intrusion and separation anxieties" (p. 125).

Roussillon (2011, p. 142) links the early experiences of pleasure and satisfaction that constitute an important element of the infant's capacity "to reflect the object within oneself", with the possibility of tolerating the object's absence and the experience of dependence on the object. The views of Roussillon and Laplanche on the primacy of the other in the foundations of the psychic structure of the child can be linked to Bion's formulation (1984, p. 36) concerning the importance of the affective component of the mother's reverie: "If the feeding mother cannot allow reverie or if the reverie is allowed but is not associated with love for the child and his father this fact will be communicated to the infant even though incomprehensible to the infant."

Roussillon makes an important differentiation between the experience of pleasure and of satisfaction; pleasure being linked to drive discharge whilst satisfaction depends on the quality of the relationship in which the pleasure can be felt to be shared. "If the pleasure echoed by the mother and by her own internal states is insufficient, her infant's affect-related pleasure may not come together, and therefore will not be experienced" (p. 143). If the linking between the sensorial and affective elements of satisfaction is insufficient, these experiences cannot develop psychic representation, leaving the individual subject to a state of narcissistic depletion that is often felt in the body.

Conrad's predominant anxiety that I would not accept and love him left him feeling small and powerless. In a somewhat defensive but poignant way, Conrad spoke about the importance of the mother's delight in the separateness and individuality of her baby, which he felt he had never received from his mother. He spoke of his curiosity about women's bodies being intensified and rejected by his mother; women's bodies were alien territory to him. He had fantasies of knifing his parents, which he linked to his feeling that his mother had murdered his sense of masculinity. But he always imagined that he would not be able to kill them properly. Through the transference and countertransference I came to understand that Conrad's experience of his mother's conscious and unconscious hostility towards his liveliness and his masculine body had interfered with the integration and binding of libidinal and aggressive drives (A. Freud 1966; Gaddini 1971). The consequences of these developmental derailments, that can be considered as forms of cumulative trauma (Khan 1974), were a fragile sense of personal and sexual identity based on defensive identifications.

I suggest that this lack of early experiences of a pleasurable affective and bodily contact with his mother formed the basis of Conrad's "savage woe"; an expression which vividly conveys the emotional and sensorial quality of his despair, the mix of suffering and rage that leads in the direction of violence and suicide. His frequently expressed fear that he was too much for me and that I was in various ways having to defend myself against him, was predicated on Conrad's inability to tolerate absence and dependence. The impossibility of negotiating a secure separation from the ambivalently internalised mother with the relative absence of a helpful father provoked self-preservative and sadistic violence (Glasser 1992).

SELF-CONSCIOUSNESS, SHAME AND DISGUST[3]

Painful self-consciousness was one of Conrad's presenting symptoms, associated with feelings of shame and disgust towards his body and its contents, which were at times barely differentiated from the contents of his mind. Conrad spoke of having read about children who believe that if they think something it is the same as doing it. He said he felt like that too, if he talked about his sexual fantasies with me: "it's dangerous because I am a man and you are a woman." He had read that concerns about dirt and cleanliness are to do with repressed feelings, which made him think of how he froze when his female tutor at University hugged him. He felt terrified of the demands of adult women that made him aware of his sense of uncertainty about his sexual identity. As a young adolescent he withdrew from contact with peers into the safety of the relationship with his mother, enduring the taunts of his brother that he was "mother's pet" and a "poof".

Shame is a powerful and painful affect involving the body and the mind, located on the border of inside and outside of the self; it always involves an observer of the self (Yorke 1990). There is an aspect of the experience of shame that gets located in the skin as it constitutes the border and "envelope" of the body self (Anzieu 1989). The skin may become "susceptible" as the result of traces of early un-pleasurable contacts that have been inscribed in and on the skin. This contributed an important element of Conrad's shame-filled experience of a fragile insufficient body boundary leaving him prey to feelings of intrusion and fears of bodily contents leaking out, associated with the threat of psychic disintegration.

Self-consciousness depends on the capacity for self-recognition and the differentiation of self from other, which normally develops in the second year within the context of the mother–child relationship and neurobiological developments. Positive self-awareness depends on repeated experiences of shared pleasure which form the basis of the capacity to play that Winnicott described as having a central function in affect regulation and symbolisation. Implicit in these developments are the beginnings of representational thinking that allow the bodily self to be taken as an object perceived by the self. Winnicott's conceptualisation of the mirror role of the mother (1949) (influenced by Lacan's paper "La Stade du Miroir") places the mother's gaze as the precursor of the mirror in the child's play. In Winnicott's view, when the baby looks at the mother's face he sees himself: "In other words the mother is looking at the baby and what she looks like is related to what she sees there" (1949, p. 112).[4] When the mother is unable to "see" the baby as separate from herself and projects her own conscious and unconscious feelings she becomes a version of the "Lorelei" mother. The maternal object which the infant introjects in this situation is frightening and overwhelming.

In "Mind and its Relation to the Psyche-Soma" (1949) Winnicott differentiates soma, mind and psyche. He defined the psyche as (p. 244): "the imaginative elaboration of somatic parts, feelings and functions, that is of physical aliveness." "At a later stage the live body, with its limits, and with an inside and an outside, is felt by the individual to form the core for the imaginative self." Winnicott's conceptualisations concerning the process of integration of the psyche-soma of the infant and the possible outcomes of environmental failures are helpful in considering Conrad's over-investment of his intellect as a defensive strategy to cope with primitive affective states related to the threat of an overwhelming and hostile maternal object. Gaddini (1987) follows Winnicott in emphasising the gradual process of integration of the initially fragmented sensorial experiences of the infant into the experience of self. Gaddini's formulation of the initiation of mental functioning also implicitly links Freud and Bion, when he describes the impact of birth in terms of the loss of the limitation/containment of the amniotic sac in the womb and the experience of "being without" as "the strongest stimulant to primitive mental functioning" (p. 129). He refers to the infant's first objective recognition of separateness as constituting the permanent loss of the omnipotent self. The consequent recognition of the extreme fragility and vulnerability of the self appears as a mutilation which Gaddini likens to Bion's notion of the "catastrophe" (1987, p. 130). The malformed baby in Conrad's mind, which emerged in the analysis at a point when he could acknowledge the conflict between his wish to merge with me in order to feel "enveloped" and his wish to be separate and independent, can be regarded as representing this internalised situation elaborated in the après-coup of later development. Conrad's attempts to control me and the process were, to an extent, expressions of a regression to anal narcissism (Shengold

1985). In the face of a narcissistic injury he experienced his body as a malformed baby, bad and worthless, full of shit and sweat coming out in an uncontrollable way.

Conrad's sense of exposure, of being seen into in a shaming way was in part based on his awareness of infantile sexual fantasies with their inevitable element of "excess". He struggled with a confused and conflated body image, in which he equated his hair growing with faeces coming from his bottom and sweat from his skin. Shame is also related to the phallic–narcissistic stage of development (Edgcumbe and Burgner 1975) when the child is faced with the task of recognising and accepting the immaturity of his own genitals alongside having to come to terms with the difference between the sexes. Conrad's intense conflicts regarding his masculine body based on castration anxiety, amplified by earlier oral and anal frustrations, inhibited the possibility for him to experience others as having their own qualities which could be appreciated and enjoyed. As he painfully expressed: "how can I allow someone to be close to me without feeling controlled, humiliated and criticised."

HAIR AND ATTACKS ON THE VITALITY OF THE BODY

Looking back on the analysis, I was struck by the extent to which Conrad's feelings and fantasies about his hair expressed his wish to control the inherent vitality of his body, and to stop the parental intercourse which produced the hated younger sibling. His intense feelings of exclusion precluded the development of the capacity to tolerate being part of a triangular relationship without being subject to intolerable negative and destructive affects. Conrad clearly gained a lot of pleasure from cutting his hair very short. I came to recognise a marked response in myself of dismay and disappointment when he entered the consulting room with another short haircut. The visual and emotional impact emphasised the castrating nature of his action, which often felt to me as a cutting short of the emergence of a softer, sensorial vitality. At these moments his almost bald head and his muscular body appeared like an exaggerated phallus which I should both admire and feel intimidated by; a condensed image conveying an aggressive primal scene in which I was the small child and he the powerful adult. Conrad spoke of his dislike of the way his hair grew wavy at the sides because his father's hair was wavy and he actively wished to distance himself from what he saw as his father's unbridled sensuality and sexuality. His mother would not allow him to touch her hair when he was a child and this was a source, one of many, of resentment towards her. The fact that his head and hair were nearest to me when lying on the couch contributed to the continuing importance and transference resonance of his treatment of his hair within the analysis.

Conrad's compulsive need to cut his hair was clearly over-determined. Whilst it was specifically focused on the hair on his head, he experienced similar feelings towards all his bodily hair. At a conscious level Conrad cut his hair in order to appear strong and repel anticipated attacks from other men. Clearly he was also attempting to ward off castration anxiety in a counter-phobic way by cutting his own hair and controlling in fantasy the anxieties evoked by the pubertal changes in his body (Laufer E. 1996). In his determination to stop his hair growing naturally, Conrad aimed to stop the forward developmental trajectory; if he could not be the girl he believed his mother wanted, then he would stay a child. There are elements of tension discharge in this compulsive behaviour that express failures of representation and symbolization of early infantile painful experiences in his body (Edgcumbe 1984).

During the analysis, I often interpreted the cutting of his hair as an expression of his need for restrictive control over his body and its vitality and over the extent of his emotional contact with me. Beneath the conscious meaning of defying his mother and his analyst lay a deeper level of conflict with the mother who denigrated his father and masculinity. But cutting himself off from his mother left him prey to fears of total abandonment. It took some arduous analytic work before Conrad could "find" his father to support his masculine development that enabled him to take pleasure in his masculine body and envisage the possibility of using his penis with a woman in a loving rather than a mutually destructive way.

THE ENDING OF THE ANALYSIS

Much of Conrad's early communication was aimed at producing a response that would seem symmetrical, to abolish the threatening difference which evoked the threat of abandonment. I felt under pressure to be acutely attuned lest any failure might provoke suicidal feelings or actions as a desperate attempt to restore his equilibrium.

I also had to recognise his need to create a distance in order not to feel overwhelmed and utterly passive, which led to his repudiation or limited use of my interpretations. He spoke of suicide as his "ultimate weapon". This was possible in the light of some hard-won analytic insight into the excitement and sadistic pleasure he obtained from his suicidal thoughts and actions.

In the last month of analysis, Conrad questioned the bill I had given him the previous day. He complained about my inflexibility; he had to rush here when I say. I said it seemed we might have different views about the number of sessions the previous month and I pointed out that he seemed to be thinking in an inflexible way, which I quickly recognised was a counter reaction on my part. He responded immediately, saying with a hint of menace in his voice: "I could get up now and beat you up that would show you how flexible I am. I could get up and break your arm." He calmed down quickly when I wondered why he felt so threatened by what I had said. He replied that he felt angry when I referred to his struggle to negotiate issues in this relationship. He felt I was being superior and making him feel weak. Later he spoke of feeling trapped and tricked by his mother. He had to put up with things and be a good boy and then he exploded as a young adult. In the final week he complained that he had never cried in a session; he felt that I had let him down and neglected this aspect of himself. I was aware that we had spoken several times about his stated refusal to cry in sessions because he felt this would be a total submission to me. I had interpreted his fear of dissolving into the couch/my body if he allowed himself to cry. Conrad now said he would feel unbearably exposed and alone if he cried, adding that some feelings of despair are beyond tears. I suggested that there was also a sexual meaning in his wish and fear to cry with me, his unrealised fantasy of a sexual union. He replied that he did not understand what I meant but he could see it was a release of bodily fluids. He would feel very close if he cried. I added: "you wonder then how you could move away." He said "yes, it's about how I experience you when I move away."

Conrad had moved considerably from his suicidal attachment to his Lorelei/mother/analyst, which he expressed in terms of no longer feeling defined by depression and feeling fuller as a person. He felt genuine appreciation towards his father and sadness tinged with anger about the unchanging quality in his contact with his mother. Inevitably, his narcissistic fragility intensified in the face of the impending ending, evoking the fantasy of attacking me to demonstrate his superior masculine strength and to defend against the continuing threat of passivity. My arm that he momentarily wished to break was both the arm which held him and the arm which shut the door in his face. The analytic work had enabled a shift in which Conrad's "problematic" concrete body that had been over-invested with un-metabolised infantile conflicts and affects, was, through the work of psychic representation, transformed into an adult sexual body in which he could experience pleasure without feeling shame or disgust, and which he could hope to use in a loving way with a woman without excessive fear of a mutually destructive entanglement.

CONCLUDING COMMENTS

Work with borderline patients always entails getting caught up in an "emotional storm" (Bion 2005). The availability of clinically useful theories provides the analyst with an orientation to weather the storm. I have made reference to theories that I have found helpful in understanding aspects of Conrad's state of suicidal depression. In so doing I also aimed to highlight some of the technical difficulties of addressing concrete bodily experiences that have yet to be transformed into psychic representations available for thought and communication. The "profound asymmetry" of early infantile life is inevitably repeated in the analytic situation which then constitutes a threatening if not unbearable experience for the borderline patient. Conrad's attacks on his body, his extreme self-consciousness and his compulsion to "hack back" his hair, all reflected an insufficient experience and representation of his body.

The session material, that in retrospect I felt constituted a turning point in the analysis, was a moment embedded in the process that began in an enactment. This was expressed in a countertransference movement towards a paternal position that initiated a process of internalisation in the patient. Conrad's violent struggle to control his body expressed his experience of infantile wishes and conflicts as unacceptable and uncontainable by his mind with its rigid defences that reflected the early lack of mutually satisfying bodily, sensorial contact with his mother and her body. The absence of pleasurable bodily experiences which can be registered at a psychic level creates an unbridgeable gap or hole that can only be "covered over" by the use of primitive defences of splitting and projection. Glasser's concept of the core complex is implicit in my understanding and interpretation of the function of Conrad's violence. This perspective recognises the patient's narcissistic need to locate projected aggression in the analyst to enable the beginning of a process of understanding. Taking this position in the transference allows the patient over time to have the experience of being in the presence of an-other who does not threaten him with annihilation, thus promoting a secure frame in which unconscious aggression can be experienced and expressed.

ACKNOWLEDGEMENTS

I would like to thank the members of the British–Italian Working group for their very helpful comments on an earlier draft of this chapter.

Notes

1 I have written about this patient elsewhere (Perelberg 1998).
2 "in the case of a great number of internal processes sexual excitation arises as a concomitant effect as soon as the intensity of those internal processes passes beyond a certain point" (Freud 1905, pp. 204–205).
3 The term self-consciousness has different meanings in English/American and European discourse, in the former it refers to a painful experience of the self as failing or being inadequate, whilst in the latter it means a positive self-awareness and self-esteem.
4 In this chapter Winnicott refers to a patient who speaks of the artist Francis Bacon liking to have glass over his pictures because "when people look at the picture what they see is not just a picture, they might in fact see themselves" (F. Bacon Catalogue raisonné and documentation. Alley 1964).

References

Anzieu, D. (1989) *The Skin Ego*. New Haven, CT: Yale University Press.
Bion, W.R. (1984) *Learning From Experience*. London: Karnac Books.
Bion, W.R. (2005) *The Tavistock Seminars*. London: Karnac Books.
Campbell, D. (1998) The role of the father in the pre-suicide state. In Perelberg, R. (ed.), *Psychoanalytic Understanding of Violence and Suicide*. London: Routledge.

Campbell, D., Enckell, H. (2005) Metaphor and the violent act. *The International Journal of Psychoanalysis*, 86: 801–824.

Edgcumbe, R. (1984) Modes of communication: The differentiation of somatic and verbal expression. *The Psychoanalytic Study of the Child*, 39: 137–154.

Edgcumbe, R., Burgner, M. (1975) The phallic–narcissistic phase: A differentiation between pre-oedipal and oedipal aspects of phallic development. *The Psychoanalytic Study of the Child*, 30: 161–180.

Freud, S. (1905) Three essays on sexuality. *S.E.*, 7.

Freud, S. (1912) The dynamics of the transference. *S.E.*, 12.

Freud, S. (1923) The ego and the id. *S.E.*, 19.

Freud, A. (1966) Obsessional neurosis: A summary of psychoanalytic views as presented at the conference. *The International Journal of Psychoanalysis*, 47: 116–122.

Gaddini, E. (1971) Aggression and the pleasure principle. In Limentani, A. (ed.), *A Psychoanalytic Theory of Infantile Experience*, 1992. London: Tavistock/Routledge.

Gaddini, E. (1987) Notes on the mind–body question. *Psychoanalytic Theory of Infantile Experience*, 1992. London: Tavistock/Routledge.

Glasser, M. (1992) Problems in the psychoanalysis of certain narcissistic disorders. *The International Journal of Psychoanalysis*, 73: 493–803.

Green, A. (2001) *Life Narcissism Death Narcissism*. London: Free Association.

Heine, H. (1827) The Lorelei. *The Complete Poems of Heinrich Heine*. Val Draper, 1982. Berlin: Suhrkamp.

Khan, M. (1974) The Concept of Cumulative Trauma in *The Privacy of the Self*. London: Hogarth Press.

Laplanche, J. (1999) *Essays on Otherness*. London: Routledge.

Laufer, E. (1996) The role of passivity in the relationship to the body during adolescence. *The Psychoanalytic Study of the Child*, 51: 377–409.

Laufer, E., Laufer, M. (1984) *Adolescence and Developmental Breakdown*. New Haven, CT: Yale University Press.

Laufer, E., Laufer, M. (1997) *Adolescent Breakdown and Beyond*. London: Karnac.

McDougall, J. (1989) *Theatres of the Body: A Psychoanalytical Approach to Psychosomatic Illness*. London: Free Association Books.

Perelberg, R. (1998) *A Psychoanalytic Understanding of Suicide and Violence*. London: Routledge.

Roussillon, R. (2011) *Primitive Agony and Symbolization*. London: Karnac.

Shengold, L. (1985) Defensive anality and anal narcissism. *The International Journal of Psychoanalysis*, 66: 47–74.

Winnicott, D.W. (1949) Mind and its relation to the psyche-soma. In Masud, M., Khan, R. (eds), *Through Paediatrics to Psycho-Analysis*. London: Hogarth Press, pp. 243–254.

Yorke, C. (1990) The development and functioning of the sense of shame. *The Psychoanalytic Study of the Child*, 45: 377–409.

11

PHYSICAL VIOLENCE AND ITS DEPICTION BY A MALE ADOLESCENT[1]

Donald Campbell

INTRODUCTION

At no other time in an individual's development are there more radical changes to their body than those that occur during puberty. While changes occur in the adolescent's primary and secondary sexual characteristics and musculature, Oedipal and pre-Oedipal anxieties and fantasies are revived. In this chapter I will present case material from my therapeutic work with an adolescent I will call Stan in order to consider the defensive use of his body in violent acts and a shift that he made with the help of therapy to sublimate his aggressive impulses in the illustration of violence. The sublimation of Stan's violence in his drawings enabled him to make a transition from violent acting out, to communicating via visual images, to using language to interact with me in therapy. Specifically, I will consider the role played by sublimation in the resolution of his relationship to his mother's body, his father's body and his own body from childhood through adolescence.

A VIOLENT ASSAULT

By the time Stan was 15 he had grown into a handsome young man of average height and build who used his reputation for violence to protect bullied classmates and intimidate anyone who threatened him. One Friday afternoon Stan was chatting with some guys in a disused garage. Grummond, a feared bully, started taunting Stan saying, "Are you still going out with that black slag?" When he didn't get a reply Grummond continued, "Is your old dog dead yet?" Stan took it all silently, but was hurt and fuming. He felt the whole group had turned against him and he was unable to say anything in response.

Stan went home and spent the weekend alone, brooding, feeling humiliated and vulnerable, unable to sleep. He knew that if he listened to *Slayer* or *Anthrax* his favourite heavy metal music would diffuse his anger, but then he would feel beaten and small, so he did not put the music on. By Sunday he knew that he had to get back at Grummond.

On Monday morning Stan took his father's hammer to school. Outside the school Grummond threw a mild verbal insult and Stan hit him on the head with the hammer several times. He was quickly restrained by a number of his friends, although he struggled to inflict more injury on Grummond.

Stan was detained for a hearing and referred for a psychiatric assessment to the Portman Clinic where I saw him four times. As is my practice, I showed my court report to the adolescent I was assessing in order to get their reactions and so they would know how I understood them and what I recommended. I had written that I thought Stan was suffering from unresolved conflicts with his mother and father that affected his self-esteem and undermined his confidence in his masculine identity. I said that he had felt shattered by Grummond's insults and had to retaliate in order to regain his self-respect. He thought words were useless and only by resorting to violence could he become powerful again. On the basis of our contact during the assessment interviews, I recommended that he be referred for psychotherapy to the Portman Clinic and not given a custodial sentence. The judge went against my recommendation and sentenced Stan to a year in a youth detention facility. He was released after six months. Stan only referred once to his experience in detention in which he emphasised the shame he felt about missing his mother so much. His weekly telephone conversation with her was the highlight of his week. He made no reference to violence or homosexual intimidation, perhaps because of shame. However, I had the impression that he was so physically intimidating that the inmates left him alone.

Stan blamed me for his prison sentence and refused to come to the Portman Clinic. Stan's mother strongly supported his involvement in psychotherapy and negotiated with Stan and through a colleague at the Portman for his return to see me. After we worked through Stan's fantasy that my report was responsible for his custodial sentence, Stan was able to begin once weekly psychoanalytic psychotherapy.

STAN'S EARLY CHILDHOOD

Stan was the first-born son of a violent father and a mother who hated being alone with him and had great difficulty cuddling him. She used to leave Stan with friends and relatives because she knew that he needed to be held and she couldn't do it herself. When Stan was four years old the next sibling, John, was born but died after only living one day. When Stan was told of John's death his mother remembers Stan asking, "Who shot him?" After John's death Stan began rocking, the earliest reported symptom. The family have been unable to mourn this loss; John's death continued to have a grip on everyone.

A year after John's death George, a Down's syndrome baby, was born. Three months after George was born Stan started school but had difficulty separating from his mother. He cried a great deal, but his mother was preoccupied with meeting the demands of her disabled son. Stan had a phobia of eating with his family. The school noticed another symptom, a phobia of buttons, which may have reflected his projected rage about his mother's breast that may have been absent for him, but vividly present for his brother George.

Stan had a repetitive dream during his early days at school of being left alone in a lighted classroom waiting for his mother to pick him up. It was getting darker and darker outside and he was all alone. Their parents had picked up all the children. He thinks the dream was actually based on real events and it has haunted him for many years. Later, I thought of this account of his mother not picking him up from school as a screen memory of a mother who literally could not pick him up and hold him as a baby. In my work with Stan I had the impression that his mother's rejection of his body and the withdrawal of her body intensified his desire for her body, subsequent incestuous anxieties associated with that desire, and his hatred of the body that had rejected him. This dynamic was displaced onto his father. Stan did not attack his mother, but was chronically fighting with his father. I think Stan's longing for his mother also aroused anxieties about her dangerousness.

Ferenczi (1952) draws attention to the child's move from the omnipotence of the womb via sleep to gestural symbols, that is the use of the body to signal mental and physical states that good enough mothers read and gratify. This reinforces a magical hallucinatory omnipotence in normal development via imaginative stories, fairy tales and later, for boys, film and comic book superheroes. My impression is that his mother's rejection of Stan's body increased his reliance on concretely physical gestures, like punching, and frustrated the development of gestural symbols, like making a threat by shaking a fist.

As a consequence, Stan's body was experienced as primary and insufficiently symbolised by Stan or his mother from a young age. However, Stan believed that he had a special relationship with his mother whom he felt was the only one who understood him. Stan's favourite moments occurred at night. With his bedroom door open and his parent's bedroom door open, Stan talked with his mother as "two voices and no bodies". Stan described this long-standing bedtime ritual in a kind of reverie. This was the way Stan represented his horizontal relationship with her.

Stan's mother took him to a Child Guidance Clinic when he was five because of his phobia of eating with the family and fear of buttons. Stan never referred to this, but I thought of this as evidence of serious disturbances in his relationships with his mother and father. I think this background left Stan vulnerable to active and passive bisexual impulses, insecurity about his masculine identity, and fears about his physical safety. Stan did not know his body, or the other's body. However, in the course of his therapy through his dreams and in his associations Stan began to "converse" with his body and his mother's body, which I will come to later.

The baby's first object of identification, its first object "choice", as it were, is the mother, particularly her breast and body. During its first year the child identifies with the mother's bisexuality, her masculine and feminine characteristics, before recognising her gender. In the case of the boy, the comfort, nurturance and safety that the baby boy derives from its contact with the mother's body will reinforce feminine aspects of its bisexuality. This feminine component of the male's original genetic template may be forgotten but is revived later much like the experience of the uncanny, which is frightening, that is not homely, *unheimlich*, and at the same time familiar like a vague sense of "home". Freud (1919) reminds us that the original home (*heim*) "of all human beings, a place where each one of us lived once upon a time and in the beginning was the female genital organs" (p. 245). The original home of all of us was an intrauterine existence, the core of the mother's femininity.

I had the impression that Stan's longing for contact with his mother's voice as he was going to sleep was an unconscious revival of sounds of his original intrauterine "home", something comforting and reassuring about the reuniting with the otherness of the other based on his earliest identification with the feminine, which leaves an unconscious residue that someone else has something he almost had, but not quite. Here you can see Stan's wish to be intimate with his mother at a distance, that is, without physical or sexual contact ("no bodies") and the accompanying inevitable incestuous anxiety.

Meanwhile, Stan and his mother denigrated his violent, underachieving father, which undermined opportunities for Stan to dis-identify from his mother and identify with his father's masculinity as part of a creative parental couple. In fact, Stan identified with his father's violence. He and his father had come to blows for as long as Stan can remember. On one occasion Stan told me that while fighting his father he grabbed a screwdriver, but restrained himself from stabbing his father with it.

In *Totem and Taboo* (1913 [1912–13]) Freud imagines a primitive horde of brothers ruled by a tyrannical father who possessed all the women. The brothers murder the father in order to take his place. However, the brother who replaced the father as the possessor of the women would be vulnerable to his brother's revenge. Instead of taking the father's position and precipitating a cycle of patricide, the brothers give up their wish to have all the women for themselves. In this way, the dead father became even more powerful by becoming for the brothers a symbol representing civilisation. Psychically, this dynamic is re-enacted symbolically in the Oedipus complex.

Perelberg (2015) draws our attention to the pathological consequences of the failure to symbolically murder the father and internalise the dead father and the incest barrier, including those patients who are violent towards their father. In Stan's case, his mother's collusion with Stan's incestuous fantasies, and his father's violence intensified Stan's body castration anxiety, which he felt he could only defend himself against physically. Consequently, the phantasy of beating his father did not take place symbolically, but was enacted in physical fights. Perelberg observed that the symbolic beating occurs on the boundary between the anal sadistic phase and the Oedipal situation. For Stan the actual beating of the father continued into his adolescence. On the one hand, Stan did not experience his father's penis as a creative link with his mother, but as a violent, threatening object – the hammer he used to assault Grummond. On the other hand, there was insufficient libidinal fusion of his aggression to constrain his violence towards his father. As a result Stan did not have an internal paternal object to protect him against narcissistic attacks on his masculinity as occurred in the garage with Grummond.

In response to his father's violence, his mother's physical withdrawal, Stan's longing, vulnerability and rage associated with his parent's behaviour, guilt about his infant brother's death, and the experience of being displaced by the most formidable rival – a damaged brother – Stan escaped into a comic book hero. Stan's first solution to this conflict about his dependence upon a murderous incestuous object was to get inside an exaggeratedly masculine identity: Ironman.

Stan had a delusional conviction that his body, like Ironman's, was made of steel. In early sessions with Stan, he recalled feeling frightened by his baby brother John's death and asked, "Who shot him?" He also remembered the more complicated feelings of hatred toward George, the second disabled sibling who displaced him, but he also felt that his parents couldn't accept his hostility towards George. Instead, Stan felt guilty and unable to vent his hostility. However, Stan's fear of retribution for the guilt he felt about the death of John and, especially, his hatred of George, left Stan with deep anxieties about the survival of his own body. Stan defended against anxiety about the vulnerability of his body by believing that he, like Ironman, was made of steel.

IRONMAN

As a child Stan would have had to make sense of a mother who produced a baby that was, in Stan's mind, murdered, and who also gave birth to a Down's syndrome son. It is likely that at an unconscious level sexual intercourse and birth would have been seen as dangerous activities. Stan's father was unable to symbolise his anger towards his son and could only enact it in physical fights. When Stan was four years old his beloved grandfather introduced him to *Ironman* (1963). In this way Stan's grandfather offered a model for sublimation of violence through an omnipotent comic book hero who fought for truth and justice. Stan adopted as his ego ideal this frighteningly powerful and nearly indestructible comic book superhero. During his therapy we came to see that the aim of Stan's identification with Ironman was to psychically get inside an omnipotent macho role model, which would keep his body safe from the object of his desire, a mother who kills and damages her children in her womb. The parental figure represented by Ironman was Stan's father.

Ironman's real name was Tony Stark. Young Stark triggered a booby trap in Vietnam and a piece of shrapnel lodged in his chest. He was captured but had only one week to live before the shrapnel penetrated his heart. With the help of another prisoner, the renowned Oriental physicist Professor Ho Yinsen, and his laboratory, Stark designed and built a suit of armour with a pace maker that would keep his heart beating after the shrapnel entered it. Yinsen sacrificed his life to give Stark time to become "activated".

Stark, as his alter ego Ironman, avenged Yinsen's death and embarked on a career of combating any force or person who threatened the security of America or the world. When Stark dons Ironman's armour he becomes impregnable and his strength is magnified to a superhuman level.

But for all his power and invincibility, Ironman does not have a fulfilling long-term heterosexual relationship. In fact, Stark was shot and crippled by a former lover who was mentally disturbed. He could, however, still function normally within his Ironman armour!

I remember watching a five-year-old boy dressed as his favourite comic book cowboy hero stare menacingly into a mirror as he drew his gun, saying, "So you're the guy who killed my brother". As he "shot" the image in the mirror, the little boy fell to the floor.

Conscious identification with superheroes is not uncommon among pre-pubertal children. On a visit to a supermarket one may see a miniature Superman or Spiderman with padded muscles swooping around the aisles. Although children take play seriously, they normally know that play is not reality. This was not the case for Stan. Stan's identification with Ironman was delusional; he actually believed he, Stan, was made of steel.

The fact that Stan's first identification with a super hero, Ironman, was mediated by a good adult male object, not his father, but his grandfather, contributed to the persistence of identifications with superheroes through his adolescence. It was Stan's way of retaining a link with his grandfather. In late adolescence, Stan sublimated his identification with a superhero through illustrations.

When Stan was about seven years old, he had a chest x-ray. Something told him not to look at the x-rays, but he did, and saw "these little ribs, no steel". His dream was shattered and he felt defenceless. Stan went on to tell me, "I used to pray, when I should have been studying, that I'd be a werewolf because I knew I wasn't a robot". Stan's anxiety and anger at the failure, in his mind, to concretely become an indestructible superhero with omnipotent powers to defeat any external threat, led him to identify with a derivative of the superhero, namely the monster of popular adolescent fiction.

THE SEXUAL BODY IN ADOLESCENCE AND THE BODY HORROR FILM GENRE

The hormonal and physiological changes initiated by puberty thrust the body's sexuality and musculature to the centre of the psychic stage and create a conflict with earlier self-images. Puberty revives conflicts and confusions linked to the individual's bisexuality. Pre-oedipal relationships are also revived along with pre-genital body images, primary process thinking and the psychotic core, which becomes a component of adolescent psychic life. It is not uncommon for adolescents to feel that their new body is an alien object, part man and part woman, with a life of its own that it cannot control; sprouting pubic hair, sudden erections, a voice that cracks. Puberty sensitises the adolescent to his or her body, a body that contradicts earlier self-images and sensations. One aspect of their interest in these horror film monsters is related to their anxieties about physiological changes that occur during adolescence, and the impacts these changes have on their sense of self. The monster of the horror film is a popular object for the projection of adolescents' anxieties about physiological changes at puberty.

The horror film sub-genre, which is very popular among adolescents and most relevant to the adolescent's anxieties associated with the change of their childhood body into an adult body, is body horror. The monster in the body horror film is not a creature external to us but one that emerges from a body like our own body. A Werewolf, which Stan had dreamed of becoming, was a human being bitten by werewolves and transformed into werewolves at every full moon. After Dr Jekyll had taken his drug in order to separate good and evil in man's personality, he became Mr Hyde. Vampires were originally human beings who were bitten by vampires and given vampire blood to drink before they expired.

Monsters who emerged from normal human beings were the progenitors of what is now referred to as body horror. The body horror sub-genre plays on the fear of one's own bodily functions (usually internal ones), their mystery and our inability to control them. Some adolescents experience their body as undergoing a metamorphosis during puberty with accompanying anxieties about loss of the familiar and worries about how to control their new body, how to use it in relationships. For these adolescents their body is a monster. In comics and films monsters graphically represent the adolescent's fantasies about their body, which generate such fear and confusion.

The Monster created by Dr Frankenstein from deceased body parts taps into the adolescents' confusion about the nature of pubertal changes. For some adolescents puberty comes as a shock. What has happened to the body of childhood? Where has the new body come from? In James Whale's 1931 film *Frankenstein*, based on Mary Shelley's (2004) novel, the monster's body is covered and anonymous before the lightning shocks it into life, perhaps like the body in latency before the shock of puberty. Developmentally speaking, we know that with the onset of anxieties about genital development and accompanying incestuous fantasies there is often a regressive revival of early body images. The first view that we have of the Monster is as he shuffles backward out of his cell towards the camera, which emphasises his massive dark shape. This is in dramatic contrast to the lonely and plaintive look in the Monster's eyes that we see when he turns to the camera. He walks like a toddler taking his first steps, or like a non-verbal person suffering from a disability for which one has pity.

VIOLENCE AS A DEFENCE AGAINST THE DANGERS OF HETEROSEXUALITY

As is apparent in Stan's violent attack on Grummond, Stan relied upon his body to protect him from threats to his narcissism and his heterosexual identity. He actively used his body to attack another person who, he believed, represented a threat to his psychic survival. Stan did not withdraw from action, nor did he withdraw from engagement with another person.

The male adolescent's impulse to achieve genital gratification in intercourse with women revives pre-pubertal repressed incestuous wishes, which, in turn, strain earlier defensive solutions. In his therapy, Stan moved back and forth between his infantile wishes to get inside his mother (a residue of the earlier wish for intimacy), and his wishes to establish a heterosexual relationship with a non-incestuous object (stimulated by his emerging adult sexuality).

Stan's conscious sexual fantasies were heterosexual. He usually had one-night affairs because of his acknowledged anxiety about "being trapped into being good with these girls if I continue with them". This would disarm him because, as he said, "I only feel safe when I am bad". The task of developing a genital relationship with the opposite sex was problematic because of his fear of being disarmed by women.

Although anxieties that he was homosexual, reinforced by shame associated with having engaged in mutual masturbation with some male friends during latency, led Stan to attack men who derided his heterosexuality, the threat to his masculinity came primarily from women. After stomping on the face of a male "yuppie" who insinuated that Stan was a homosexual, Stan ran back home and bitterly reminded his mother that when he was young she became "mad, dead, and couldn't leave the house". This memory of an emotionally unavailable mother demonstrated the link in Stan's mind between his uncertain masculinity and a mother who couldn't support him. Later that night Stan dreamt that a vagina cut off his penis.

Wishes to have intercourse with his mother became conscious and acknowledged in his sessions. The lifting of the repression of his incestuous wish aroused fears that he would be trapped inside his mother and increased his anxiety about his father's retaliation. These fears dominated the transference for some time and led him to feel threatened by me. Interpretations were often experienced as my attempts to take him over, like his experience of the "uncanny", and to seduce him homosexually. In the outside world, Stan saw all women as dangerous. Stan wrote a polymorphous perverse story about a "penis flytrap" from which he managed to extract his bleeding penis.

VIOLENCE AS A DEFENCE AGAINST EXCESSIVE PASSIVITY

In spite of Stan's anxieties about being taken over by women and his fears about his father's retaliation for his incestuous fantasies, Stan engaged in intercourse with several women. However, intercourse stimulated passive wishes to merge with the woman, on the one hand, and anxieties about being trapped, on the other, which can be illustrated with some material from Stan's psychotherapy.

Early in a session Stan told me that he elected to stay the night with Betty, his girlfriend, when his mates left the pub. He got drunk with Betty and then went back to her flat for sex. After intercourse he dreamt of Grace Jones, a pop singer and movie star who presents herself as a dangerous phallic woman. He mounted her and then woke up with a start. When he went back to sleep he dreamt of Grace Jones mounting him.

Stan went on to say that the next night he had another dream about getting his mate Paul out of hospital. They wouldn't let Stan leave and took his clothes. He grabbed a bathrobe, put it on, ran down corridors and crawled through ventilation ducts to get outside and away. But then he had no money.

I linked the second dream to coming along to see me today and wondered if it was related to his disappointment with me last week and his expressed belief that only a residential setting, the hospital in the dream, could help him. I added that being held, as in the hospital, also carried with it the threat of being trapped. I wondered if today he was worried about being trapped by me. I thought the dream also disguised a pleasure in escaping into a woman just as he had begun the session by telling me he had gone off to have sex with Betty rather than going off to a nightclub with his mates.

Stan associated to how Paul says he is his best mate but Stan can't say it back. Paul "slags off" his cousin by disparaging his penis as too small. He remembers how his ex-mates always knocked girls. He was slagged off because he was the only one in his group who got laid. Some of the other guys went out with younger girls and he thinks it's repulsive. He can recall his own fear of being seen as queer by others when he's out with his mates. Perhaps that was why he wanted to get away from them. He wondered if they're queer. Stan was beginning to get quite angry at me; his face reddening, his muscles tensing and his breath coming in shorter gasps. He hit his fist into the palm of his hand and said, "All you psychoanalysts think about is sex." I was anxious about my physical safety. I took up his anxiety about his own masculinity and suggested that he shifted his insecurity on to me and his mates and then saw them as envious of him.

Following this sequence of material as it emerged in the session, it appeared that his dreams of Grace Jones, which occur after having sex with Betty, represented an attempt to gratify a sexual wish that also aroused anxiety when he penetrated Betty. When he assumed the dominant position with Grace Jones, anxiety became unbearable, interrupted the dream and he awoke. However, anxiety did not interrupt sleep when he dreamt of assuming a passive feminine posture with Grace Jones.

The session seemed to reflect Stan's anxiety about being active with a dangerous phallic woman, Grace Jones, retreating to a male (Paul) who belittled a man (e.g. turned him into a boy with a "too small penis") and regressing to an infantile relationship (getting inside the mother/hospital) from which he must escape. The consequence of this regression was the loss of his potency (e.g. ending up without any money) if he actually succeeded in returning to his mother's womb (losing his clothes and crawling through the ventilation ducts), and an increase in his homosexual anxiety if he gave up his penis in favour of a passive asexual relationship with his mother. The shift in the material from a dangerous phallic woman to a man who is not so much castrating as narcissistically wounding (that is, turning him into a little boy) represented Stan's experience of his mother and father. My association to the ventilation ducts was to an intrauterine image and Stan talking to his mother at night as "two voices and no bodies".

Stan was in a bind. To become active and penetrative with a woman aroused castration anxiety. But to surrender to a passive role with a woman confirmed his feeling of helplessness and passivity, which he equated with being like a baby again. Metaphoric language had failed to contain and communicate primitive anxieties in an "as if" context. Fears about his passivity and heterosexual relations were experienced viscerally and threatened Stan with breakdown. Stan's violence stood between the threats posed by heterosexuality, on the one hand, and passivity, regression and breakdown on the other hand. Violence, Stan's only defence against breakdown, enabled him to maintain a precarious foothold on reality. As he said, "if I wasn't violent, I would cry like a baby".

STAN'S ILLUSTRATIONS

As Hanna Segal (1947) said of Proust, "It is when the world within us is destroyed, when it is dead and loveless, when our loved ones are in fragments, and we ourselves are in helpless despair, it is then that we must re-create our world anew" (p. 189). Stan began drawing comic strips during latency when his delusional conviction that he was Iron Man collapsed. Initially, any threat to his heterosexuality was experienced as a threat to his psychic survival. Stan used his body to physically attack or intimidate anyone in order to protect himself. When Stan started therapy, depiction of violence coexisted with perpetrating it.

As therapy progressed Stan's growing capacity to think about interpretations, which focused on his anxieties arising from his wish for and fear of being taken over by his mother, contributed to a gradual shift from acting out his violent fantasies, to struggling to keep himself from getting into fights, to sublimating his violent fantasies in comic strips. Drawing played an essential role in this transition because it offered Stan a means of moving from action to symbolisation, and to a more differentiated state of mind (Muller, 1999, p. 108). Following Winnicott, Podro (1998) notes that depiction unconsciously revives an infantile experience of "a transitional space in which the external and internal pass into each other; correspondingly, depiction occupies a transitional space between literal presence and what is imagined in it" (p. 149). Through the medium of the comic strip Stan did not have to physically assault a threatening object but he could attack it in his imagination.

In the second half of Stan's therapy he brought his illustrations done in comic book form into his sessions. The panels on each page provided containment for bisexual and violent images, and windows, which framed the images and invited the viewer to look into the page. He laid the illustrations on the desk between us, never commented on them or referred to them during a session. The drawings were not given to me directly, but left behind. I placed them on the desk before his next session and invited his thoughts about them and suggested he was leaving them behind for me to consider how they might reveal something about him. I made many comments about Stan's drawings, which he listened to, but did not take up. Instead he would go back to whatever was on his mind from his on-going life. The emergence of Stan's drawing during the latter part of his therapy confirms Freud's view that sublimation can only be achieved "after psychoanalytic work has lifted the repressions" (Putnam, 1971, p. 121).

Freud wrote that sexual curiosity can "be diverted ('sublimated') in the direction of art". I would add that for Stan's sublimation functioned to triumph over his castration anxieties associated with intercourse. The incestuous nature of Stan's fantasies was projected and triggered violent castration images in his illustrations.

ILLUSTRATIONS DEPICTING VIOLENCE BASED ON *JUDGE DREDD*

During a period when a homosexual transference was particularly acute, Stan brought drawings based on the American superhero *Judge Dredd* (1977) comic. Stan was quite enthusiastic about the Judge Dredd stories and told me all about the dystopian future Earth where law and order was maintained by Street Judges who patrolled Mega-City One and acted as police, judge, jury and executioner. Joseph Dredd, the most famous of the Street Judges, had the power to instantly convict, sentence and execute offenders. His omnipotent power was represented by the advanced technology of his weapons, which appeared in Stan's drawings. Although Stan did not include the setting, background or story lines in his illustrations, he was clearly excited by the corrupt and violent impulses rampant in the urban environment, and identified with the character of Judge Dredd who personified a powerful and efficient super-ego. Judge Dredd was often more vicious than the criminals, corrupt politicians and evil robots who were his enemies.

Stan was one of those people that Hanna Segal described as being in communication with their unconscious (Segal, 1957, pp. 57ff), but he was also someone who resists the other's scrutiny. It is the implicit nature in a work of art, it's complexity, that leaves room for fantasy in the viewer (Podro, 1998, p. 174). Stan's drawings are explicit and, as such, do not draw us more deeply into the subject matter. In the drawings based on *Naked Lunch* it is difficult to find a narrative. Stan does not create a world and invite us in. Instead, there is a familiar relentless pace without catharsis or completion that is, therefore, doomed to repetition. Again, in the *Judge Dredd* pictures, Stan is obsessed with the male body. Again, there is great attention to anatomical detail. The body and its action is the canvas for his mind. Stan gives away the tongue-in-cheek nature of this exercise in his title of the piece Judge Dredd in *Dredd and the Art of Motor Psycho Maintenance*. In the midst of violence, mayhem, blood and gore, the viewer can see that Stan has drawn, in a fainter line than the one he uses to depict violent adults, a little boy who is curious and maybe a bit worried, but is untouched and not frightened.

The monster in one of the drawings is a caricature of a human monster that incorporates piercings, mechanical body parts, and massive wounds in his chest where bullets have passed through. However, Stan grabs the viewer's attention with playfulness and humour. Flowers burst out of a man's head. There is an Uncle Sam figure, probably representing me, who is more ludicrous than frightening. Stan is not disgusted but curious about his mind and his body – the medium of his violence. Like the Japanese Manga comic strips that inspired him there is great movement across every page, and fluidity in his layouts. There is no let up, no release, and no peace. The sublimation of his violence on the page demonstrates that he has to fight to survive. But neither the monster's violence, nor, indeed, his own violence, destroys him. In a panel on its own is an electric chair that is empty, and Uncle Sam is laughing.

Stan's intense desire to be taken over by his mother made it difficult for him to think about himself as an active heterosexual male and aroused chronic homosexual anxieties. He reported a dream in which his right arm was amputated at the shoulder. There was no pain when a metal rim and fitting was attached to the stump. Then a mechanical arm was fitted to it. Later, this castration image displaced from his penis appeared in a drawing from a series based on the superhero *Judge Dredd* (1977). Stan's phallic power resided in his drawing hand. As Stan said, "I'd be fucked without my right arm. Couldn't draw". During Stan's therapy there developed an internal representation of his hand as an organ of mastery as he moved from the gross movement of his upper body in swinging the hammer to the fine motor control of drawing with a pencil. Stan's capacity to sublimate his violence in drawing enabled him to move from action to thought, and to move from anxiety about castration to mastery of this anxiety.

Stan's associations to the drawings led him to see how he had recreated his experience of me in his sessions as a monster who attacked his mind. The dream of the man with the mechanical arm became the source for the illustration of a character mechanical right arm and only a stump for a left arm. In the session we returned to his previous association that he would be fucked without his right arm to draw with in order to see how he used his drawing, just as he used his violence against others, as a counterattack against me when he felt I was planting homosexual wishes into his brain.

I thought the disintegrating image of Mega City represented Stan's internal world. I had the impression that Stan's sadism was, at least in part, excited by the corrupt and violent impulses rampant in the urban environment, on the one hand, and Judge Dredd's dominating violence, on the other hand. At the centre of the fight with a depraved-looking criminal was Judge Dredd who personifies a powerful and efficient super-ego. Judge Dredd has a long knife pointed at the crotch of the ne'er-do-well who is shrinking back in terror.

I think the viewer's experience of Stan's illustrations parallels Stan's efforts to sublimate his aggression. In Bion's terms, Stan's drawings graphically illustrate his process of translating violent unrepresentable visceral beta elements into integrated and contained alpha elements that are represented not verbally but pictorially. The viewer's first reaction to the visceral violence may be one of shock and revulsion. However, a second look reveals a context and rudimentary narrative that integrates the action. In spite of the relentless almost audible violence, there is massive formal control. Each page includes framed images, that is, images within images, which boundary the narrative and contain the violence.

Bearing in mind Stan's experience of his mother as "dead", it is not surprising that women rarely appear. However, what was surprising to me was that when women do appear they are kept whole, still and quiet, and are drawn with soft, gentle strokes, as though Stan intended to protect the women from the viciousness of his aggression. This suggests that Stan found enough aliveness in his mother to feel some containment and safety, perhaps in those moments of communicating as two voices and no bodies.

The intrauterine origin of the ego contributes to an experience of the uncanny, that is an unconscious reference to his original home – his mother's body. His drawings not only depict the intensity of the violence between Stan and his father, but also the rage he felt towards his "dead' mother that is displaced onto his father. This displacement functioned to protect that part of Stan's mother that loved her son, understood that he needed help and supported his therapy.

Horror has such sublimatory potential because traditionally horror is depicted as arising out of what is familiar and initially recognisable in the everyday ordinary world, which is transformed into a nightmare. Our first impression is that we feel safe because we have a reference point that is familiar, which counters that which attacks the familiar. I think Stan's art is derivative because he needed to have a familiar point of reference from which to depict the horrific. When looking at Stan's illustrations two influences come to mind: the graphic depiction of violence in Japanese manga art, and Salvador Dali's surrealism used to represent his conscious fantasies. Manga has a formal pattern and repetition of images that breed familiarity. The precision itself restrains the artist's hand. The viewer experiences control inherent in the sometimes chaotic violent images. There is something of the outlandish, "over the top" quality to Stan's illustrations that reminded me of Dali's narcissism and posturing as a one-person cult outside the group.

Increasingly, Stan dedicated himself to drawing his favourite action heroes, who, in various narratives, triumph over death and destruction. Stan's mother gave him the impression that she valued him over his underachieving father. This fed his infantile omnipotent fantasies, on the one hand, but increased his castration anxieties, on the other. Stan not only identified with superheroes who possessed indestructible phalluses, he depicted them.

The superhero was not only a manifestation of his frustration, anxiety and fear that his penis would not function properly with a woman, but was also the vehicle for the projection of these anxieties into the viewer. Stan needed witnesses of his physical attack on Grummond, just as he needed me and others to witness the violence of his internal world that he depicted in his comic book illustrations. This need to be seen is emphasised by the way Stan depicted the action within the frame and squarely in the face of the viewer. There is no exit for the observer, which graphically represents the inescapability of Stan's internal world. The play on the word dread in the use of *Judge Dredd* comes to mind. However, none of the characters in Stan's drawings look at the viewer. The gaze of his objects is turned away or focused on another character. So, despite the sense of closeness to the violence, Stan keeps us at a distance from the subjects. We have no role beyond that of the bystander. The transference object can be played with, but he also needs to be kept at a safe distance. There is also a reparative quality in Stan's work that protects us from the violence. The sheer repetition of the violence dulls its impact. The exaggeration of the graphic detail makes the violence appear ludicrous. We shift from shock to curiosity – like the little boy.

Violence, perhaps more than any other delinquent act, compels the environment to manage the adolescent (Winnicott 1956). In fact, Stan's violence had alerted the police and the courts to his need for holding and containment. However, neither Stan nor the authorities were aware of Stan's unconscious need for a father who would contain him while protecting him from a mother he feared would take him over (Campbell, 1995).

Ken Gemes (2009) drew my attention to another observation that Freud makes about sublimation in his 1915 paper "Repression" (1915) regarding the "ideational" component of a drive and its "quota of affect" (p. 152). While viewing Stan's drawings of violent acts it is clear that his homosexual conflicts are repressed but break through in the content of the images. However, it is also clear that Stan's drawing, the sublimatory activity, has released the repressed energy associated with his homosexual conflicts. Work in Stan's therapy enabled *enough* lifting of the repression of incestuous phantasies and *enough* resolution of castration anxieties for the repressed infantile *energy* to be available to drive his graphic representations of his fantasies and anxieties. This is not to say that the sublimatory process of drawing was therapeutic in and of itself for Stan, but that his illustrations exposed unconscious preoccupations that could be interpreted and worked through, particularly those related to his mother's rejection of his body and his father's assaults on his body.

UNDERSTANDING THE VIOLENT ASSAULT

During Stan's psychotherapy he came to believe that he attacked Grummond because he had been upset by Grummond's derogatory remarks about his masculinity. However, it was Grummond's wish that his dog die that profoundly disturbed Stan. We know that animals often represent children or infantile aspects of ourselves. Stan was identified with his dog. He told me that he could trust only three people: his mom, his granddad and his dog. In wishing his dog dead, Grummond had unwittingly attacked the vulnerable child in Stan. With his psychic survival at stake, Stan fought back with his father's hammer. Stan's use of violence, in identification with his father and supported by an omnipotently destructive ego ideal, rescued the helpless little boy inside the adolescent Stan.

CONCLUSION

Stan derived considerable secondary gain from his drawings, which were very popular at school. In addition, Stan's gift for drawing and his use of it to depict his violent fantasies offered him an alternative to violent enactments. Sublimation was not therapeutic in itself, but it facilitated the therapeutic process. Stan's use of sublimation created a transitional space within which extreme acts of violence could be imagined instead of acted out. In this way his drawing bought him some relief by sparing him the trauma, paranoia and shame that accompanied his violence.

The violence in Stan's illustrations, especially in the Judge Dredd series, not only represented his attempt to master the trauma of his encounter with Grummond, but aesthetically recreated an *après coup* in me of the impact that Grummond's insults had on Stan's narcissistically vulnerable self-esteem. Stan's depiction of the horrible anxieties he felt about his body gave him a sense of control over those anxieties, and communicated to me something of his internal world even though his drawings did not implicitly invite me in. I understood that Stan needed to keep me, the parental transference figure, at a safe distance. Just as action replaced symbolisation in the assault, depiction replaced metaphor to convey affects and object relationships that I used to help Stan work through early experiences, the impact of Grummond's insults, and his adolescent anxieties about his passivity and heterosexuality.

By the end of Stan's eight-year therapy he had sufficiently worked through his paranoid anxieties about his father and incestuous fantasies about his mother to be able to hold a full-time job and rent a flat with his long-term girl friend.

ACKNOWLEDGEMENTS

I am grateful to my colleagues, past and present, in the British-Italian group whose comments on previous drafts have been used to clarify my thoughts in this chapter.

Note

1 Most of the clinical material in this chapter was first published in Campbell (2000).

References

Campbell, D. (1995) The role of the father in a pre-suicide state. *The International Journal of Psychoanalysis*, 76: 315–323.

Campbell, D. (2000) Violence as a defence against breakdown in adolescence. In Wise, I. (ed.), *Adolescence*. London: Institute of Psychoanalysis, pp. 11–20.

Ferenczi, S. (1952) *First Contributions to Psychoanalysis*. London: Hogarth Press and the Institute of Psychoanalysis, pp. 1–131.

Frankenstein (1931) James Whale.

Freud, S. (1913 [1912–1913]) Totem and taboo. *S.E.*, 13: 7–162.

Freud, S. (1915) Repression. *S.E.*, 14: 141–158.

Freud, S. (1919) The uncanny. *S.E.*, 17: 217–256.

Gemes, K. (2009) Freud and Nietzsche on sublimation. *Journal of Nietzsche Studies*, 38: 38–59.

Ironman (1963) Marvel Comics.

Judge Dredd (1977) London: Fleetway.

Muller, J.P. (1999) Modes and functions of sublimation. *Annual of Psychoanalysis*, 26: 103–125.

Podro, M. (1998) *Depiction*. New Haven, CT & London: Yale University Press.

Perelberg, R. (2015) *Murdered Father Dead Father: Revisiting the Oedipus Complex*. London: Routledge.

Putnam, J.J. (1971) *James Jackson Putnam and Psychoanalysis*, N. Hale (ed.). Cambridge, MA: Harvard University Press.

Shelley, M. (2004) *Frankenstein*. London: CRW Publishing.

Segal, H. (1947) A psychoanalytic approach to aesthetics. In *The Work of Hannah Segal*. London: Free Association Books, pp. 189ff.

Segal, H. (1957) Notes on symbol formation. In *The Work of Hannah Segal* (1981). London: Free Association Books, pp. 57ff.

Winnicott, D. (1956) The anti-social tendency. In *Collected Papers: Through Paediatrics to Psychoanalysis*. London: Tavistock, 1958.

12

THE HIDDEN SECRET – EGO DISTORTION IN FACIAL DEFORMITY

Some reflections on the analysis of an adolescent boy

Bernard Roberts

> When we put bits into the mouths of horses to make them obey us, we can turn the whole animal. Or take ships as an example. Although they are so large and are driven by strong winds, they are steered by a very small rudder wherever the pilot wants to go. Likewise, the tongue is a small part of the body, but it makes great boasts. Consider what a great forest is set on fire by a small spark. The tongue also is a fire, among the parts of the body. It sets the whole course of one's life on fire.
> (From a sermon On Taming the Tongue, James 3: 1–12, *Bible: New International Version (NIV)*)

INTRODUCTION

In this chapter I explore some of the ego effects of a disfigured infantile body in the adolescence and adulthood of a boy born with a facial disfigurement. The disfigurement was both internal and, for the first four years, visible externally. It became externally invisible as a result of surgery but left profound traces in the ego. I discuss these problems as they appear in the boy's life, reflected in the transference and countertransference, to illustrate the dynamics generated in the minds of the patient and analyst.

My patient, Peter, was born with an enlarged tongue eventually necessitating surgical treatment. The trauma of disfigurement in childhood, the further trauma of interventional treatment and the associated unconscious impulses and defences, can become organised in pathological ways early in adulthood, all the more likely when the disfigurement persists. Peter's congenital condition remains active, needing surgery from time to time. As the tongue is core to primitive ego development my patient's condition has considerable developmental implications.

My fundamental theoretical formulation starts with Freud's bodily ego (1923). In chapter II of "The Ego and the Id", when he is discussing the differentiation of the id from the ego Freud points out that "A person's own body, and above all its surface, is a place from which both external and internal perceptions may spring …. has a special position among other objects in the world of perception". He concludes that, "The ego is first and foremost a bodily ego; it is not merely a surface entity but is itself a projection of a surface". Freud refers the reader to the "cortical homunculus" of the anatomist. In this homunculus, the higher sensory area, it can be seen that the tongue, oro-pharynx and lips occupy an area larger than the thumb and forefinger indicating hugeness of the influence of the oral cavity on sensory life.

Another of Freud's contributions that also brings this case to life for me appears in his short paper, "Some Character Types Met with in Psychoanalytic Work" (Freud, 1916). Freud uses Richard III, the hunchback king, to illustrate a character problem born out of physical deformity – that a birth defect entitles one to evade the ordinary problems of mourning the loss of infantile omnipotence, in favour of retaining a lifelong grievance about the deformity. The bearer of the deformity is entitled to hurt all the envied normal people, who are in debt to him forever.

I reference the work of Rene Spitz (1955) "The Primal Cavity: A Contribution to the Genesis of Perception and its Role for Psychoanalytic Theory" and Augusta Bonnard (1960) "The Primal Significance of the Tongue in Normal and Aberrant Conditions".

Mo and Eglé Laufer developed Freud's ideas in their approach to the analysis of adolescents (1984). In their formulation, one of the major aims of analysis in adolescence is to keep open the unconscious developmental pathways long enough for resolution of unconscious conflicts, and to increase possibility of a functional flexibility in the defensive structures.

MAIN DIFFICULTY FOR THE ANALYST, THE COUNTERTRANSFERENCE

The main difficulty for me, as the analyst, is the countertransference and how to make use of it. I find the patient deeply upsetting. It is a mixture of concern for the fragility of the boy with the deformity and feeling traumatised and invaded by the material so that my mind is paralysed and I cannot think. I often feel shocked, saturated, confused and dominated by a mixture of pity and revulsion, sometimes feeling forced to watch a pornographic scene. This toxic mixture makes it hard to think clearly and to sort out what the patient has that is good and can be built on from what has been damaged and needs to be mourned.

It brings to mind Freud's earliest formulation of the "countertransference", arising in the analyst as a result of the patient's influence on his unconscious feelings. Freud describes himself as "inclined to insist that the analyst shall recognise this countertransference in himself and over come it".

It may be that the repeated intrusions into the patient's mouth have been as traumatic as the underlying physical condition. Mental structures built up to manage primitive anxiety about these intrusions have broken down a number of times under stress; there has been a psychotic breakdown during the analysis and my patient's mental life is governed by a profound paranoid delusion.

HISTORY

Peter and his brother, who is four years younger, lived with their Irish immigrant parents. Peter's birth was a normal full-term first delivery to parents who wanted children. The tip of Peter's tongue protruded from his mouth at birth.

Peter was breast-fed and his mother reported that he was able to feed well even though his tongue swelled and filled his mouth by the end of his first year. The swelling was intermittent and, gradually, it became apparent that the process of swelling was itself accompanied by pain. By three and a half years, at nursery school, Peter had an obviously protruding tongue. It often became dry and cracked, inflamed and painful with uncontrollable dripping of saliva. At this later stage it is likely that Peter could smell his own tongue. Peter remembers at nursery school being repulsive to look at and other children shrinking from him, some mocking and some pitying him. As the swelling of his tongue waxed and waned he was often unable to keep solids in his mouth and food had to be pureed. As far as Peter understands, nobody knew exactly what was wrong with his tongue until his third year. The parents confirmed this.

Diagnosis was not immediate because Peter has a rare congenital non-malignant tumour of one of the components of the tissue of the tongue. The condition is thought to arise spontaneously rather than being genetically determined. Somewhat confusingly for Peter, there is another individual in his wider family with a more common non-malignant skin tumour for which there is a familial predisposition.

In the second half of his fourth year two significant events occurred. Peter's brother was born, a baby also without any physical deformity. The arrival of the sibling was particularly traumatic for Peter who became aggressive, sometimes hitting the baby. These attacks led to a devastating loss of his close relationship with his father. His previously warm father regarded him as a danger to his brother. Indeed Peter's aggression to his brother featured in the first three years of the analysis. Peter has expressed sorrow and guilt at his violence and the major breakdown during the analysis occurred a few months after his brother was offered the university place that eluded Peter.

Within six months of his brother's birth Peter underwent surgery to amputate a considerable portion of the extensible front part of his tongue, leaving a relatively immobile stump. Pain relief was administered by rectal suppository. Peter remembers feeling frightened, deeply humiliated and outraged, physically resisting the rectal insertion and having to be restrained. From time to time cysts reform, the edge of tongue stump has tiny frond-like cysts on it, the tongue swells painfully and the cysts can burst. Peter had further surgical operations on his tongue, the latest just before the start of the analysis, and as the condition is intrinsic to the tissue of the tongue it cannot be eradicated.

After surgery Peter's face appeared normal and he started primary school, a cute-looking freckly boy. Inside his mouth, however, is the stump of a tongue that swells intermittently. Peter had speech therapy and his speech is almost normal but for slight difficulty pronouncing the letter 't', a consonant requiring a flexible tongue tip to be held in extension on the hard palate.

Peter cannot clean his teeth with his tongue, lick his lips or use his tongue to move food around his mouth. He has to use his fingers to clean his mouth or swill it with water, and food sometimes spills out of it, so he is self-conscious about eating with other people. He feels that kissing a girl exposes him to a repeat of the repulsions of his childhood.

Peter struggles with being rotten to the core, to the genes in his every cell. His are "killer cells". This is the core paranoid construction, maintained into adulthood with delusional intensity.

Peter turns his hatred on to his body when he is in emotional difficulties, cruelly attacking it with criticism of his spotty face, misshapen jaw, lopsided face, puny muscles, dry skin, receding hair – implicitly condemning his parents whom he holds responsible for his deformity. This state of affairs is not to be confused with psychosomatic illness. I do not think I have a psychosomatic patient. Peter can symbolise enough to enable vivid communication of his inner world and his feelings.

UNRESOLVED PRE-LATENCY CONFLICTS

Peter's internal world remains dominated by the preoperative disfigurement. The surgery, which coincided with the birth of his younger brother, led to a heightening rather than diminution of Oedipal anxieties. The conflicts re-emerged in an overwhelming way in mid-adolescence.

The pre-operative state dominates the mind. The picture is that of a living gargoyle. Peter felt he was "repulsive" during the first four years of his life. As a further complexity, Peter feels he was presumed "normal" post-operatively, as if he had never suffered. He felt expected to behave as though he had always been normal, a negation of his experience.

This internal scenario was lived out in the analysis in many different ways. There was the pattern of Peter's attendance. Peter was late and missed many sessions in the first years. The problem persisted, inviting either a sadistic reproach or a masochistic collusion. Accompanying the provocation in Peter's persistent "just a bit" or "I don't care" about lateness there was in his mind a continuous stream of hateful raging against his mother for having intercourse with his genetically dangerous father. In hatred and revenge Peter would rather do nothing that would please his parents even if that meant sacrificing his own happiness. This was projected into his friends and into me so that his objects, in projective identification, could become hurt, disappointed, damaged and vengeful and seek to extract themselves from Peter's company whilst dissembling in order to cover up the pain and hostility. This structure had served for many years as a refuge from a much deeper sense of despair in his conviction that he was not properly human, unfit as a partner and parent.

THE BREAKDOWN IN ADOLESCENCE

Peter was referred to an NHS child and adolescent psychiatrist at the age of sixteen. The developmental breakdown featured abusive verbal attacks on his friends leading to intense shame and withdrawal. Instead of entering the sixth form when he was considered to be top university potential, Peter dropped out of school, took to his bedroom, and wanted to die. This constellation replicated the sense of imprisonment and isolation of the little kid locked in with his earlier disfigurement. His psychiatrist prescribed antidepressants and referred Peter to a Psychoanalytic Centre for Young People where he was admitted to the adolescent exploratory interviewing programme. He engaged well in weekly interviewing and was referred for an analysis that started four months before his eighteenth birthday.

"What I had was facial disfigurement" said Peter when he was twenty. "Kids with facial disfigurement get ostracised – people find you disgusting to look at – doctors want to stick needles into you to find out what you have got. They prop open your mouth so that students can look into it. People who love you can't bear you. They can't bear to see you. It's a fucking nightmare. Children don't hide their feelings. It's like being caged in a zoo. People stare at you. At nursery school I sat by myself. Nobody wanted to play with me because my tongue was hanging out. I said nothing; but I painted. The paintings were of storms that I made with my fingers. No one knew what I had or what to do about it for SO long. My parents were hunting about for ages, getting nowhere. I became the object of my parents' frustration and sadness and the object of other children's disgust. Once I had the operation I went to normal in their eyes; and no one knows what it is like to have had four years of hatred from everyone. I am a freak. I am someone only a mother could love."

At twenty-one Peter observed, "My personality has grown like ivy around the specialness of my disfigurement. How can I give that up and still feel myself to be special and individual? The ivy will be torn off and I will be left with nothing."

A central concept of the philosopher Brian O'Shaughnessy, expressed in one of his major works, *The Will* (1980) captures the essence of this painful picture. O'Shaughnessy came to the view that the ego cannot fully retreat into the mental realm devoid of contact with the physical body. This is summed up in his statement that "The mind looks to be irremediably infected with the body".

O'Shaughnessy's thinking reflects the psychoanalytic formulations of primitive development in the work of Rene Spitz and Augusta Bonnard. Spitz, 1955, describes the body ego originating from sensory experiences inside the oral cavity. The mouth fulfils the conditions being both the inside and the outside, simultaneously an interoceptor and an exteroceptor, bridging the gap between internal and external perception, like no other region of the body.

Bonnard uses a neuro-anatomical pictorial visualisation of the sensory and motor cortex of the brain to compare the vastness of the representation of the tongue and lower face, including the oral cavity with that of the rest of the body. Through her use of the phrase, "The tongue's relationship with the baby", she describes the tongue as the "primal organiser of the self", "the primal bridge of the combined subject–object relationship". Bonnard notes the precision and versatility of the tongue's fine muscular movement, such as for directing the flow of breast milk and later for speech, and the quantity of sensory information gathered that makes the tongue the seat of ego development. The tongue is used to explore the inner and outer mouth, to learn about vertical, horizontal and circular movement, becoming "the rudder" of spatial awareness. She talks of an "archaic lingualisation of the body" and "the symbolic displacement downwards towards the genitalia".

O'Shaughnessy's "mind infected with the body" concept, so richly informed by Spitz and Bonnard's work, seems to me to illustrate the tenacity of some of the problems so vivid in Peter.

At twenty-three Peter explained that when he approached people he liked, especially girls, he became embarrassingly upset, near to bursting into tears as he had in nursery school. He does not actively remember his tongue upsetting him then. "That was me, I knew nothing different", but remembers sobbing, both when alone and often when others played with him.

At twenty-five, after seven years of analysis, Peter felt happier than at any other time in his life, in his job in a clothes shop. It was a sort of social life where people talked to him. He was at the same time profoundly despairing, feeling stuck in his development, no longer eighteen like the starters, but unable to function as a sexually mature adult. He had, in his own words, "plateaued", with some life but too overwhelmed with anxiety to move on. Peter still felt near to tears a lot of the time when he was involved with other people of his age. He felt ashamed and embarrassed and withdrew to hide his shame.

THE ANALYSIS

Peter started analysis four months before his eighteenth birthday. He is an average height, acceptable looking young man in his twenties, quite physically robust. He is clean, well kempt and fashionably dressed. He has always talked a lot.

Vivid enactments at the opening of Peter's analysis dramatised both the bodily intrusions and the unresolved pre-latency conflicts. When Peter had to wait outside the consulting room just before his first session I heard the bathroom door open and close, followed by the kitchen door and the door of my colleague's consulting room, interrupting another patient's session. My colleague came out of his consulting room to talk to Peter. It was obvious that he had opened all these doors and looked inside. I had a powerful experience of my personal space and body being intruded into. With the knowledge of his history I could say to Peter in the first session that I thought he was showing me with this behaviour how anxious he was that the analysis would repeat how he had felt when his body had been intruded into without his being able to prevent it.

At the end of the same session, after leaving the consulting rooms, there was a knock on the front door. I opened it to see Peter running off down the corridor – I had been subjected to the "knock-down-ginger" game of latency in which children knock on a door and run away. The knocking creates anticipation in the householder, only for the anticipation to be dashed, being replaced with the sense of feeling tricked and humiliated. This constellation, repeated as it has been in different ways over the years, has many resonances. It reflects the experience of a mother whose anticipation of her infant was rudely intruded into or that of an infant seeing in his mother's eyes the dashed hopes of pleasure of expecting a normal baby. The scenario came to be repeated later in an extreme way in an outbreak of frank psychosis during the analysis. In the repetitions Peter either seduces and disappoints or becomes identified with the disappointed and humiliated object.

In the unfolding analysis the elements of this enactment were manifest more generally, unconsciously and sometimes more consciously affecting his relationships in the outside world. When Peter first started regular work he managed well. People liked him, wanted to get to know him and invited him to their social events. He would become anxious, turn up late or accept invitations and then not attend. Naturally he began to feel disliked, to be shunned, and not to be invited to after work events. This was echoed in the analysis in runs of sessions when he came on time, a build-up of expectation and interest in me, dashed by lateness or where I am sadistically left dangling. As Peter would say, he cannot express his aggression in a normal way.

THE BREAKDOWN DURING THE ANALYSIS

Just before Peter's twenty-first birthday, his younger brother had an offer of a place at university, the offer that has eluded Peter. It came just before the summer break, which includes his birthday. I found myself feeling that I was a mother abandoning him at birth for my better, normal children.

At a party Peter and a girl took drugs. Over the next three days he became increasingly manic, paranoid and deluded. He acknowledged taking drugs and then told me the girl had injected him with heroin, that she was HIV positive and they had shared the needle. He attended his sessions becoming increasingly paranoid and agitated, then convinced that the girl had injected him in the tongue and anus. Peter described a beautiful feeling of submission to the girl injecting him.

He wandered the streets without eating and sleeping and appeared at sessions increasingly unkempt and smelly. He needed admission into the local mental hospital. The confidentiality of the analysis was compromised. I had to fight for the privacy of the analytic space. His mother came to the consulting room to take him to the hospital. While she was outside Peter tried to insert his body between the mattress and the cover of the couch. I felt he was both terrified and desperate to be inside my body to protect him from his profound paranoia. When Peter was in hospital his father made several phone calls, text messages and emails wanting to speak to me. I had one conversation with him in which I recognised the anxiety any parent would have about their child in this situation. This was accompanied by a vivid experience of which Peter complained, of a compulsive, relentless intrusiveness of his father, reminiscent of Peter's intrusiveness on his first day of analysis. With Peter's agreement I spoke with his psychiatrist. Opiates and Viagra were found in his urine.

He returned to analysis within days of the admission and was discharged within ten days. For the next three years he was an outpatient of an Early Intervention in Psychosis Service, with a care coordinator.

THE AFTERMATH OF THE BREAKDOWN

In one of the first sessions after the admission Peter reported a dream that made him feel uncomfortable.

It was a session of his analysis. He had brought his laptop and propped it open on the bookshelf where we could both see the porn that was on it. He heard me, his analyst, undressing and turning around in my chair, offering him my anus. He could now penetrate me.

One constellation in the dream is a sexual organisation that carries excitement invested in an addiction. It is very difficult to give up.

My countertransference was of shock, invasion and this time with a feeling of complicity as if I too was involved in the watching and, thus, joining in the acting out of a pornographic scene. It seemed to be an experience of turning a good analysis into a perverse drama.

ONE YEAR AFTER THE BREAKDOWN

When Peter goes out with a girl the repeated pattern is to feel attracted to her and then find something that makes her unattractive. At a party he'd been with Ella who had been friendly. Ella obviously likes him. He says she is pretty but her breath smells. Peter heard Ella tell another boy to get away because he was hurting her. Peter did not bother to intervene. Ella was upset with him for not helping her. So while Peter tells me that his objects are damaged, in fact he neglects them, treats them cruelly and, when they respond accordingly, he claims they do not like him. By then it is often accurate because other people do give up on him. I looked for this attitude in the transference and within himself in relation to his internal objects. With respect to Ella's "bad breath" I have interpreted to Peter how his "just a bit late" to sessions (and work) leaves a metaphoric "bad taste'" in peoples' mouths – and that he is invoking such a response in me. I link this with the surgery.

My countertransference is to feel upset when I hear of Peter's moving attempts and failures at making friends, especially with girls. He can understand that he may have been upsetting and worrying to his mother right from the beginning, as an infant at the breast, and how scared she may have been that he would choke and die. He senses his parents' terror that he would live his life with his tongue protruding until, at the age of four, they found a surgeon to treat him.

A FRIDAY SESSION AFTER MISSING THURSDAY WHICH IS AN EARLY MORNING SESSION

As Peter lay down he said, "Sorry about yesterday; didn't get enough sleep. I could have come here for a bit but I just couldn't be bothered".

After a pause he said he had a weird dream on Tuesday, a nightmare. The early morning sessions are really difficult for him to get to. There is a work "do" (party) planned for Sunday evening at a restaurant in the West End. It is a bit informal. You just turn up. That is awkward for him. Ella and Jamie are sort of not his friends any more. Maybe he should just move stores and try to get work in another branch, with people who are not as young.

I say that he is not sure whether I want to be bothered to hear his dream now that he didn't come to his session yesterday.

He asks me if I know the film, *I Am Legend* – it's where people become zombies after being bitten by alien mad dogs. Then he tells me the dream.

Peter is in the film with his family. There are zombie dogs, infected with a deadly disease, and they come out at night and bite people. It is very scary because someone has to go out and get food for the family. The dogs are waiting at the doors and windows. They come into the garden and some of them have bitten his mum. The dream gets worse and worse.

His Tuesday night dream was a proper nightmare from which he had awoken really scared and disturbed – he'd felt persecuted by it and he smelled bad, a bit mad, just like the mad people in the psychiatric ward smell – "You know the smell of mad people". He said it was all about him trying to go about his life, trying to avoid the zombie dogs – but, basically, they had broken through his defences. They ate me and my family – everywhere I went they broke through. "The dream itself is like an allegory of my mind", he said. "I try to go about my life but the paranoid feelings and thoughts are bad and I can't do what I would like. I have to sedate myself every day."

I said he was really scared, maybe describing an infected dog part of himself that bites the sane him that knows he needs his sessions (the food). I think he feels he is biting the mother me too, provider of the analysis, when he says he "can't be bothered". It's hard to face his struggles, his weirdness and awkwardness, and how he can throw himself to the dogs.

He replies that he really wants a girlfriend but girls don't like him enough – he doesn't know how to do it, like he doesn't know how to drive. He can drive at 30mph but on the dual carriageway he finds himself drifting; he gets nervous and cannot keep the car going straight, in the right direction.

I said that he seems to not know how to keep on the straight road of knowing that he needs to look after himself. Perhaps he drifts because he hates himself for needing to work harder than other people or me, who he perceives to be not as easily disturbed as he is.

There was more in the dream. He was on the back of a motorbike. One of the dogs was mauling his mum. The dogs became gorillas and he used the body of a baby gorilla, on his hand like a glove, to beat off the adult ones.

He felt dangerous. He linked the motorbike with me. (He knows I have a motorbike – he once said to me that surely my wife and children would be worried about me riding a motorbike.)

I thought he feared the excitement of his own aggression. As a consequence, he was passive in relation to it, like saying, "I can't be bothered", just as he had been passive with Ella, letting her be hurt without actively protecting her. I thought he was scared that if he was active with his aggression it might consume and destroy everything good in him.

He recognises passivity with Ella but he cannot process things. He knows that he shuts down, especially if someone is aggressive. It is worse if it's someone he wants to be friendly with. Now he's afraid of losing Ella and Jamie. Actually he thinks he has lost them.

I thought the motorbike part of the dream was about fear of losing me just when he is aware of how much he wants from me.

He added to the dream, saying that the motorbike had been driven by Will Smith. They were shooting at the dogs. They drove to Kentucky Fried Chicken, got the chicken and killed the dogs.

This seemed a picture of a helpful me – if he eats the analytic food I give him it will rescue him from his hatred.

Just before leaving he wants something from me but is not sure if he should say so – something he wishes that I would do. He tells me pleadingly that he wants me to let him off the hook of being "borderline PD". He wants me to tell him he has no mental health problems, can get a girlfriend, go to university, and everything will be fine.

I say that it is hard to bear knowing he has such problems. He wants me to know what it is like to really wish I could just say that everything would be fine.

SOME EXTRACTS FROM A SESSION SEVEN YEARS LATER

Some material from a session seven years later demonstrates a great deal of development, both in the quality of Peter's life and his thoughtfulness. And yet it continues to be suffused with graphic bodily images. It is only a small vignette but it shows both development and the continuation of a very troubled internal world.

Peter has a girlfriend, Helen, with whom he has been in a relationship for over a year. This is a very significant development. He would often spend a great deal of his session time describing his sexual life with his girlfriend in extensive and graphic anatomical detail, describing his body parts and bodily feelings, without the filter of shame or self-respect.

The session material

Peter was talking about his weekend with Helen in his session and said that actually he had had a dream about her the previous night. He was not sure how good that was.

In his dream he was penetrating Helen's backside with a courgette in a sexual way. They were then riding bicycles around the outskirts of a city where the Dolce Vita nightclub used to be. He was really worried because the bike they were on did not seem to have any brakes.

By way of association he said that Helen was eating courgettes to lose weight. Also his penis did not always work when he was having sex with her. He was thinking of using Viagra. After a thoughtful silence he added that maybe he was anxious about being so behind in his life. He was worried, too, because even after Helen was angry with him and they had made up his penis still did not work very well.

I commented on how the bodily reference in Peter's dream, the backside, a behind, and the failing penis, represented his feeling behind and how scared he is when he feels the pressure to move forwards with his life and powerless in the face of the pressure.

Peter asked me in an ironic tone whether that was a metaphor. There has been an on-going dialogue about metaphor that he sometimes refers to in a sardonic and defensive way. He knows he feels ashamed of being with a girl who is younger and seems better at life than he is. He can then feel anger and hatred for her.

DISCUSSION

Freud's concept of the ego as a bodily ego has been core to my understanding of how my patient's distorted oral and facial anatomy has shaped his self-perception and defensive organisation throughout his life. It has affected each stage of his life when the tension between developmental pressure and defensive organisation has led to breakdown in mental functioning. Self-perception and defences had to be adapted and re-organised in a cumulative way to accommodate the original anatomy, the changing anatomy, the intrusions around surgical examination and diagnosis and the physical and emotional trauma of surgical intervention. Bonnard's observations of the tongue as both an internal and external organ, the seat of spatial orientation and the idea of "lingualisation" of the body add specificity to the centrality of the tongue in ego development.

The presence of the early bodily disfigurement itself remains unintegrated, so that the disfigured body image seems to infect the mind, leading to repeated developmental breakdown. This aspect is particularly insidious in adolescence when the mind is struggling to adapt to the volcanic upheavals of bodily growth and sexuality. The challenge of identification with the normally growing adolescent body is made all the greater when the mind is pre-infected with anatomical and defensive distortion.

The mention of the rectal suppository in the narrative of the surgical process indicates the preponderance of anal aspects of the defensive organisation. Anal quality persists in Peter's obsessive focus and attention to his body, lack of generosity and stuckness. There is a failure of sublimation so that Peter is unable to use his mind in creative and imaginative ways. To link up with the biblical quotation at the opening of the chapter Peter is blinkered in his life; he appears to have a limited emotional awareness of the effect of himself on other people. He knows, however, how stuck he is in relationships with others. He cannot, so to speak, get the bit of life between his teeth and feels he is caught up in fighting with it and blaming the parents for putting it there rather than running with it.

I would argue that concreteness of the anatomy and the surgery and its anatomical after-effects have made symbolisation itself difficult to achieve. It is perpetually difficult to disentangle anatomy and altered anatomy from the emotional trauma. There is a palpable in between-ness in the emotional muddle of the body zones. The fact of the perseveration of body parts and early sensory experience into everyday language is evidence for this. The same quality of body part language infiltrates into dream life too, where again it is not being metabolised. The dreams have their own re-traumatising effect akin to the recurrent dreaming of the trauma in post-traumatic stress disorder.

The psychological impact of the timing of the amputation of Peter's tongue taking place in his fourth year and coinciding with the birth of his brother cannot be under-estimated. The likelihood of the surgery becoming experienced in his mind as an act of castration was increased by the sometimes-punitive approach of the father to his aggression towards his brother. Peter has not recovered from either element. They have persisted in life in fights with his father and hostility to his brother. Both elements are also projected and in projection have been identified with by the father. In the more primitive pre-oedipal configuration Peter experienced the arrival of his brother as signifying expulsion from his mother's body. It seems that in the relief of discovery of the diagnosis and a surgical operation that made Peter look normal, the need for psychological understanding and help was missed. The effect, too, of the continuing swelling and pain in the remaining tongue tissue was not taken into account.

I show in the clinical material how Peter through adolescence and adulthood remains the boy with the disfigured body and how this is revealed in the use of his body and in his verbal communications. As Peter becomes a young adult the language of his narrative remains infiltrated with bodily parts and the trauma has not been fully symbolised.

Peter's progress with life has been very slow but he has, after all, managed to hold down work and make progress in the complexity of working with other people, becoming a team leader. He has been able to develop an intimate relationship in which he experiences and exchanges pleasure, though remaining very troubled. He and his girlfriend talk about whether their relationship could endure and could they become parents.

All of these elements were repeated in the transference and countertransference. My concern and pity for the disfigured boy sometimes led me to ignore the sadism. I found myself thinking in bodily part–object ways as if my own mind was blocked with something like the sensation of a big tongue filling my mouth. If I asked myself the question of who was I in the transference I sometimes felt I was the little baby with something big filling my mind so that there was no room for thoughtfulness. That could switch rapidly to feeling like a mother upset at the sight of and unable to comfort a disfigured and distressed baby. I had to consider whether I was a mother who hated Peter for the disappointment of not being the normal baby that would feed and grow or, as an analyst, hated Peter for not being the more normal patient who could use the analysis to develop. In the father transference the sense of trying to help Peter harness the internal developmental drive could be experienced as cruel, heartless and bullying and an insensitive partner to the mother. This represented one of the technical problems for me in how to help my patient mobilise his reparative use of the analysis.

CONCLUSION

The appearance of a baby at the end of the zombie dog dream epitomises the ongoing challenge for patient and analyst. It is vital not to think of Peter with only destructive and vengeful impulses. The dream contains the wish for a magical repair or rebirth into a world with a normal body and a mother able to fend off the paranoid state of mind. The continuing work of the analysis is in this very area. The guilt of having damaged developmental objects of the past and hurting those in the present, including the analyst in the transference, can be overwhelming. At such times the pull to retreating into a paranoid enclave of recriminations with the omnipotent fantasy of rebirth can be tempting.

References

Bonnard, A. (1960) The primal significance of the tongue – in normal and aberrant conditions. *The International Journal of Psychoanalysis*, 41: 301–307.

Freud, S. (1916) The exceptions, in some character types met with in psychoanalytic work. *S.E.*, 14: 311–315. London: Hogarth Press.

Freud, S. (1923) The ego and the id. *S.E.*, 19: 19–27. London: Hogarth Press.

Laufer, M., Laufer, M.E. (1984) *Adolescence and Developmental Breakdown: A Psychoanalytic View*. New Haven, CT and London: Yale University Press.

O'Shaughnessy, B. (1980) *The Will*. Cambridge: Cambridge University Press, Volume 2, Chapter 15, p. 229 and Obituary in *The Guardian*, 14 July 2010.

Spitz, R. (1955) The primal cavity: A contribution to the genesis of perception and its role for psychoanalytic theory. *The Pychoanalytic Study of the Child*, 10: 215–240.

Afterthoughts

Donald Campbell and Ronny Jaffè

Argan: "Why will you not believe that a man can cure another?"
Béralde: "For the simple reason, brother, that the springs of our machines are mysteries about which men are as yet completely in the dark, and nature has put too thick a veil before our eyes for us to know anything about it."

(Molière, 151, 1669)

Molière was suffering from tuberculosis and, during the fourth performance of the play, he had a violent coughing attack at the theatre. Brought back home, he died a few hours later. Trick of fate, physiological death, failure to contain one's emotions during the performance or even writing a play with the title "The Imaginary Invalid" as a defence against a real ailment; all of them are plausible assumptions that remind us of the mystery of the relationship between the body and the mind.

When the Body Speaks aims to make a contribution to the understanding of this complex somato-psychic machine of ours, which accompanies all of us on our journey through life; a machine, in Molière's 17th-century eyes, that stimulates psychoanalytic research into the mind–body relationship, and through an on-going dialogue with other disciplines, particularly with neuro-sciences. This book affirms that it is possible for another man – in this case the psychoanalyst – to shine a light in the darkness, thereby disproving the answer given by Béralde 352 years ago. If Béralde were alive today we would remind him that the mind–body relationship had been the subject of inquiry at the time of Plato and Aristotle, and that in the Middle Ages that debate was the core of philosophic and medical speculations. For example Grmek noticed that "The relationships between soul and body were thought to be so tight and interconnected that the disease was necessarily considered a psychosomatic entity" (Grmek, 1998). According to their clinical experience, the authors of *When the Body Speaks* recognize, although with different nuances, that the treatment of the somato-psychic condition has its foundation in the mind–body unity and argue that this foundation is embodied in the mother–child relationship. Freud pointed out over one hundred years ago that while going through the vicissitudes of childhood and adolescence, the infant is at the same time biologic and psychic. However, there is an essential nuance, i.e. "the body has no absolute need of a mental activity, whereas the latter is unconceivable without an existing and functioning body" (Gaddini, 1989). Therefore, we have to take into account that the beginning and the early stages of life are characterized by a physiological and natural dissymmetry and that it is the mother's mind–body unity that contains the child's body and makes it possible for the child to create mental representations of its body.

We can understand from infant observation and infant research, that an infant's body can have the most harmonious and integrated development when it has the support of a mother's mind that is capable of containing it with her arms, her gaze, her listening to its rhythms and primary needs. If the infant is in the presence of a sufficient holding and containment that favours an adequate development and shaping of the body structure, it has the possibility of integrating somatic development and psychic evolution. However, without containment and maternal reverie, or when they are insufficient, discontinuous or unpredictable, the child is seriously at risk of feeling thrown into a dimension of emptiness – Bion's (1965) no-thing – and melancholy. This can find its representation in an amorphous, melancholic and inexpressive body, a nothing-body, incapable of expressing itself and remaining silent, as Thanopulos has poignantly pointed out with the expression "silence of the body": a body that is motionless, non-present, apparently anaesthetized, closed in an autistic envelope, narcissistically dead, with reference to André Green's conceptualization of "the dead mother".

Sometimes a silent body, perhaps less showy but no less disturbing, can be a mimetic body when a subject camouflages itself as another's body. This depersonalization phenomenon is accompanied by an ephemeral sense of body representation due to an idea of perfection that hides an uneasiness about the body belonging to oneself. The modus vivendi is based on the fragile defence mechanism of appearance, which can suddenly be shattered and which the subject tries to avoid by compulsively resorting to aesthetic surgery, vigorexia, anorexia, as the expression of an emulation of top models. Others resort to full-body tattoos which may aim to affirm a sense of identity, or conceal a shell-skin and soma.

Instead of dealing with the amorphous, melancholic and inexpressive body, on the one hand, or the mimetic and fictitious body, on the other, the analyst may find themselves engaged with untethered, disharmonic, agitated, writhing bodies. Instead of harmonic gestures expressing a conscious intention towards the other, we observe a dishevelled and apparently purposeless way of gesticulating, the expression of a somatic marasmus often revealing the unconscious need to draw the other's attention in order to be sheltered or contained. Such body states may function as primitive defence mechanisms aimed at avoiding an icy emptiness, and can be expressions of psychotic states. In any case, a body showing a somatic marasmus is a speaking body, a body which is alive despite its suffering.

We may also be in the presence of a body that is the medium for perverse enactments. Bodybuilding may represent a wish to demonstrate a sense of omnipotence, in order to scare the other, or to enact physical acts of violence on the other. A speaking body can express itself through more customary behaviours such as tics and compulsive gestures aimed to control nameless terrors, anxieties about death, suicidal or homicidal phantasies.

Livia was abandoned by her mother at four, and set against her mother by her father. Around 20 years of age Livia was caught in a compulsive enactment of continuous comings and goings in order to control homicidal wishes against her mother, other female figures, and the analyst, when she would hear inside her head her father's voice urging her to kill them. In order to walk a couple of kilometres from her home to the analyst's practice she would need about two hours. Only if the last step was made with her right foot would she feel less dangerous and be able to ring the door bell. Livia's body movements would harness and attack every possibility of constructive thought whenever there was the possibility of an encounter with the other.

Lighter somatic disorders can have an impact on our ability to think, or can create anxieties over more serious illnesses or anxieties about death. Painful body signals, although bearable, can be, in Dostoevsky's terms, "notes from a psychic underground" characterized by anxieties, fears and obsessions of different origins that need to be understood in the analyst's consulting room.

If Gilbert, a physically healthy man, happens to have a simple flu, he enters into a state of deep anxiety which prevents him from moving, so he remains motionless in bed for fear that any movement should cause his death. After two years of psychoanalytic work, memories emerged of a child left alone in his bed, often with a temperature, in the grip of fears and nightmares, without warm and caring attention, except for the obligation to take medication and eat soup and boiled vegetables.

A speaking body, a screaming, murmuring, silent body were common threads in the various chapters of this book and represented by its title, *When the Body Speaks*, taken from Luigi Caparrotta's clinical work in Chapter 8. Our book concentrated on clinical cases in which the body speaks because it is suffering and sick. However, we want avoid the risk of a misunderstanding by reminding the reader that the speaking body is also a healthy body, which expresses its wishes and emotions and makes them known through the five senses and its own drives. Some authors have referred to dysfunctions of the sensory and sensual dimension where we are in the presence of a live and relational body which is trying to cope with the malfunctioning of its senses or organs in an attempt to recover ways to look, listen, smell and feel its own and the other's body.

The British–Italian group has shared a commitment to the study of detailed accounts of psychoanalytic sessions in its search for evidence. Although the first resource for both British and Italian analysts in their efforts to conceptualize the nature of the body/mind continuum was Freud, Italian colleagues were additionally influenced by their background in Greek philosophy. British analysts, for their part, benefited from their background in child and adolescent development.

A useful compass for the British–Italian group as it discussed the complex meanderings of the body was a distinction between "Korper, i.e. the real body, the material and visible object, the biologic object and the rock on which the psychic dimension develops ... and Leib, i.e. the body as vital substance" (Conrotto, 2003, p. 44). *Körper* indicates the pure biologic dimension, meant as the real body made of matter that has the potential to be mentalized and thought of with the help of the parental function first and the reflective function later according to Italian theoretical paradigms. Italian analysts referred to phenomenologists from Husserl to Merleau-Ponty to Levinas who have dealt with this distinction from a philosophic viewpoint, arguing that the Korper can be connected with Descartes' *res extensa*, a body occupying a space, limited by the boundary of the skin wrapping it. A body that can be separated or in contact with another's *Körper*, as is the case with two objects in a room, which can physically come together or be separate. Therefore, it is a matter of bodies, objectified and passive, characterized by an exclusive biologic concreteness which is completely different from the notion of *res colitis*, which implies a thinking mind that is able to interact with the other. This thinking mind is connected with the notion of the body as *Leib*, which bears the marks left by experiences, memory traces, history, emotions, sexual instinct that can be intercepted by the other's *Leib*.

Stressing the difference between *Körper* and *Leib* is, in our opinion, very important because it makes it possible to understand the difference existing between being a body and having a body, and this means being able to grasp such difference within the relational dimension and the analyst–patient relationship. Being a body implies a subjectivity, being in close contact with one's own senses, desires, drives and disorders as well, whereas to say that one *has* a body can lead towards a sense of estrangement and alienation from the body that occurs most severely in pre-suicide states (Campbell and Hale, 2017). However, even in common linguistic usage we say, "I have a headache. I have a stomach ache. I have a cough. I have a cancer." As though these disorders were detached from our minds.

If, in the analyst's consulting room, we go beyond listening to the common linguistic usage and enter a deeper way of listening, we can understand whether a subject – the patient – means "I have a headache" as a pain outside himself, or as a disorder belonging to him, being inside himself as a part of his subjectivity. This allows us to understand how much a subject is in contact with his suffering body, or how much he thinks the bodily pain is something that hails from outside and therefore can be scarcely integrated and digested within oneself.

Saying "I am sick" and "I have a disease" is not the same thing. In the second instance, the disease is a sort of object which is other than the self and can produce states of depersonalization, dissociations and dismorphophobias that make one perceive one's body as a heavy and cumbersome object dominating one's mind, a body that could put the mind in checkmate.

For this to be possible we need to remember that the analyst himself, in the consulting room, is a body that can be used to calibrate the gaze, the closeness/distance, the tones and colours of the patient's voice. In this connection, we are impressed by Plato's remark "that the *logos* makes the thought visible through the voice" meaning by that "that the verbalizing operation presided over by the *logos* consists in a sound visualization of the thought" (Frontisi-Ducroux and Vernant, 1997, p. 96).

We view thought, body and sensoriality together to be an expression of the patient's mental state through manifest words. The mind and body underpin communications, sensory and bodily expressions in the dialectics between conscious, unconscious, preconscious, between visible and invisible, shadows and contrasts.

The child achieves a global mental representation of his body around two years of age and acquires at the same time the sense of a border between his own internal space and the surrounding space. In the very early stages of life, the child has a bi-dimensional representation of this space, as we can also observe in his early graphic representations, usually circles in which various unconnected body fragments are scattered. These circles are the first rudimentary mental representation of the bodily self.

In the early stages of development, the possibility of knowing one's own body is based on a long process of "aggregation of fragmentary sensory experiences" (Gaddini, 1980, p. 480), at first scattered and disconnected from each other, which in the course of time might become coordinated with each other, as has also been pointed out by Ferrari (1982) from a different theoretical perspective. The child can have tactile and visual experiences of bodily fragments such as arms or legs or belly. However, it must be stressed that he can only have tactile and not visual sensations where the face and the rear parts of the body are concerned because the organ of sight cannot directly look at the face and the rear parts of the body. Therefore, in the early stages of life, tactile routes and sensations, but not sight, allow us to experience the space and boundary of our body.

What are the elements allowing us to give our body a sense of completeness, to conceive the notion of tri-dimensionality, to represent ourselves as a sphere and not a simple bi-dimensional circle as in the early graphic representations of the child? In our view, there are three elements:

1. the phylogenetic transmission of an inborn pre-conception that our body is not bi-dimensional but tri-dimensional.
2. the child, through the contacts established by the five senses, e.g. touch, sight, hearing, smell and taste, experiences its mother's body as tri-dimensional. Consequently, through processes of imitation and primitive identification, the child realizes that his own body, like the mother's, is characterized by tri-dimensionality although she/he cannot see it with their own eyes. It is with the mind's eyes that she/he can hallucinate, fantasize, dream, and represent their envelope as the bodily sphere.
3. through the child's psycho-physiologic development she/he adds to the world of sensations the world of perceptions, which will allow them to "perceive the shape of her/his own body in space" (Gaddini, 1980), and to carry such shape within him or herself through the memory traces which have been activated and formed since their early moments of life.

In our view, it's clear that the child can therefore know by intuition his own face, his own tri-dimensionality, his own space in the world. However, in order to have not only an intuitive, but a concrete knowledge on which memory traces can be built, it is necessary to resort to an external element. Socrates asked Alcibiades: "And what are the objects in looking at which we see ourselves although we still see them?" Alcibiades replied, "Clearly, Socrates, in looking at mirrors and the like" (Plato, *Alcibiades*, 132 b.c. from Frontisi-Docroux and Vernant 1997, 125). "It's impossible to see ourselves without a mirror," says Aristotle (Aristotle, *The Great Ethics* II, XV, 7, 1213). "Mirrors," writes Seneca, "have been invented for man to know himself" (Frontini-Ducroux and Vernant 1997, p. 125).

Following the metaphor of seeing as insight, we must paradoxically resort to an object outside the subject, an external object, which is not made flesh but is appointed to reflect the carnal dimension. Without a mirror, parts of us – face, back, anus – might remain forever invisible to our gaze, thus remaining in the realm of imagination and intuition. We believe that this invisible, intuitive and imagined dimension plays a role in what is the enigmatic and obscure side of our thought made flesh, which goes beyond what is manifest, what is visible and conscious. The body's visibility and invisibility seem to have a correspondence with Freud's conscious–preconscious–unconscious psychic apparatus that has structured and illuminated the British-Italian group's study of its clinical material, which we have identified and discussed in the chapters of *When the Body Speaks*.

References

Aristotle (2013) *The Great Ethics* II, XV, 7. Milan: Mimesis, 2014.
Bion, W.R. (1965) *Trasformazioni*. Rome: Armando, 1973.
Campbell, D., Hale, R. (2017) *Working in the Dark: Understanding the Pre-Suicide State of Mind*. London: Routledge.
Conrotto, F. (2003) Corpi e contro corpi. *Rivista Psiche il Saggiatore*, 1.
Ferrari, A. (1982) *L'eclissi del corpo*. Rome: Borla, 1992.
Frontisi-Ducroux, F., Vernant, J.P. (1997) *Ulisse e lo Specchio*. Rome: Donzelli, 2003.
Gaddini, E. (1980) Note sul problema mente-corpo. In *Scritti*. Milan: Cortina, 1989.
Gaddini, E. (1989) *Scritti*. Milan: Cortina.
Grmek, M.D. (ed.) (1998) Il concetto di malattia. In *Storia del Pensiero Medico Occidentale*. Bari: La Terza, 1998.
Molière (1673) *The Imaginary Invalid*, translated by Charles Heron Wall (2017). Dumfries & Galloway: Anodos Books.

Index

abscess 186
absent body, hyper-presence of 137
access to embodied unconscious through reverie and metaphor 105–122
acoustic-musical reverie 155
acoustic reverie 155, 164
adult sexuality, emerging 10, 238
aesthetic reciprocity, between mother and child 14
affect(s): definition 129–130; as psycho-somatic states 34; sensory registration of, translation of 10
affect attunement 10, 151, 171
affective reverie 158
affective states, traumatic 109
affective symbolization 151
affect regulation 109, 220; mutual dyadic 151
aggregation of fragmentary sensory experiences 271
Aisenstein, M. 85, 171
Alcibiades 272
Alien 8, 110–111

alienating identification, with maternal imago 201
alpha-elements 122, 150, 244
alpha-function 64–65
altruistic surrender 174
amenorrhoea 11, 182
amniotic membrane 192
anaclitic object choice, vs. narcissistic object choice 33
anal mastery 12, 203
anal narcissism, regression to 221
analyst: bodily reactions and countertransference of 3; body–mind unit of 3; body of, transference wish to penetrate entrails of 7; homosexual attachment to 176; olfactory memory of 70–74; physical vulnerability of 13; reverie of 122
analytical field, sensorial communications in 5
analytical process, analytic process, development of, within analytic setting 163; role of smell in 6

Index

analytical relationship, bodily language in 53–54
analytic consulting room, mind–body problem in, British-Italian conversations on 159–164
analytic couple, dreaming together of 163
analytic encounter 171–173; bodily communications in 2; body in 146–164
analytic field 8, 74, 122, 147, 157, 161
analytic function, loss of 9
analytic setting, development of analytic process within 163
analytic work, corporeal dimension in 147
Anderson, F. S. 142
angioma 77
Anna Freud Centre 211
anorexia 31, 52, 106–107, 268
anorexia nervosa, as melancholia 31
Anthrax 230
anthropology 20, 41
Antinucci, G. 3–4, 16, 19–39
anxiety(ies): archaic 193, 194, 196, 203; castration 15, 242–246; catastrophic 159; identity 115; incestuous 233; internal sources of 34; intrusion 193, 197, 218; Oedipal 13, 229, 253; paranoid 247; pre-Oedipal 13, 229; primitive 28, 39, 251; psychotic-type 195; pubertal 198; about sexual body 11; about sexuality, impact of puberty 13
Anzieu, A. 203
Anzieu, D. 2, 80, 87, 196, 203, 212; formal signifiers 194;

skin as coat of arms 75; skin as envelope of body 220; skin ego 12, 192, 206; skin fusion 6, 76
archaic anxieties 193–194, 196, 203
archaic identifications 7
Aristotle 267, 272
Arlow, J. A. 106, 121
Arnetoli, C. 152
Aron, L. 108–109, 125, 142
asthma 211
attachment 151; secure 171
Auerbach, J. S. 173, 177
Aulagnier, P. 194
autistic envelope 267
autistic nutritional organization 31
autistic withdrawal 86
autoeroticism 26–28, 32; infantile 27
Autonomic Nervous System 128

baby: hate of, towards mother 5; ruthless love of, for mother 5, 48; subjectivity of, essential structure of 4; *see also* infant
Bacon, F. 226
Badoni, M. 75, 107
Barale, F. 114, 122
Baranger, M. 68
Baranger, W. 68
basic mental organization 160
Bateman, A. 173
Benjamin, J. 108, 109
Benveniste, D. 105
beta-elements 65, 122, 150, 244
betalomes 114
Betjeman, J. 170
Bion, W. R. 6, 9, 68, 75, 139, 141, 146, 160, 221; alpha-elements 150; alpha-function 64, 65; beta-elements 65, 122,

276

150, 244; caesura 100; concept of reverie 151; container–contained model 63, 64; embryological intuition 64; emotional storm 225; maternal reverie 54, 218, 267; negative capability, analyst's 155; no-thing 267; proto-mental system 150; reverie 55
bio-psychic body, silent, spontaneous body as 47
birth, as castration 35
bisexuality, psychic 15
Blatt, S. J. 173, 177
Bleger, J. 160
Bloch, E. 20
bodily ailments, as unconscious communication 181–186
bodily communications, in analytic session 2
bodily fragments: Gaddini's concept of 66–67; as lack of continuity 67; listening to 67–68; as sensorial communications 5, 64, 66, 67, 271
bodily influences, dependence of psychic phenomena on, and somatic processes 8
bodily matrix of self, psyche rooted in 2, 9
bodily reactions, analyst's 3
bodily reverie 158
bodily self 68, 105, 150, 158, 220, 271; acquisition of, role of imitation in 10; mental acquisition of 66, 171; spots of, as sensorial communications 5, 67
bodily sensations, ego derived from 11

bodily states: countertransferential elaboration of 153; use of metaphor with 7
body: analyst's, as instrument and heart of cure 9; in analytic consulting room 146–164; bio-psychic, silent, spontaneous body as 47; centrality of, in psychoanalysis 2; clinical manifestations of 147; clinical use of, and psychoanalysis 52–55; and dream 153–154; hysterical 5, 37, 41, 43, 51, 53, 148; *Körper* 2, 105, 269, 270; lack of expressiveness by 5; *Leib* 2, 105, 270; libidinal 3, 27, 126; listening to 151–154; as metaphorical source of all metaphors 7; and mind, dialectic movement between 163; as original matrix of mental function 8; and psyche, bond between 42; psychic 4, 43, 47, 53; in psychoanalysis 125–143; psychoanalytical 41–61; relational 5, 55, 269; sick 75, 136, 148; silence of 5, 267; surface of, mental projection of 38, 170, 191; symbolic 5, 148; vital and expressive 148; vitality of, attacks on 209–226; wellness/illness of 2
body boundaries 191, 199
body countertransference 141
body defect, congenital 15
body ego 170, 192, 255; early organization of 12; ego as 12, 38, 191, 209, 250, 262; emergence of 194; and sensory experiences in oral cavity 15; shadow falling upon 30

Index

body horror 236, 237
body image, disfigured 263
body language 5, 51, 152, 160; in analytical relationship 53–54; unconscious 181
body scars: analyst's 6; Hautmann's concept of 65–66; as sensorial communications 5, 64, 65, 69
Bollas, C. 152, 153, 160
Bolognini, S. 162
Bonnard, A. 15, 250, 255, 262
borderline pathologies 193
borderline patient 12, 225
borderline personality disorders 172
Botella, C. 22
Botella, S. 22
boundaries: body 191, 199; psychic 191, 193, 201; skin, and feminine sexuality 191–207
Bowlby, J. 151
breakdown, fear of 195
breast, infant's illusory creation of 46
breast cancer 133
British–Italian conversations, on mind–body problem in analytic consulting room 159–164
British–Italian group, cultures and psychoanalytical traditions within 9
bronchial colic 130
Bronstein, C. 2, 3, 126
Brown, D. 185
Bruno, W. 71, 72, 73
Burgner, M. 222
Burroughs, W., *Naked Lunch* 15, 242

caesura 33, 34, 37, 100
Campbell, D. 1–16, 106, 160, 162, 212, 215, 229–247, 266–273

Caparrotta, L. 1, 10, 13, 169–188, 269
Cartesian body–mind dualism 8, 126
Cartesian *mens* 126
castration anxiety(ies) 13, 15, 86, 213, 222, 223, 233, 240, 242–246
Castriota, F. 68, 129
catastrophic anxieties 159
cathexis 12, 37, 43
Ceroni, G. B. 1
Charcot, J.-M. 23
Chiarelli, R. 68, 129
Chiland, C. 203
child analysis 9, 122, 148; body in 157–159
Child Guidance Clinic 232
Chiozza, L. 128
clinical evidence, attention to 161
clinical examples: Conrad (attacks on vitality of body, and suicidality) 209–226; Cristina (dreams involving skin) 11–12, 16, 194–205; Eugenia (psychotic patient) 55–59; Federico (olfactory memory of analyst) 69–75, 81; Gilbert (illness causing deep state of anxiety) 269; Giulia (infecting sensory transmission) 75–82; Giulia (intrusion of unprocessed traumatic parental aspects) 110–121; Hayley (bodily ailments as unconscious communication) 10, 11, 181–186, 187; Justin (sexual identity conflict and self-harm) 10, 11, 13, 174–181, 185–187; Livia (homicidal wishes against mother)

Index

268–269; Ms T (patient's perfume and analysts lack of ability to smell) 87–103; Peter (boy with facial deformity) 249–267; Stan (violent male adolescent) 13–15, 229–247; T (presence–absence of body) 133–137
Colazzo Hendriks, M. 1, 3, 6, 7, 84–103, 157
comic strip 241
comic strip illustrations, patient's 241–246
communication(s): intentional 46, 47, 50–52; nonverbal 152; verbal 186, 264
complementary identifications 99
compulsive thoughts 180
co-narrative transformations 155
concrete originary object 150, 160
concrete thinking 121
Conrotto, F. 270
constancy principle 28
container–connector function, of analyst's body 8
container–contained model 63–64
containment, maternal 107
continuity, lack of, bodily fragments as 67
core complex 187, 217, 226
core identity 160
corporeal countertransference 140
corporeal dimension, in analytic work 147
corporeality, erotics of, and maternal love 32
corporeal self, constructions of 132
corporeal states, understandable within interaction matrix 8
Corrao, F. 155

Corsa, R. 86
cortical homunculus 250
counteridentification(s), projective 97–98
countertransference: analyst's 3; bodily 6–8, 132, 159; body 141; corporeal 140; decodifying bodily events 153; as main difficulty for analyst 251
cranial trauma, suffered by analyst 84–85
cumulative trauma 219
cyst 182

Dali, S. 245
Damasio, A. R. 129
Davies, S. 1
defence(s): omnipotent modes of 210; phobic 203; violence as, against dangers of heterosexuality 237–238
defensive identifications 219
degeneracy, medical category of 20
delusional thinking, psychotic 206
depersonalization 191, 268, 271
Dermen, S. 16
Descartes, R. 126, 142, 270
De Toffoli, C. 131, 149
Deutsch, H. 128
development, phallic–narcissistic stage of 222
developmental failure, pre-oedipal 187
developmental infantile trajectory, blocked at imitation phase 169
dialectic movement between body and mind and between self and object 163
Di Benedetto, A. 155
Di Chiara, G. 155

disbiosis 37, 38
disidentification 38, 206
dismorphophobias 271
dissociation(s) 51, 153, 176, 271; defensive use of 187
distraction, as expressive communication 59
Dora (Freud's case) 24–29, 38, 81
Dostoevsky, F. 269
double consciousness, of hysterical patients' presentation 20
Down's Syndrome 14
dream(s): analysis of 53; and body 153–154; function of symbolism in 53; as metaphors 106; navel of 60; skin in, and dreams as skin 194–198; space for 153
dreaming: talking as 164; transformation in 164
drive(s): as borderline concept between body and psyche 42; concept of 43; as concept on frontier between psychic and somatic 42; as psycho-somatic states 34
drive theory 28
Dr Jekyll and Mr Hyde 237
dynamic intersubjectivity 163
dysmorphic fantasies 180

Early Intervention in Psychosis Service 16, 258
early mother-baby relationship, and concept of wish 43–46
early traumatic experiences, absence of registration of 22
eating disorders 106
economic model, Freud's 3
eczema 195
Edelson, J. T. 121

Edgcumbe, R. 222, 223
ego: as bodily ego 12, 38, 191, 209, 250; intrauterine origin of 244; as projection, of surface 60, 191, 250; sensory floor of 160
ego development, centrality of tongue in 255, 263
ego distortion, and facial deformity 249–265
ego dystonic obsession 175
ego ideal 113, 235, 247
ego-instincts 29
Eissler, K. R. 175
embodied unconscious, access to via reverie and metaphor 105–122
embryological intuition 64
emotion, definition 52–53
emotional storm 225
emotion–reason dichotomy 129
Enckell, H. 7, 106, 212
enigmatic signifier 218
epistemological foundation, of psychoanalysis 4, 43
Erikson, E. 177
erotic attachment, pre-Oedipal 10
erotic homosexual transference 178
eroticized transference 13
erotogenic zones 199
erotomania 176
Escher, M. C. *Drawing hands* 132
expressive gesture, baby's 47–48, 51–52, 54, 59
expressive intentionally communicating body, and hysterical identification 48–52

facial deformity, ego distortion in 249–265
facial disfigurement 249, 254

280

father transference 264
Fechner, T. 28
female sexuality, and bodily orifices 199
feminine sexuality: boundaries, and skin 191–207; development of 191
Fenichel, O. 170
Ferenczi, S. 27, 72, 86, 98, 128, 130, 132, 232
Ferrari, A. 9, 68, 128, 150, 160, 166, 173, 271
Ferraro, F. 5, 9, 66, 152
Ferro, A. 68, 114, 122, 141, 164
figurability, psychic work of 22
Fivaz-Depeursinge, E. 109
Fliess, W. 31, 86
Fonagy, P. 108, 173
Foresti, G. 155, 163
formal signifiers 194
Fraiberg, S. 114
Franchi, F. 68, 129
free association(s) 22, 27–28, 75, 172
Freud, A. 174, 219
Freud, S. *passim*: affect 129; autoeroticism 26–28; conscious–preconscious–unconscious psychic apparatus 273; countertransference 251; Dora 24–29, 38, 81; drive(s) 42, 150; drive theory 28; early object relationship; economic model 3; ego as body ego 12, 38, 170, 191, 209, 250, 262; ego derived from bodily sensations 11; femininity 38; internal censor, concept of 34–39; Oedipus complex in women 39; pressure technique 23, 25, 27; primacy of oedipal structure 27; primal seduction 218; psychical as unconscious 147; psychic development 193; psychic processes 81; psychosomatic states, origin of 4; quota of affect 52, 246; Rat Man 86; structural model 30, 33–34; sublimation 246; theory of subjectivity 19–39; topographical model 3, 24–26, 27–30, 39; transference as playground 210; trauma model 23, 29, 39; trauma theory 25; wish, concept of 43–46; woman, psychosexual development of 35
Frontisi-Ducroux, F. 271, 272
fusion 162
fusional–confusional dyad 206
fusionality, good 161

Gaddini, E. 3, 9, 11, 47, 64, 127, 150, 171, 192, 219, 221, 267, 272; aggregation of fragmentary sensory experiences 271; basic mental organization 160; bodily fragments 5, 64, 66–67, 271; bodily self, role of imitation in acquisition of 10; imitation, concept of 22, 170; mind everywhere in body 146
gallbladder infection 182
Garma, A. 128
Gemes, K. 246
genital development, anxieties about 237
Gergely, G. 171
ghosts in nursery, transgenerational transmission of 114
Gill, M. M. 107, 162

Glasser, M. 187, 217, 220, 226
Godfrind, J. 158
Goethe, J. W. von 28, 38
going on being 140
Golse, B. 159
good-enough mirroring 108
Green, A. 3, 23, 75, 85, 125, 126, 194; boundaries, and borderline pathologies 193; dead mother 70, 267; dear mother 101; intrusion anxiety 193; trusting passivation 218
Grieve, P. 11, 12, 16, 191–207
Grinberg, L. 97, 98
Grmek, M. D. 267
Groddeck, G. 128
Grotstein 2, 125, 164
Guerrini Degl'Innocenti, B. 2, 7, 8, 16, 105–122

hair, ripping out 6, 92–93, 101, 102
Hale, R. 270
hallucinatory omnipotence, magical, infant's 232
Harris, A. 132, 141
Hautmann, G. 5, 64, 65, 69
Heimann, P. 193
Heine, H., *Lorelei* 13, 209, 213, 221, 224
Heisenberg, W. 163
Hermann, I. 86
heterosexual identity 237
Hirst, D. 183, 184
hives 11, 182, 186
holding, maternal 267
holding environment 193; failures in 195; maternal 12, 192
homicidal impulses, patient's 13
homosexual anxieties 243

homosexuality: cultural meaning of 20; primary 98
homosexual transference 242; erotic 178; narcissistic 179
horror films 236–237
Husserl, E. 270
hypnotic–somnolent state of mind, analyst's 13, 185
hysteric, psyche-soma of 20
hysterical body 5, 37, 41, 43, 51, 53, 148
hysterical conversion 52, 59, 128
hysterical identification: and intentionally communicating body 48–52; pathological vs. physiological 49
hysterical language 5, 10

I Am Legend 259
iconic codes of thinking 152
idealization 70
identification(s): alienating, with maternal imago 201; archaic 7; complementary 99; feminine 10; with fictional destructive and omnipotent monsters 14; hysterical 48–52; masculine 198; with phallic mother 59; primary 22, 65; primitive 6; primitive symbiotic 7; projective 65, 98, 122, 152, 162, 254
identity, sense of 172, 174, 268; poor 187
identity anxieties 115
identity barriers, "porosity" in 98
identity conflicts 112, 114, 173
imitation: concept of 22; role of, in acquisition of bodily self 10; stage, as fundamental developmental step 170

imitation-value, of perception 21
implicit relational knowledge, patient's and analyst's
implicit thinking 152
incest barrier 233
incestuous anxiety 233
incestuous fantasies 15, 233, 237, 239, 246–247
incipient third 109
infant: illusion of self-sufficiency of 31; magical hallucinatory omnipotence of 232; omnipotent self of 221; psyche-soma of, integration of 221; *see also* baby
infantile autoeroticism 27
infantile internal world 23
infantile omnipotence, loss of 250
infantile sexuality 28; conceptualization of 24
infecting sensory transmission, in analytic relationship 78–79
intentional communication 46–47, 50–52
interaction matrix 132; corporeal states understandable within 8
inter-bodily communications, between analyst and patient 9
interbodily dialogue 157
internal censor, concept of 34–39
internal objects: parental 210; split, analyst's 68; splitting of 67
interpretation(s): embodied 68–69; transference 102, 155; unsaturated 155
introjected mouth, and introjected breast, exchange between 64
introjection 12, 64, 127, 170–171; process of 150
intrusion anxiety(ies) 193, 197, 218

Italian psychoanalysis (*passim*): polyphonic aspect of 162
Ironman 234–236, 241
Isaacs, S. 9, 192, 194

Jaffè, R. 1–16, 63–82, 266–273
Johnson, M. 105
Jones, E. 131
Jones, G. 239, 240
Judge Dredd, illustrations depicting violence based on 242–247
Jung, C. G. 99

Kaës, R. 78
Kahn, L. 42
Kandinsky, V., Bleu de ciel/Sky blue 47
Keats, J. 146
Khan, M. M. R. 152, 219
Kilborne, B. 177
Klein, M. 67, 139, 193
Kohut, H. 176
Körper 2, 105, 269–270

Lacan, J. 221
Lakoff, G. 105
language: bodily 53, 160; body, *see* body language; development of 10; hysterical 5, 10; mentalistic 142; protosymbolic 5, 10; symbolic 53, 105; use of to communicate affects, absence of an experience of 10
Laplanche, J. 2, 27, 105, 193, 218
Laufer, M. 175, 180, 210, 223, 250
Laufer, M. E. 175, 180, 210, 223, 250
Lausanne Group 109
lazy eye 182, 186
Le Doux, J. 129

Lehtonen, J. 170
Leib 2, 105, 270
Lemma, A. 107, 110, 136
Levinas, E. 270
libidinal body 3, 27, 126
Limentani, A. 177
linear causality 127
lingualisation, of body 255, 263
linguistic metaphor 106
lipothymia 128
listening: to body 151–154; deeper 270
Lombardi, R. 16, 141, 153, 173
Lorelei mother, analyst as 213–215

magical hallucinatory omnipotence, infant's 232
magical thinking 178, 180
Manga comic strips, Japanese 243, 245
Mangini, E. 163
marasmus, somatic 268
Marty, P. 125
masculine identification 198
masculine identity, insecurity about 232
masochism, primary 49
maternal care, pre-symbolic registration of 29
maternal containment 107
maternal erotics 24, 32
maternal function 36, 61, 67, 75; theory of 35, 192
maternal holding, deficit of 79
maternal love, and erotics of corporeality 32
maternal object: surrender to, dread of 210; symbiotic, fusing 116
maternal projections, introjection of 12

maternal reverie 54, 218, 267
Mathew, M. A. F. 159
Matte Blanco, I. 52, 61, 129
Matthis, I. 146, 149
McDougall, J. 6, 76, 148, 167, 218
Meltzer, D. 14, 155
mental development, initial stages of 3
mental differentiation, initial stages of 3
mental function, body as original matrix of 8
mental functioning, level of, symbolic and presymbolic 152
mentalistic language 142
mentalization 65, 105, 109, 127
mental reverie 158
Merleau-Ponty, M. 132, 270
meta-ego 160
metaphor(s): access to embodied unconscious through 105–122; linguistic 106; loss of 7; body as metaphorical source of 7
metapsychological psychoanalysis 19
Milner, M. 139, 160
mind, dark zones of, secret parts of the self encapsulated in 158; development of 66, 164, 171
mind–body dualism, Cartesian 8, 126
mind–body integration 152
mind–body question 147; in analytic consulting room 159–164; British-Italian conversations on 159–164
mind–body relationship 1, 3, 9, 147, 163, 173, 209, 266–267; development of 217–220; dualistic view of 127; historical review 149–151

Index

mind–body unit: analyst's 3; mother's 267; as single holistic unity 9
mirroring 109, 112, 173, 180; caregiver's 8; failing 8, 111; good-enough 108; maternal 171
mirror-neurons, neuro-scientific discovery of 22
mirror role, of mother 221
Mitrani, J. 159, 160
mnemic symbols 35
mnestic trace 60, 158
Moccia, G. 158
Modell, A. H. 106, 107
Molière, "The Imaginary Invalid" 266
monistic position 8
mother: baby's hate towards 5; baby's ruthless love of 5, 48; capable of sufficient holding and containing 267; and child, aesthetic reciprocity between 14; dead 70, 267; early holding and containing of, function of skin as mediator of 11; engulfment by, pre-Oedipal anxieties about 13; high anxiety of, intrusion of 12; infantile libidinal tie to 199; phallic, identification with 59; pre-inscription of relationship with 4, 45; primal seduction by 218; regressive pull into 13; as seducer 28
mother–baby relationship, early, and concept of wish 43–46
mother–child dyad 2, 151
mother–child relationship 2, 151, 220, 267
mother–daughter skin, shared 203

mother–infant, affect attunement of 10
mother–infant communication, spontaneous gestures in 46
mother–infant interaction, mutual imitation in 171
mouth cavity, as cradle of perception 170
Muller, J. P. 14, 241
Mushatt, C. 128
musical grammar, deep 155
mutual dyadic affective regulation 151
Mycenean civilization 27

Nacke, P. 32
Nancy, J-L. 37, 38
narcissism 27
narcissistic compensation 86
narcissistic object choice, vs. anaclitic object choice 33
narcissistic regression 86
narcissistic wound 99
nascent transference 158
navel of dreams 60
negative capability, analyst's 155
negative transference 91
Neri, C. 78, 155, 161
nettle-rash 77–79
neurotic psychopathology 193
Nicolosi, S. 64
Nietzsche, F. 143
noninterpretive interventions 155, 161
nonverbal communications 152
non-verbal representational meanings, elaboration of, via psychoanalytical metaphor 7
no-thing 267
nutritional autism 31–32

object, shadow of 32, 35, 37
object cathexis 37
object choice, narcissistic vs. anaclitic object choice 33
object relationship: early 19; primacy of 34
Oedipal anxieties 13, 229, 253
Oedipal configuration 75
Oedipal conflict 114
Oedipal father, trauma model 29
Oedipal identifications 13
oedipal structure, Freudian primacy of 27
Oedipus complex 39, 203, 233
Ogden, T. 106, 109, 121, 140, 149, 155, 160, 161, 164
olfactory memory, of analyst 70–74
omnipotence, infantile, loss of 232, 250
omnipotent fantasies, infantile 245
omnipotent modes of defence 210
omnipotent self, infant's 221
ontogenesis 29
oral cavity, sensory experiences in, and body ego 15
orifices, bodily, and female sexuality 199
O'Shaughnessy, B. 15, 255

pain: physical 29, 81, 148; psychic 2, 148
papilloma virus 154, 203
paranoid anxieties 247
paranoid delusion 251
Parat, H. 32
parental aspects, unprocessed traumatic, intrusion of 8, 111
parental internal objects 210
passivity, excessive, violence as defence against 239–240

patient: and analyst, inter-body dialogue and communication between 9; body of, hyper-presence of 3, 9; concrete absence of, felt as hyper-presence of ill body 9; deep and archaic psychic layers of, understanding 7
penis, as potentially destructive intruder 201
perception: imitation-value of 21; mouth cavity as cradle of 170; sympathy-value of 21
Perelberg, R. 215, 226, 233, 234
personalization 191
phallic identification 185, 186
phallic mother, identification with 59
phallic–narcissistic stage of development 222
phantasies, unconscious 22, 127, 128, 194
phobic defences 203
physical violence, depicted by adolescent male 229–247
Piovano, B. 1, 2, 9, 16, 146–164
Plato 126, 142, 267, 271, 272
pleasure principle 31
Podro, M. 241, 242
polyphonic aspect of Italian psychoanalysis 162
Ponsi, M. 105
Porcelli, P. 128
Portman Clinic 230
positivization 158
post-traumatic stress disorder 263
potential space 139
Pozzi, M. E. 159
pre-genital conversion 128
pre-inscription, of relationship with mother 4, 45

pre-latency conflicts, unresolved 253, 256
pre-Oedipal anxieties 229; about engulfment by mother 13
pre-Oedipal developmental failure 187
pre-Oedipal erotic attachment 10
pressure technique 23, 25, 27
pre-suicide states 270
presymbolic level of mental functioning 152
pre-symbolic order 3
pre-symbolic register 22
primal scene 34, 197–198, 207, 218, 222
primal seduction 218
primary homosexuality 98
primary identification 22, 65
primary masochism 49
primary maternal object 3
primary object 30, 35–36, 159; child's bodily relationship with 158; role of 151
primary process thinking 236
primitive anxiety 28, 39, 251
primitive defence mechanisms, analyst's 86
primitive ego, tongue core to 250
primitive identification 272
primitive infantile states, theory of 35
primitive mental functioning 192, 221
primitive unconscious phantasies 194
primordial nuclei of experience, formation and encoding of 21
procedural thinking 152
projected counteridentification 97

projection(s) 38, 64, 127, 196, 201, 245, 264; primitive defence of 226; role of, in ego's experience of body 11; of surface, ego as 60, 191, 250
projective counter-identifications 98
projective identification(s) 65, 98, 122, 152, 254
protective shield, analyst's 115, 138
proto-mental system 150
protosymbolic language 5, 10
Proust, M. 241
psyche: and body, bond between 42; rooted in bodily matrix of self 2, 9
psyche-soma 19–20, 33, 85, 131, 150–151, 221
psyche-soma integration 151
psychic apparatus, development of skin as 11
psychic body 4, 43, 47, 53
psychic boundaries 191, 201; loss of 193
psychic development 193; significance of skin in 206
psychic energy 42
psychic experiences, somatic incarnation of 163
psychic layers, deep archaic, patient's, understanding 7
psychic life: beginnings of 192; origin of 22
psychic organizations, vs. somatic organizations 3, 125
psychic pain 2, 148
psychic phenomena, bodily influences on 130; and somatic processes 8
psychic registration 22

psychic representation, formation of 4
psychic skin 192, 194; development of 207
psychic structuring, failure in 171
psychoanalysis: body in 125–143; centrality of body in 2; and clinical use of body 52–55; epistemological foundation of 4, 43; metapsychological and relational, polarization between 19; relational 19
psychoanalytical body 41–61
psychoanalytical metaphor 106; elaborating non-verbal representational meanings 7
psychoanalytic knowledge, development of 66
psychoanalytic treatment, body always present in 85
psychological self 105
psychopathology, neurotic 193
psychophysical organization 152, 154
psychosexual development of woman 35
psychosis, as silence of body 5
psychosomatic diseases 2, 52, 191
psychosomatic pathology 154
psychosomatic phenomena 126
psychosomatic states, origin of, Freud 4
psychosomatic unit 2
psychotic delusional thinking 206
psychotic patient, silent body of 54–55
psychotic states 268
psychotic-type anxieties 195
pubertal anxieties 198

puberty, psychological impact of bodily changes 210; long-term consequences of 10; on anxieties about sexuality 13
Putnam, J. J. 242

Quine, W. V. O. 142
Quinodoz, D. 155
quota of affect 52, 246

Racalbuto, A. 150, 155, 163
Racker, H. 99
reality principle 170
reflective function 7–8, 105, 107, 270; lack of 111, 112, 115
reflective thinking 107
registration, psychic 22
regression, narcissistic 86
reintrojection, of affect or sensation 11
relational body 5, 55, 269
relational knowledge, implicit, patient's and analyst's
relational psychoanalysis 19
relational vicissitudes, early, infant's 19
representational meanings, non-verbal, elaboration of, via psychoanalytical metaphor 7
representational thinking 220
repression, organic basis for 86
resonant listening 155
reverie(s): access to via embodied unconscious 105–122; acoustic 155, 164; acoustic-musical 155; affective 158; analyst's 122; analytic use of 121; bodily 158; concept of 151; maternal 54, 218; mental 158; as metaphors 106; sensorial 155, 164; visual 155, 164

Index

Richard III 250
Riolo, F. 100
Roberts, B. 15, 16, 249–265
Rocchi, C. 3, 8, 9, 16, 125–143, 148
Rosenfeld, H. 172
Roussillon, R. 162, 194, 218, 219
Russo, L. 97
ruthless love, baby's, for mother 5, 48–49

sadomasochism 97
sado-masochistic transference 217
Salpêtrière 23
Sandler, A. M. 170
Sandler, J. 22, 170, 174
Savitt, R. A. 128
Scarfone, D. 22
Schächter, J. 12, 13, 14, 16, 209–226
Schore, A. J. 109
Schwartz, H. J. 86
second skin 91
seduction: primal phantasy of, enactment of 27; transference–countertransference 25
seduction phantasies 27
Segal, H. 67, 84, 241, 242
self: self, secret parts of, encapsulated in dark zones of mind 158; and object, dialectic movement between 163; sense of: formed through bodily self and psychological self 105; fragile 193
self-harm(ing) 102, 169, 172–173, 175–176, 180
self-identity, poor 187
self-image, poor 187

self-mutilation 176
self-reflective capacity, foundations of 125
Semi, A. A. 20
Seneca 272
sense of self, fragile 193
sensoriality, analyst's and patient's 84
sensorial minus 7, 99
sensorial reverie 155, 164
sensorial self, child's 158
sensory channels, analyst's 7
sensory deficit 99
sensory floor of ego 160
sensory memories, working-through process of 72–74
sensory registration of affects, translation of 10
sensory states, transmission of, in psychoanalytic relationship 63–82
separation anxiety(ies) 11, 180, 218
separation–individuation 138
sexual body: adolescent, and body horror film genre 236–237; anxiety about 11
sexual identity 172, 174, 215, 219, 220
sexuality, anxieties about, impact of puberty on 13
shadow of object 32, 35, 37
Shelley, M., *Frankenstein* 237
Shengold, L. 221
sick body 75, 136, 148
silence: of body 5, 267; as curative factor 156
silent communication, mother–infant 46
Silver, A.-L. S. 86
sinusitis 11, 182, 186

289

skin: boundaries, and feminine sexuality 191–207; as coat of arms 75; development of, as psychic apparatus 11; in dreams, and dreams as skin 194–198; function of, as mediator of mother's early holding and containing 11; mother–daughter, shared 203; second 91; significance of, in psychic development 206

skin ego 12, 192–194, 197, 203, 206; holes in 199

skin fusion 6, 76

Slayer 230

Smadja, C. 171

smell, sense of 75, 85–86, 170; countertransferential role of in analysis 6, 70–76; loss of, analyst's 7, 84

Socrates 142, 272

Solano, L. 149

Solms, M. 129, 130

somatic disorders 269

somatic marasmus 268

somatic memories 192

somatic mnemic traces 35

somatic organizations, vs. psychic organizations 3, 125

somatic pathologies 147

somatic processes, and bodily influences 8, 130

somatic sensations 11, 28, 32

somatic-sensory sediments 9

somatic states, transmission of, in psychoanalytic relationship 63–82

somatic symptomatology, unconscious conflicts underlying 23

somatization 129

somatizing patient 149

Speziale-Bagliacca, R. 136

Spira, M. 5, 64, 67, 68

Spitz, R. 15, 170, 250, 255

split-off bad object, body experienced as 14

splitting: of internal objects 67; primitive defence of 226

spots of bodily self 64; as sensorial communications 5, 67

Steckel, W. 100

Stern, D. N. 8, 10, 108, 109, 151, 155, 156, 171

stomach pain, as communication 141

Strachey, J. 30, 33, 35

Straker, G. 109

structural model 30, 33, 34

subjectivation: process of 19, 22; somatic, intra-psychic and interpersonal dimensions of 19

subjective object 12, 46, 193

subjectivity: baby's, essential structure of 4; self-fulfilment of 8

subject–object relationship 3, 21, 23, 147, 151, 255

sublimation: of aggression, socially acceptable 14; failure of 263; integrating function of 14; and processing disparate aspects of sexuality 15; role of 229; use of 14, 247; of violence 229

suicidal fantasies 14

suicidality 209–226

suicide attempt(s) 12, 210, 211, 215

superego, internal censor as 34

surface of body, mental projection of 38, 170, 191

symbiotic mechanisms 6

symbolic body 5, 148
symbolic functioning; deficit in 107; mental 152
symbolic language 53, 105
symbolic representations 105, 152, 194
symbolization 65–66, 69, 109, 223, 263; vs. action 241, 247; affective 151; bodily and interactive roots of 149; capacity for 10, 110, 153, 155, 187; and capacity to play 220; processes of 147, 149, 151, 159
sympathy-value, of perception 21
symptoms, as metaphors 106

tachycardia 156
Tagliacozzo, R. 156
talking cure 140, 154–157
Thanopulos, S. 2, 4, 5, 16, 41–59, 66, 158, 267
thing-presentation 23, 26
thinking: iconic codes of 152; implicit 152; procedural 152; reflective 107; verbal, linear codes for 152; visual 152
thumb-sucking 25
Todarello, O. 128
tongue: centrality of, in ego development 263; core to primitive ego 250; as primal organizer of self 15; as seat of ego development 255
topographical model, Freud's 3, 24–25, 27, 30, 39
touching cure 154–157
transference: eroticized 13; homosexual/narcissistic 179; interpretation of 161; nascent 158; negative 91

transference–countertransference seduction 25
transference interpretations 102, 155
transitional area(s) 121, 159–160, 213
transitional object 53
transitional space 241, 247
transpersonal infection 78
trauma, cumulative 219
trauma model 23, 29, 39
trauma theory 25
traumatic experiences, early, absence of registration of 22
triangular relationship 222
trichotillomania 6, 85, 87
Tronick, E. Z. 151
trusting passivation, infant's 218
Tuckett, D. 155
tussis nervosa 25
Tustin, F. 160

uncanny, the 22, 114, 153, 232, 238, 244
Un Coeur en Hiver 74
unconscious communication, bodily ailments as 181–186
unconscious phantasies 22, 127–128, 194; primitive 194
undifferentiation 162
unmentalized states of mind 160
unrepresented affects, bodily expressions of 169–188
unsaturated interpretations 155
urinary tract infections 182, 186
urticaria 195

vaginismus 12, 199–202
Valéry, P. 80
verbal communications 186, 264

verbal thinking, linear codes for 152
Vernant, J. P. 271, 272
Viagra 258, 262
Vigneri, M. 148
vigorexia 268
violence: as defence against dangers of heterosexuality 237–238; as defence against excessive passivity 239–240; use of body illustrate 14
vis-à-vis analysis 152
visual reverie 155, 164
visual thinking 152
vitality of body, attacks on 209–226

Werewolf 236, 237
Whale, J. *Frankenstein* 237
Winnicott, D. W. 11, 12, 30, 54, 84, 98, 108, 149, 199, 202, 246; bodily self 150; body ego 191; breast, infant's illusory creation of 46; capacity to play 220; environment, mother as 55; fear of breakdown 195; going on being 140; intrusion anxiety 193; mirror role of mother 221; neonate inseparable from mother 151; potential space 139; psyche-soma 131; ruthless love, infant's for mother 5, 48; silent communication, mother–infant 46; skin and ego distress 206; skin as limits of self 191–192; spontaneous gestures, in mother-infant communication 46; transitional area 121, 159–160, 213; transitional object 53; transitional space 241, 247
wish: and early mother-baby relationship 43–46; Freud's concept of 43; meaning of concept of 43; as psychic derivative of drive 44
woman, psychosexual development of 35

Yorke, C. 220